ELEMENTARY

Language
LEADER
COURSEBOOK
and CD-ROM

PEARSON
Longman

Ian Lebeau Gareth Rees

Language Reference and Extra Practice by John Hughes

CONTENTS

Listening	Speaking / Pronunciation	Scenario	Study & Writing skills
Interviews in a language school TV programme	Asking personal questions Asking questions about different cities Pronunciation: contractions, schwa	On the Street Key language: Saying where places are Task: Describing where places are	Using your dictionary (1) A description of a city Adjectives Linkers: and
Interview with a student	Reporting on someone's job/study Discussing jobs Pronunciation: word stress	In an office Key language: Asking for information Task: Asking and answering questions	Using your dictionary (2) A CV Capital letters
TV interview about deserts	Talking about water and deserts Asking questions about routines and habits Pronunciation: showing interest	At a festival Key language: Making suggestions Task: Making and responding to suggestions	Classroom language Description of a process Linkers: Sequencing phrases Pronouns it and they
Interviews with members of a health club	Talking about films Guessing game Pronunciation: weak or strong vowel, linked sounds	At a travel agent's Key Language: Asking for information, saying no politely Task: Exchanging basic information	Working with numbers A description of a table or bar graph Approximation
People talking about transport	Choosing a car Discussing different means of transport Pronunciation: vowel sounds, stress in compound nouns	At a ticket agency Key language: Buying a ticket Task: Booking a travel ticket	Planning your written work: Organising information Description of a transport system Paragraphs, Topic sentences, Ordering ideas Linkers: but
Interview about eating habits	Describing photos Discussing food problems Pronunciation: intonation	At a conference Key language: Requests and offers Task: Talking about numbers and quantities	Correcting your writing: Making mistakes A restaurant review Commas in lists

CONTENTS

LANGUAGE LEADER ELEMENTARY

Listening	Speaking / Pronunciation	Scenario	Study & Writing skills
A radio programme: discussing online shopping	Talking about shopping habits Discussing shopping preferences Pronunciation: stressed words	At a meeting Key language: Giving advantages and disadvantages Task: Describing places	Giving a short, informal talk: Making notes An informal email Linkers: *because, so*
Short presentations on technology and cultural changes	Talking about ancient civilisations Discussing change in culture, lifestyle Pronunciation: Vowel sounds, linked sounds	At a museum Key language: Polite requests Task: Finding out important information	Learning new words: Managing new vocabulary, Working with vocabulary A description of an objects Pronouns and Demonstratives – *it, this, these*
Radio interview: Medical inventions	Discussing famous inventors Talking about personal experiences Pronunciation: Verb endings, stressed words	On the radio Key language: Giving reasons Task: Giving a short presentation	Taking notes while reading: Recording notes A short biography Linkers: during, later
A talk: Information to foreign students about safety in the UK	Talking about different ways of spending and saving money Pronunciation: Stressed words	In my opinion Key language: Asking for and giving opinions Task: Expressing thoughts and opinions	Taking notes while listening: Introducing extra information A formal letter Linkers: *that*
Audio interviews from website	Describing where you live Talking about leading a green life Pronunciation: contractions, stressed words	At an accommodation agency Key language: Checking understanding Task: Asking for information about accommodation	Examination skills An informal letter Directions Linkers: *when*
Interview with a 'global nomad' A lecture on using technology to learn English	Talking about experiences	Around the world Task: giving short talks	Learning outside classroom: Using technology to learn A postcard Adjective intensity

Audioscripts (p146–157) • Phonetic Charts (p158) • Irregular Verb List (p159)

1 Cities

1.1 CITY FACTS

> *The city is not a concrete jungle, it is a human zoo.*
> **Desmond Morris, 1928– , British biologist and writer**

VOCABULARY: cities, adjectives

1 Look at the photos A–D on pages 6 and 7. Choose the names of the cities from the box. (There are two extra names.)

| Istanbul   Kraków   London |
| New York   São Paulo   Tokyo |

2 Match adjectives 1–8 with their opposites a–h. Then choose two or three words for each city in the photos.

1 good	a) hot
2 old	b) dry
3 big	c) quiet
4 cold	d) new
5 wet	e) expensive
6 noisy	f) ugly
7 beautiful	g) bad
8 cheap	h) small

London – big, …

READING

3a Read the text and choose the correct answer.
São Paulo is …
1 big and noisy.
2 small and quiet.
3 cold and expensive.

Ten facts about
São Paulo

1 It's in the south of Brazil.
2 It's a big city.
3 It isn't the capital of Brazil. (Brasilia is the capital.)
4 It's 75 kilometres from the sea.
5 In summer, the weather is hot and wet.
6 It's famous for coffee!
7 The restaurants are good.
8 São Paulo and Corinthians are football clubs in the city. They're famous in South America.
9 It isn't a quiet city. In fact, it's very noisy.
10 The buses aren't expensive.

3b Are these sentences about São Paulo true or false?

1 It's in Brazil.   *true*
2 It's small.
3 It's the capital of Brazil.
4 It isn't in the north of Brazil.
5 The summers are dry.
6 The football clubs aren't famous in South America.

GRAMMAR: *to be*

4 Look at the text *Ten facts about São Paulo*. Complete the table.

Affirmative (+)	Negative (–)	Question (?)
I'm (I am)	I'm not (I am not)	am I?
he's (he is)	he isn't (he is not)	is he?
she's (she is)	she isn't (she is not)	is she?
¹ *It's* (it is)	it ³ _____ (it is not)	is it?
you're (you are)	you aren't (you are not)	are you?
we're (we are)	we aren't (we are not)	are we?
² _____ (they are)	they ⁴ _____ (they are not)	are they?

➡ Language reference and extra practice, pages 122–123

5a Choose the correct form.

1 London *is/are* the capital of the UK.
   It's/He's an old city.
2 Istanbul *aren't/isn't* the capital of Turkey.
3 São Paulo and Brasilia *am/are* in Brazil.
4 Kraków and London *aren't/isn't* hot in winter.

5b Write one or two sentences about your city or town.

My city is cold in winter.

6 Look at these questions and choose the best answer.

1 Is your city beautiful?
   Yes, it is. / No, it isn't.
2 Are you a student?
   Yes, I am. / No, I'm not.
3 Are the restaurants in your city bad?
   Yes, they are. / No, they aren't.
4 Is your teacher from the UK?
   Yes, he/she is. / No, he/she isn't.

> **GRAMMAR TIP**
>
> Notice the short answers:
> *Is London old?*
> – *Yes, **it is**.*

7 Put the words in the right order to make questions. Then ask and answer the questions with a partner.

1 good in your city   coffee   Is   ?
   Is coffee good in your city?
2 expensive in your city   Are   the buses   ?
3 in Europe   Is   New York   ?
4 Tokyo   a big city   Is   ?
5 you   in your city   happy   Are   ?
6 famous   in your city   you   Are   ?

LISTENING

8a [1.2] Listen to two conversations and answer the questions.

1 Are the conversations between:
   a) two students?
   b) two teachers?
   c) a teacher and a student?
2 The situation is:
   a) on the phone.
   b) in a class.
   c) in a café.

8b Now listen again and fill the gaps with one word.

Kraków

1 small, beautiful, *old*
2 in the _____ of Poland
3 _____ in winter

Istanbul

4 big, beautiful, _____
5 _____ in winter
6 _____ mosques

SPEAKING

9a Practise the conversations in Exercise 8. Look at Track 1.2 on page 146.

9b Now work with a partner and make similar conversations between a teacher and a student.

VOCABULARY: places in a city

1a Match the words in the box with the photos on pages 8 and 9.

> an airport   a beach   a bridge   a canal
> a church   a cinema   a fountain
> a harbour   a mountain   a museum
> a park   a temple   a theatre

1b Think of more buildings and places in a city.

A   B   C   D

READING

2 Read the article about famous cities from an in-flight magazine. Put these words in the correct gaps in the text.

> beaches   films   ~~music~~   water

3 Read the article again and complete the sentences.

1 Sydney Opera House is a famous *building*.
   a) park   b) cinema   c) building

2 Sydney is a good place for _____.
   a) films   b) water sports   c) museums

3 Mumbai is a _____ city.
   a) small   b) busy   c) quiet

4 Bollywood films are from _____.
   a) Los Angeles   b) Mumbai   c) Venice

5 Venice is a _____ city.
   a) big   b) noisy   c) small

6 Venice isn't a good place for _____.
   a) cars   b) people   c) boats

Famous cities

E   F   G

In all cities there are large buildings, parks, museums and schools, but a lot of cities are famous for other things.

Sydney, city of ¹*music* and city of ²____

Sydney is in the southeast of Australia. The population is four million. In Sydney there's an opera house and there are a lot of lovely beaches. Bondi Beach is famous for surfing. Sydney is a fun city.

Mumbai, city of ³____

Mumbai is in the west of India. It's a big city with over ten million people – it's a busy city. There isn't an opera house, but the city is famous for films. In Los Angeles, there's Hollywood; in Mumbai, there's Bollywood. In Mumbai there are a lot of cinemas – over 200! It's an exciting city.

Venice, city of ⁴____

Venice is in the northeast of Italy. It isn't a big city – the population is under 500,000. In Venice there aren't any buses or cars. Venice is a city of water. There are 150 canals and a lot of boats. It's a beautiful city.

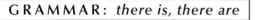

H **I** **J**

GRAMMAR: *there is, there are*

4a Complete these sentences from the article.

1 In Sydney *there's* an opera house.

2 In Mumbai _____ _____ a lot of cinemas.

3 (In Mumbai,) _____ _____ an opera house.

4 In Venice, _____ _____ _____ buses or cars.

There is (There's) / There are introduces a place or thing. It tells us what is in a city, building, room or place.

4b Look at sentences 3 and 4 in Exercise 4a. When do we use *any* in a negative sentence?

5 Complete the table with the correct words.

| is̶ is are are any not isn't |

	Singular	Plural
+	There's a cinema. (There ¹ *is* a cinema.)	There ⁵_____ 200 cinemas.
−	There isn't a theatre. (There is ²_____ a theatre.)	There aren't ⁶_____ theatres. (There are not any theatres.)
?	³_____ there a park? Yes, there is. No, there ⁴_____.	Are there any canals? Yes, there ⁷_____. No, there aren't.

➡ Language reference and extra practice, pages 122–123

6 Choose the correct form of *to be*.

1 In London, there *is* / ~~are~~ an opera house.

2 There *is* / *are* two international airports in New York.

3 In Edinburgh there *isn't* / *aren't* any canals.

4 There *isn't a* / *aren't any* harbour in Mexico City.

5 *Is* / *Are* there any temples in Paris?

6 Are there any museums in Nairobi? – Yes, there *are* / *is*.

GRAMMAR TIP

a lot of = a large number of

*In Mumbai there are **a lot of** cinemas.*

SPEAKING

7 Work with a partner to find out about different cities.

Student A: Look at the table on page 110 and ask your partner questions.

Student B: Look at the table on page 114 and ask your partner questions.

LISTENING

8a `1.3` *I love my city* is a TV programme. Listen to the programme and match the people with the cities.

1 Yukako   a) Cape Town
2 Pablo   b) Lima
3 Stefan   c) Kyoto
4 Peter   d) Chicago

8b Listen again. Tick (✓) the correct sentences.

1 Kyoto
  a) There are a lot of new buildings.
  b) There are a lot of old buildings. ✓

2 Lima
  a) There are a lot of cars and buses.
  b) There are a lot of cafés.

3 Chicago
  a) There are a lot of temples.
  b) There are a lot of museums.

4 Cape Town
  a) There's a beautiful fountain.
  b) There's a beautiful mountain.

pronunciation

9a `1.4` Contractions Listen. Tick (✓) the sentence you hear.

1 a) I'm from Chicago. ✓
  b) I am from Chicago.

2 a) They are very quiet.
  b) They're very quiet.

3 a) There is a beautiful mountain.
  b) There's a beautiful mountain.

9b Listen and repeat the three sentences.

WRITING

10 Write about your city. Then tell the class.

My city is in the north/southeast of … The population of my city is … My city is famous for … In my city, there are …

PREPARATION

1 Match the places in the box with the symbols 1–14 below.

> ~~bookshop~~   building site   bus station   car park
> college   gardens   library   market   post office
> public toilets   railway station   shopping centre
> swimming pool   tourist information centre   zoo

1 *bookshop*
2
3
4
5
6
7
8
9
10
11
12
13
14
15

2a [1.5] Listen to six sounds from a city. Match them with places in Exercise 1. Write the places.

1 – railway station

2b Are the sounds in Exercise 2a 'nice' sounds or 'nasty' noises?

3a Think about your city. Which places are noisy? Which places are quiet?

3b Ask and answer questions with a partner about places in your (area of the) city or your capital city, using the words in Exercise 1.

Is there a university?
– Yes, there is. / No, there isn't. / I'm not sure.

Are there any gardens?
– Yes, there are. / No, there aren't. / I'm not sure.

4 Complete the text with the words in the box.

> ~~England~~   famous   gardens
> language   population   students

5 [1.6] Listen to a talk. Where are the people? At a university? At an English language school? On a tour bus?

CITY FOCUS
Cambridge

King's College

Cambridge is a famous university city in the UK. It's in the east of ¹ *England* , 80 kilometres north of London. It's a small city with a ²_____ of 110,000. Cambridge is a beautiful old city, and very green, with many parks and ³_____ . There are 31 colleges in the University of Cambridge – King's and Trinity are two ⁴_____ colleges. There are 17,000 ⁵ _____ at the university. There are also a lot

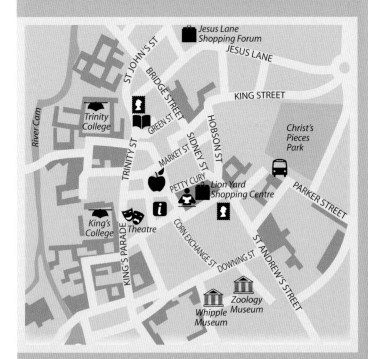

6 Listen again and tick (✓) the words you hear.

colleges ✓   shopping centre   railway station
bookshop   car park   library
post office bus station   tourist information
university   public toilets   centre
market   park   zoo
                               gardens

7a Listen again and choose the best words to complete the sentences.

1 The bookshop is
   a) in Trinity College.
   b) opposite Trinity College.
   c) next to Trinity College.

2 The market is
   a) next to Trinity College.
   b) in the shopping centre.
   c) between Trinity College and the main post office.

3 The bus station is
   a) next to the park.
   b) opposite the main post office.
   c) between the main post office and the market.

4 The library is
   a) opposite the bus station.
   b) in the shopping centre.
   c) between King's College and the tourist information centre.

7b Now check your answers on the map.

KEY LANGUAGE:
saying where places are

8 Look at the map of Cambridge and make true sentences. Use the table to help you.

The small post office		between	Trinity College.
The theatre	is	next to	The Whipple Museum.
The library		in	King's College and the tourist information centre.
The Zoology Museum		opposite	the shopping centre.

The library is in the shopping centre.

pronunciation

9a [1.7] Schwa Work with a partner. Listen to these words. How do we say the underlined part? Practise saying the words.

stat<u>io</u>n   opp<u>o</u>site   fam<u>ou</u>s   Engl<u>a</u>nd

We call this sound the *schwa* /ə/.

9b [1.8] Underline the parts of the words below with the *schwa*. Listen and check, then repeat the words. One word has two schwas.

canal   fountain   library   cinema   quiet   million

TASK: describing where places are

10 Work with a partner to find places on a map.

Student A: Look at the information below.

Student B: Look at the information on page 114. Do not look at the map below.

Student A
On the map below there are six places with no name. Ask your partner questions about the places, then write the names of the places on your map.

Is there a/an … ?

fountain   theatre   park   railway station
opera house   shopping centre   university
tourist information centre

Now use your map to answer your partner's questions. Say where the places are.

Yes, there is. It's between / opposite / next to the … / in …
No, there isn't.

OTHER USEFUL PHRASES
It's on the left/right of the map.
It's on the left/right of the library.
It's at the top/bottom of the map.

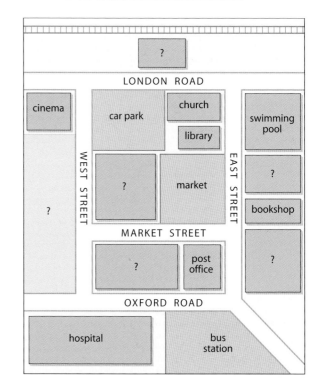

1 **1.9** The alphabet What is the first letter of the English alphabet? What is the last letter? Listen and repeat the alphabet. Look at page 146.

2 **1.10** Complete the groups 1–7 with these letters. Listen and check.

C̶ E J K L N O P T U X Y

1 /eɪ/ A H _ _
2 /iː/ B C̲ D _ G _ _ V
3 /e/ F _ M _ S _ Z
4 /aɪ/ I _
5 /uː/ Q _ W
6 /əʊ/ _
7 /ɑː/ R

3 Which letters are these? Try to say them aloud. Use the phonetic chart on page 158.

1 /siː/ C̲   4 /dʒeɪ/ _   7 /waɪ/ _
2 /dʒiː/ _   5 /kjuː/ _   8 /zed/ _
3 /eɪtʃ/ _   6 /juː/ _

4a Listen to your teacher spell some words. Write the words.

4b Work with a partner and spell words. Write your partner's words.
Student A: Look at page 110.
Student B: Look at page 115.

5 Number these words in alphabetical order. You have 30 seconds.

yes	☐	is	☐
famous	☐	café	1
market	☐	music	☐
chair	☐	harbour	☐
no	☐	cold	☐
city	☐	park	☐
mountain	☐	museum	☐

6a Work with a partner and do a word race. Find these words in your dictionary. Write the next word from your dictionary. Who is first?

under grass map head sea food radio thing English

6b Compare your words and your partner's words. Are they the same?

7 Listen to your teacher and write down the words you hear. Check your spelling in your dictionary.

8 A dictionary entry Look at the dictionary extracts below. Write the labels from the box in the correct place.

definition pronunciation example grammar part of speech   different meanings of the word

a _____

po•ny /ˈpəʊni $ ˈpoʊni/ *noun, plural* ponies
a small horse

b _____

po•ny•tail /ˈpəʊniˌteɪl $ ˈpoʊniˌteɪl/ *noun*
long hair tied at the back of your head so that it hangs down: *Kim's hair was pulled back in a ponytail.* ⇨ *see picture on page 353*

pool¹ /puːl/ *noun*
GRAMMAR
a pool of something
1 a place that has been made for people to swim in: *They have a pool in their garden.*
2 a pool of water, blood etc is a small area of it somewhere: *There was a pool of oil under the motorbike.*
3 [no plural] a game in which you use a long stick to hit numbered balls into holes at the edge of a table. You play or shoot pool.

c _____

d _____

poor /pʊəl $ ˈpʊr/ *adjective*
1 Someone who is poor has very little money and does not own many things ⇨ *opposite* RICH (1): *My family was very poor.* | *I came from a poor background* (= from a family that has very little money or an area with a lot of poor people).
2 something that is poor is not as good as it should be: *His schoolwork has been poor recently.*
3 *spoken* used to show that you feel sorry for someone: *Poor Ted had no idea what was happening.*

e *part of speech*

f _____

from Longman Wordwise Dictionary

9 Parts of speech
The underlined words in sentences 1 and 2 are *nouns*. The underlined words in sentences 3 and 4 are *adjectives*.

1 There is a <u>harbour</u> in Sydney.
2 There is a <u>museum</u> in my city.
3 Mumbai is a <u>busy</u> city.
4 My city is <u>big</u>.

Which words below are nouns? Which words are adjectives? Use your dictionary. Write *n* or *adj* next to the words. (Dictionaries often use *n* for nouns and *adj* for adjectives.)

1 international *adj*   7 quiet
2 kilometre   8 shop
3 lovely   9 small
4 noisy   10 station
5 peaceful   11 university
6 port   12 zoo

WRITING SKILLS:
a description of a city

City Factfile: **TORONTO**

1 _____

Toronto is in the southeast of Canada, in Ontario. It is on Lake Ontario.

2 _____

In the summer Toronto is warm (25°C) and in the winter it is very cold (–10°C).

3 _____

Toronto is a big city. The population is 2.5 million.

4 *General description*

Toronto is a modern and busy city. There is a beautiful harbour. There are a lot of museums, theatres and restaurants.

5 _____

Chinatown – there are a lot of restaurants and Chinese shops here.

The CN Tower – there is a restaurant and a theatre at the top of the tower. The views are wonderful.

Niagara Falls – this beautiful tourist centre is 160km from Toronto.

The CN Tower

Niagara Falls

CANADA

Toronto •

Lake
Ontario

Niagara •

USA

10 Look at the Toronto City Factfile for tourists. Match these headings with the correct section 1–5 of the factfile.

- General description
- Location
- Tourist attractions
- Size
- Climate

11a Adjectives Adjectives make descriptions interesting. Which of these words are adjectives and which are nouns? Use your dictionary.

1 beautiful *adj*	6 summer
2 busy	7 view
3 Chinese	8 warm
4 modern	9 wonderful
5 population	

11b Write an adjective from Exercise 11a next to the correct description. Use your dictionary to help you and to check your answers.

1 It isn't hot, it isn't cold.   It's *warm*.

2 It's new.   It's _____.

3 It's full of people, cars and noise.   It's _____.

4 It isn't ugly.   It's _____.

5 It's very good.   It's _____.

12 Linkers We use *and* to join two sentences or ideas. Look at the examples, then join the pairs 1–6 below.

*Toronto is a modern city. + Toronto is a busy city. = Toronto is a modern **and** busy city.*

*There is a restaurant at the top of the tower. + There is a theatre at the top of the tower. = There is a restaurant **and** a theatre at the top of the tower.*

1 London is a big city. + London is an expensive city.

2 There are museums in the city. + There are theatres in the city.

3 Venice is a small city. + Venice is a beautiful city.

4 There are canals in the city. + There are a lot of churches in the city.

5 Sydney is a large city. + Sydney is a noisy city.

6 There is an opera house. + There is a beautiful harbour.

13 Write a factfile for your city or another city.

- Note information about the city.
- Put the information into sections, e.g. *Location, Climate …*
- Write sentences for each section. Use adjectives. Use *and*.

2 Work and study

In this unit

Grammar
- present simple

Vocabulary
- places of work

Scenario
- In an office

Study skills
- using your dictionary (2)

Writing skills
- a CV

2.1 WORKING LIFE

The only place where success comes before work is in a dictionary.
Vidal Sassoon, 1928– , British hair stylist

VOCABULARY: jobs and places of work

1a Match the nouns below with the photos A–G on this page.

> an accountant   a doctor   a lawyer
> a businessman/businesswoman
> a lecturer   a pilot   a web designer

A – a web designer

1b Where do the people in photos A–G work? Choose from the words in the box.

> in a court   in a hospital   in an office
> on a plane   in a shop   in a university

A – in an office

2 Do you know anyone who does these jobs? What jobs do people in your family do?

I'm a businesswoman.

My father is a lecturer.

READING

The businesswoman Youna Kim

Youna is a fashion buyer. She's 31 and she lives in Seoul, in South Korea. She works for a big clothes shop. She says, 'I love my job. I go to a lot of countries and I buy clothes. But I don't wear them. They're for the shop – it sells the clothes.' Youna meets a lot of people in her job, but she doesn't meet any famous fashion designers!

The pilots Jos van der Linde and Marco van den Berg

Jos and Marco are pilots. Jos is 38 and Marco is 42. They live in Amsterdam, in Holland. They fly from Amsterdam to airports in Europe – for example, London, Rome and Frankfurt. They don't fly to the USA or to East Asia. Jos says, 'We like our jobs. We speak a lot of English and – in good weather – we see beautiful mountains, lakes and beaches.'

3 Read the articles on page 14. Are these sentences true or false?

1 Youna is 28.   *false*

2 Youna works for a small clothes shop.

3 She doesn't sell clothes.

4 She designs clothes.

5 Jos and Marco fly to Rome.

6 They don't speak English.

4 Who says these things – Youna or Marco?

1 'The clothes aren't for me.'   *Youna*

2 'I go to two or three countries in one day.'

3 'I don't live in Europe.'

4 'I see a lot of blue sky.'

5 'In good weather my job is great.'

GRAMMAR: present simple

We use the present simple tense to talk about:

a) things that are generally/always true.

b) things that happen again and again.

5 Match sentences 1–4 with a) or b) above.

1 I *go* to a lot of countries.

2 We *like* our jobs.

3 They *live* in Amsterdam.

4 Youna *meets* a lot of people.

6 Find verbs in the articles on page 14 to complete the sentences.

1 Youna *works* for a clothes shop.

2 She says, 'I _____ clothes.'

3 She _____ _____ any famous fashion designers.

4 Jos and Marco _____ in Amsterdam.

5 They _____ _____ to East Asia.

6 Jos says, 'We _____ beautiful mountains.'

7 Complete the table. Use the articles and Exercise 6 to help you.

Affirmative (+)	Negative (–)
I meet	I ³ _____ _____ (do not meet)
he / she / it ¹ *meets*	he / she / it ⁴ _____ _____ (does not meet)
you meet	you don't meet (do not meet)
we ² _____	we don't meet (do not meet)
they meet	they ⁵ _____ _____ (do not meet)

➡ Language reference and extra practice, pages 124–125

8 Choose the correct form.

1 Irina *live/lives* in Frankfurt.

2 Pilots *fly/flies* planes.

3 Carlos *doesn't/don't* like doctors.

4 Accountants *doesn't/don't* work in a court.

5 A web designer *use/uses* a computer.

6 Lecturers and lawyers *don't/doesn't* work in a shop.

9 Make true sentences about yourself, using the verbs in brackets.

1 My parents _____ Spanish. (speak)

2 My mother _____ in an office. (work)

3 I _____ a lot of coffee. (drink)

4 I _____ a lot of clothes. (buy)

5 I _____ in East Asia. (live)

6 My friends _____ to the beach in summer. (go)

SPEAKING

10a Write about yourself. Then give your notes to a partner.

My name is _____

My job is _____

I live _____

I work/study _____

I like _____

I don't like _____

I _____

10b Tell the class about your partner.

Anna lives in Moscow. She's a student. She studies at Moscow University. She likes clothes and music, but she doesn't like opera. She …

> **GRAMMAR TIP**
>
> Verbs ending in -*y*, for example *to fly* or *to study*, usually change to -*ies* in the present simple after *he / she / it*:
>
> *She flies. He studies. (But She buys.)*
>
> **Note:** for more spelling changes, see Language reference, page 124

CENTRAL AUCKLAND UNIVERSITY

Education for life

| About us | Main Courses | Students | ▼ | Staff | Clubs and Societies | Application |

Students

>> Summer schools

>> Student Services

>> Accommodation

>> Student Life

International Students' Office

The top eight student questions

a ....
You need an IELTS or TOEFL qualification with the following minimum scores: IELTS 6.0. TOEFL 550.

b ....
Yes, it does. We give you an official letter to help you.

c ....
No, it doesn't. We have short one-month courses but we don't have one-year foundation courses.

d ....
Yes, it does. These are available for all foreign students. We also have study skills classes.

e ....
Yes, there are. The exams are in June every year.

f ....
No, they don't. Students live in the halls of residence on campus and in private flats off campus.

g ....
Yes, they do. The kitchens have everything you need. Ten people share each kitchen.

h ....
Yes, they do. Students work in cafés, bars and shops.

READING

1a Look at part of a page from a New Zealand university website. Is it for lecturers, students from New Zealand or foreign students?

1b Look at the blue boxes. Find links to the information below.

1 The history of the university   *About us*

2 The student football teams

3 Lecturers and professors

4 Flats and halls of residence

2 Read the web page. Match questions 1–8 with the answers a–h on the page.

1 Does the university have a foundation course?   <u>c</u>

2 Does the university help with my visa application?

3 What qualifications do I need?

4 Do all the students live in halls of residence?

5 Are there exams every year?

6 Does the university give extra English language classes?

7 Do students have part-time jobs?

8 Do the halls of residence have kitchens?

3 Read the web page again. Are these sentences true or false?

1 An IELTS score of 7.5 is good for this university. *true*

2 The university writes a visa letter for students.

3 Students do a one-year course before their main course.

4 The university gives classes to help you study.

5 There are exams every year.

6 Students live in different places.

7 Students do not cook in the halls of residence.

8 Students do not have time to have a job.

GRAMMAR: present simple questions

4a Look at the questions in Exercise 2 and answers on the web page. Choose the correct word.

1 We form present simple questions with *do* or *is/does* + verb.

2 The verb is in the infinitive, <u>with/without</u> to.

3 In short answers with *yes*, we use <u>do</u> or <u>does</u>; in short answers with <u>no</u>, we use <u>do/don't</u> or <u>doesn't</u>.

4 We <u>use / don't use</u> the verb *do* with *to be*.

2.2

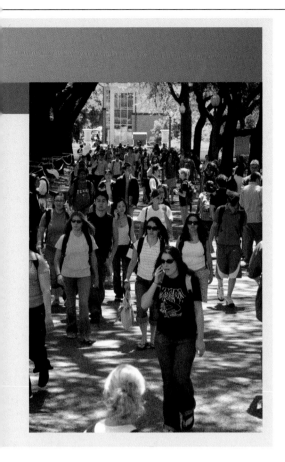

4b Complete the table with the correct words. Use the verb *to teach*.

Yes/No
1 _Do_ I / you / we / they ____ in a university?
2 ____ he / she ____ in a university?
Question word
3 What subject ____ I / you / we / they ____?
4 What subject ____ he / she ____?

➡ Language reference and extra practice, pages 124–125

5 Complete the questions with *do* or *does*. Then underline the correct answer for you.

1 _Do_ you like English?
– Yes, I do. / No, I don't.

2 _____ your brother go to university?
– Yes, he does. / No, he doesn't.

3 _____ your mother work?
– Yes, she does. / No, she doesn't.

4 _____ you have a lesson this afternoon?
– Yes, we do. / No, we don't.

5 _____ your parents speak English?
– Yes, they do. / No, they don't.

6 What languages _____ you study?
– English, Chinese, Arabic and Spanish.

6a Put the words in the right order to make questions.

Questions about work

1 do What you job have ? *What job do you have?*

2 Do work for you a small company ?

3 in a normal day do do What you ?

4 you your like job Do ?

Questions about study

5 go to school, Do college or university you ?

6 What study subjects you do ?

7 course you Do like your ?

8 live Do you hall of residence in a ?

6b Work with a partner. Does he/she work or study? Ask the questions from Exercise 6a.

LISTENING

7 [1.11] A language school in the UK wants to know about the lives and habits of its students. Listen to an interview with Gina, a student, and complete the questions in the survey.

Survey of English Language Students		*Gina*
Study habits 1 Do you _study_ English at the weekend? 2 Do you _bring_ a dictionary to class? 3 Do you ____ a computer? 4 Do you ____ the library and study centre?	*yes*	**More information** *Sunday, an hour*
Work, travel and home life 5 Do you also ____ a job? 6 Do you ____ to school by train, bus or car? 7 Do you ____ alone, with family or with friends?		
Free time 8 Do you ____ your classmates outside school? 9 Do you ____ sports? 10 What other things do you ____ in your free time?		

8 Listen again. Complete the survey for Gina.

SPEAKING AND WRITING

9 Your college wants to find out about the lives of its students. Use the questions from Exercise 7 and interview other students. Make notes of their answers.

10 Write sentences about different students from your survey.

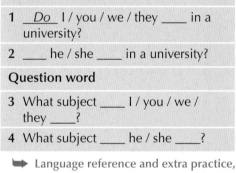

David studies English at the weekend. He doesn't bring a …

1 What do people do in an office? Complete the phrases with the verbs in the box.

> answer   do   go to   organise
> send   use   ~~write~~

1 _write_ / _____ a letter / an email
2 _____ a letter / an email / the phone
3 _____ a computer / the Internet / a photocopier
4 _____ a meeting / lunch / work
5 _____ the filing / the photocopying
6 _____ a meeting / an event

2 Discuss these questions with a partner.
1 Do you have a job?
2 Do you work in an office?
3 What work do people do in an office?

3a Match the phrases a–e with the phrases 1–10. Use each phrase twice.
a) communication skills   b) computer skills
c) qualifications   d) salary   e) working hours

1 write good letters   _a_
2 a school certificate
3 use the Internet
4 a degree in chemistry
5 Saturdays, from 10 to 6
6 20,000 euros per year
7 Monday to Friday, from 9 to 5
8 talk at a meeting
9 2,000 dollars a month
10 use a database programme

3b Complete the questions with words from a–e in Exercise 3a. Work with a partner and ask and answer the questions.
1 Do you have good computer _skills_?
2 Do you have good _____ skills?
3 What is a good _____ in your country?
4 What school _____ do you have?
5 What are your working _____?

4 [1.12] Petra wants a new job. She goes to an employment agency. Listen to the conversation and tick (✓) the information she gets. Does she want the job?

location ✓   company address   working hours
holidays   salary   work duties

5 Listen again and complete Petra's notes below.

Office Assistant

Company name: DP Computer Export
Location: 1 _city_ centre
Transport: good
Working hours: 2 _____ a.m. to 5.30 p.m.,
Monday to 3 _____
Salary: 4 _____ per month

Work duties
- 5 _____ the phone, write and send
  6 _____ and 7 _____
- do the 8 _____ and the photocopying

Qualifications/Skills
- school 9 _____
- basic 10 _____
- good computer and communication skills

KEY LANGUAGE: asking for information (1)

6 **1.13** Complete these questions. Listen and check.

1 What *information* do you want?
2 Where is _____?
3 Is it in the _____ centre?
4 What are the working hours and _____?
5 What does an _____ assistant do?
6 What are the work _____?
7 What _____ do I need?
8 What _____ do I need?

pronunciation

7a **1.14** **Word stress** There are three syllables in the word *Internet*:

In - ter - net

Write the number of syllables in each word. Then listen and check.

1 duties
2 Internet   _3_
3 information
4 office
5 salary
6 qualification

7b **1.15** Listen again to the pronunciation of *Internet*. How do we pronounce it?

a) Ínternet   b) Intérnet   c) Internét

7c Listen again to the other words from Track 1.14 and mark the word stress. Practise the words with a partner.

8a Look at Track 1.12 on page 146. Listen to the conversation again and mark the word stress on the words in italics.

8b Practise the conversation with a partner.

TASK: asking and answering questions

9 Work with a partner to find out about different jobs.

Student A: You work at an employment agency. Answer your partner's questions about the project manager job on page 110.

Student B: You want a job. Find out about the project manager job. Use the Key language to ask your partner for information and complete the notes below.

Job Title:
Company name:
Location:
Transport:
Working hours:
Salary:
Work duties
•
•
•
Qualifications/Skills
•
•

Swap roles. Do the role-play again.

Student A: Find out about the administration officer job.

Student B: Answer your partner's questions about the administration officer job on page 115.

10 Choose a job for you (the office assistant job, the project manager job or the administration officer job). Tell your partner why you want that job.

I want the administration officer job. The hours are good and the salary isn't bad. There's good transport.

I don't want the office assistant job. The salary isn't good and I think it's boring.

STUDY SKILLS: using your dictionary (2)

1 `1.16` **Word stress** Listen and choose the correct word stress.

1 employ·ment   employ·ment

2 lec·ture   lec·ture

3 or·gan·ise   or·gan·ise

4 pho·to·copy   pho·to·copy

2 Look at the dictionary entries for these words. How does the dictionary show word stress? Is this the same as your dictionary?

> **em·ploy·ment** /ɪmˈplɔɪmənt/ *noun* [no plural] *formal* **work that you do to earn money**: *Students had to leave school and find employment.*

> **lec·ture¹** /ˈlektʃə $ ˈlektʃɚ/ *noun* a talk to a group of people that teaches them about a subject: *What time is the lecture? | a lecture on Beethoven*
> **lec·ture²** *verb* to teach a group of people about a subject: *Dr Marks lectures in biology.*

> **or·gan·ise** /ˈɔːgənaɪz $ ˈɔrgəˌnaɪz/ *verb*
> to plan or arrange an event or activity: *The school has organised a trip to the sea.*

> **pho·to·cop·y¹** /ˈfəʊtəʊˌkɒpi $ ˈfoʊtəˌkɑpi/ *noun, plural* **photocopies** a copy of a document that you make using a photocopier: *Send a photocopy of your certificate to the college.*
> **pho·to·cop·y²** *verb* **photocopied, photocopies** to make a copy of a document using a photocopier: *Could you photocopy this article, please?*

from Longman Wordwise Dictionary

3a What is the word stress of these words? Put them in the correct columns (A–D). Then check in your dictionary.

| accountant company complete |
| design designer email location |
| ~~organise~~ pilot visit |

A	B	C	D
••	••	•••	•••
		organise	

3b `1.17` Listen and repeat the words.

4 In the dictionary entries in Exercise 2, why are there numbers after the words *lecture* and *photocopy*?

5a Which of the words in Exercise 3a are verbs, nouns or both? Work with a partner to complete the table. Check in your dictionary.

Student A: Check the words in columns A and B in Exercise 3a.

Student B: Check the words in columns C and D in Exercise 3a.

Verb	Noun	Verb and noun

Which word is a verb and an adjective?

5b Complete these sentences with the correct form of a word from the table above.

1 An <u>accountant</u> manages a company's money.
2 I send about 50 _____ a day.
3 The office is in a good _____, near the station.
4 In his job, he _____ a lot of different countries.
5 The architect _____ a building, then the builders build it.
6 She works for a famous _____ – Nike.
7 Sarah is a _____. She works for British Airways.
8 _____ the form. Then, send it to the company.
9 In his job, he _____ the meetings for his boss.
10 The fashion _____ chooses the colours.

WRITING SKILLS: a CV

6 Read this job advertisement and Nina Cassidy's CV on page 21. Do you think she is a good person for the job? Why / Why not?

> ### CONRAD WEB DESIGN
>
> **Conrad Web Design** needs a **Project Manager** for their Paris office
>
> **Duties:** manage a team of web designers
>
> **Skills/Experience:**
> - excellent communicator
> - manage project accounts/money
> - university education
> - organise meetings and visits to clients
> - project/event management
>
> **Salary:** €27,000 per year
>
> Email your CV to Conrad@ConradWebDesign.fr

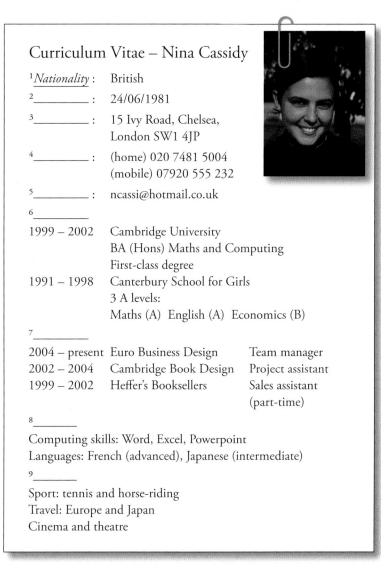

Curriculum Vitae – Nina Cassidy

[1]*Nationality* :	British
[2]_____ :	24/06/1981
[3]_____ :	15 Ivy Road, Chelsea, London SW1 4JP
[4]_____ :	(home) 020 7481 5004 (mobile) 07920 555 232
[5]_____ :	ncassi@hotmail.co.uk

[6]_____

1999 – 2002	Cambridge University BA (Hons) Maths and Computing First-class degree
1991 – 1998	Canterbury School for Girls 3 A levels: Maths (A) English (A) Economics (B)

[7]_____

2004 – present	Euro Business Design	Team manager
2002 – 2004	Cambridge Book Design	Project assistant
1999 – 2002	Heffer's Booksellers	Sales assistant (part-time)

[8]_____

Computing skills: Word, Excel, Powerpoint
Languages: French (advanced), Japanese (intermediate)

[9]_____

Sport: tennis and horse-riding
Travel: Europe and Japan
Cinema and theatre

7 Fill the gaps 1–9 on the CV with these section headings.

Address	Interests
Date of birth	~~Nationality~~
Education/Training	Other Skills
Email	Telephone
Employment	

8 Are these sentences about Nina true or false?

1 Nina lives in the UK. *true*
2 Her degree result is not very good.
3 She is good at maths.
4 She has experience of work in a bookshop.
5 She has basic French.
6 She likes to stay at home.

9a **Capital letters** Look at Nina's CV. Which types of word have a capital letter at the beginning?

people's names   cities   languages   sports   companies   countries   streets   school and university names   nationalities   levels of language (e.g. beginner)

cities – London

9b Look at this information from another CV. Which words need capital letters? Correct the capitalization.

martin jeffers – *name*
canadian
22 rose street, london
london metropolitan university
ma (business and computing)

world computer company
russian (elementary)
football
music: guitar and piano

10 Now match each piece of information with a section heading from Exercise 7.

11 Write your CV. Remember to put something in each section.

3.1 WET AND DRY

Water, water, everywhere
Nor any drop to drink.
Samuel Taylor Coleridge,
1772–1834, English poet

READING

1 Read this quiz and answer the questions with a partner. Check the answers on page 121.

What do you know about water?

1 When is it good to drink a cup of hot water and lemon?
a) early in the morning   b) late at night

2 What percentage of an iceberg is under the water?
a) 70 percent   b) 90 percent

3 At what temperature does water boil?
a) 50 °C   b) 100 °C

4 Which town doesn't have a lot of rain?
a) Antofagasta, Chile   b) Reykjavik, Iceland

5 Who uses about 500 litres of water a day?
a) a Chinese person   b) an American person

6 Why do people need to drink a lot of water?
a) because a lot of our body is water
b) because water has a lot of vitamins

7 Where in the world is there almost no water?
a) in the mountains   b) in the deserts

8 How do people in the desert wash their dishes?
a) with sand   b) with water

VOCABULARY: verbs connected with water

2a Which of these verbs are connected with using water? Check new verbs in your dictionary.

boil change cook drink find freeze
make sleep stop swim wash waste

2b Complete these questions with one of the verbs in Exercise 2a.

1 Do you _drink_ a lot of tea in the morning?

2 Do you _____ water to make coffee?

3 Do you _____ in the sea or in a swimming pool?

4 Do you _____ dinner in the evening?

5 Do you _____ your car every week?

6 Do you _____ two litres of water every day?

2c Now ask and answer the questions with a partner.

Do you drink a lot of tea in the morning?
– No, I don't like tea.

LISTENING

3a What do we call a place with almost no water? (Look at the quiz in Exercise 1.) Match photos A–E with these words.

| cactus | camel | plant | rock | sand |

3b Do you know the names of any deserts? Where are they?

4a `1.18` Dr Steve Simmonds is on a TV programme about deserts. Before you listen, tick (✓) the things you think he talks about. Then listen and check.

rain temperature the sea lemons animals
food money

4b Listen to the interview again and tick (✓) the ideas you hear.

1 Deserts are not all the same.
2 There's almost no water in deserts.
3 Life in deserts is difficult.
4 Dangerous animals live in deserts.
5 People don't live in deserts.
6 Desert people don't stay in one place.

4c `1.19` Listen to the first part of the interview and complete the sentences with a number.

1 In hot deserts, the temperature changes from _____ degrees in the day to _____ at night.
2 Only _____ percent of the world's deserts are sand.
3 Deserts have a maximum of _____ millimetres of rain a year.

4d `1.20` Listen to the second part of the interview and complete the notes.

Life in the desert

Animals: a lot of them ¹ _sleep_ in the day. They ² _____ for food at night.

Plants: the Saguaro cactus ³ _____ five tonnes of water in its body.

People: they ⁴ _____ from place to place. In Australia they ⁵ _____ desert plants and ⁶ _____.

GRAMMAR: question words

5a Look at the quiz in Exercise 1 and Track 1.18 on page 147. Underline the question words, for example *What*.

5b Complete the seven question words in the box. Then use them to complete sentences 1–7.

| wha_t_ whe_ whe__ wh_ wh_ h__ whi__ |

1 *What* asks about a thing or an idea.
2 _____ asks about a person.
3 _____ asks about a place.
4 _____ asks about time.
5 _____ asks about the way we do something.
6 _____ asks about the reason for something.
7 _____ asks about a choice between two or more things.

> **GRAMMAR TIP**
>
> We sometimes use *What ... ?* and *Which ... ?* with a noun:
> *What percentage ... ? Which languages ... ?*

➡ Language reference and extra practice, pages 126–127

6 Choose the correct question word to complete these questions. Then ask and answer the questions with a partner.

1 *When / Who / Where* do you live?
2 *How / What / Who* do you study English?
3 *Which / Why / What* do you want to learn English?
4 *How / Who / Why* do you remember from your first school?
5 *Who / Where / What* do you meet your friends?
6 *Where / Which / How* hand do you write with, your left or your right hand?
7 *Why's / What's / When's* your favourite city?
8 *What / Who / When* do you drink coffee?

SPEAKING

7 Work with a partner to find out some more facts about water.

Student A: Look at the information on page 110.
Student B: Look at the information on page 115.

3.2

<table>
<tr><td>**VOCABULARY:**
words connected with water</td></tr>
</table>

1a Put these words in the correct column in the table.

dive dolphin float jump ~~lake~~ ocean penguin sea seagull shark tuna whale

Animals	Places	Actions (verbs)
	lake	

1b Now complete the sentences with words from Exercise 1a in the singular or plural form.

1 Hawaii is in the Pacific *Ocean*.

2 Dolphins _____ out of the sea.

3 _____ live in Antarctica.

4 _____ is a popular food all over the world.

5 _____ are very noisy birds.

6 _____ are dangerous fish.

7 The River Nile enters the Mediterranean _____.

READING

2 Look quickly at the information leaflet for a whale-watching trip. Then answer the questions.

1 Where is the tour?

2 When are there trips?

3 Which types of whale do people see?

3 Read the leaflet and number the names of these five animals in order of size, from big to small.

minke whale   humpback whale   ~~fin whale~~ killer whale   bottlenose dolphin

1 fin whale

4 Read the leaflet again and answer these questions.

1 Which animals are good singers? *humpback whales*

2 Which animals have long lives?

3 Which animals do not swim in large groups?

4 Which animals are a danger to other whales?

5 Which animals are good for photographs?

6 Which animals don't visit the North Atlantic Ocean?

West Ireland
WHALE WATCH

Daily trips, 1 p.m. and 5 p.m.
On our trips we see a wide range of whales, dolphins and sea birds. Use this information leaflet on your trip.

Humpback whales
Length: 15m
Weight: 30 tonnes
These whales are famous for their long songs and big jumps. We sometimes see them, about three times a week, but they're never around for long, so be ready to take a photo.

Killer whales
Length: 8m
Weight: 8 tonnes
These animals eat 400 kilograms every day and they often eat other whales. We occasionally see them, about twice a month: let's hope we're lucky.

GRAMMAR: adverbs of frequency

5a Look at the leaflet and complete the two sentences with a), b) or c).

a) 100 percent   b) 50 percent   c) 0 percent

1 They see bottlenose dolphins on _____ of their trips.

2 They see grey whales on _____ of their trips.

5b Which words in the leaflet give this information? Complete the sentences.

1 We _____ see them. We guarantee great photos!

2 We _____ see them because they live in the Pacific Ocean.

Words like *always* and *never* are adverbs of frequency. We use them to talk about routines and habits. We use these adverbs to answer the question *How often … ?*:
How often do they see grey whales? – Never.

Minke whales
Length: 10m
Weight: 10 tonnes
These creatures usually swim alone, but they sometimes feed in pairs. We usually see them because they like cold water.

Fin whales
Length: 20m
Weight: 80 tonnes
Fin whales live for up to 100 years. They are common in the North Atlantic and we often see them near Ireland.

Bottlenose dolphins
Length: 3m
Weight: 500kg
These dolphins are very active and jump very high. We always see them. We guarantee great photos every day!

People often ask us about grey whales, but we never see them because they live in the Pacific Ocean.

6 Find three more adverbs of frequency in the leaflet and complete the table.

We see	Adverb	
bottlenose dolphins	*always*	100%
minke whales		
fin whales	*often*	
humpback whales		50%
killer whales		
grey whales	*never*	0%

➡ Language reference and extra practice, pages 126–127

7a Complete these sentences from the leaflet.

1 … we _____ see them near Ireland.

2 … they're _____ around for long, so be ready to take a photo.

3 … we _____ see them because they live in the Pacific Ocean.

7b Does the adverb of frequency go before or after *to be*? Does it go before or after other verbs?

8 Look at these expressions of frequency. Put them in order.

every day ☐1 once a year ☐ weekly ☐
twice a month ☐ three times a week ☐

9a Find expressions of frequency in the leaflet. Do we put them:

a) after the verb and other words?

b) after the subject, before the verb?

c) before the subject?

9b Put the words in the right order to make sentences.

1 We … see never blue whales
   We never see blue whales.

2 Dolphins … groups live in usually large

3 Baby fin whales … every day 230 drink litres of milk.

4 Blue whales … out of never the water jump

5 Humpback whales … for dive 45 minutes occasionally

6 Killer whales … fish sometimes eat

7 Blue whales … travel to once a year the Arctic

8 Grey whales … in the Pacific Ocean are near America often

10 Add an adverb or expression of frequency to these sentences and make them true for you.

1 I swim in the sea.
2 I eat tuna.
3 I drink coffee.
4 I visit my grandmother.
5 I use the Internet.
6 I travel by boat.
7 I go to the cinema.
8 I play sport.
9 I read a newspaper.
10 I play computer games.

1 I often swim in the sea.

SPEAKING AND WRITING

11a Ask a partner about his/her routines and habits. Use the ideas in Exercise 10 and your own ideas. Use the question *How often … ?*

How often do you play sport? – Every week.

11b Write sentences about the differences between you and your partner.

Irina plays sport every week but I play sport once or twice a month.

A

B

PREPARATION

1 Read about the water festivals and match the photos A–C with the festivals 1–3.

1 **The Songkran Water Festival**
This traditional festival is the start of the Thai New Year in April. On day one, Thais clean their houses, visit temples with food and visit old relatives. Day two is the famous 'water-throwing day' when people throw water at each other. No one is safe – not even police officers! On day three, there are dance shows and music concerts.

2 **The Abu Dhabi F1 Water Festival**
This five-day festival in December is part of the World Powerboat Championship. There are a lot of races and competitions (powerboat, water ski jumping and jet ski) for international teams. The festival starts with a big parade, there is a large boat show and there is a lot of international food.

3 **The Vilagarcia Water Festival**
This festival takes place on August 16th in northern Spain. After a parade, people in the houses throw water on the people in the streets. After this, there is a drum dance and then the people jump in the sea!

C

2 Complete the first three rows of the table with information about the festivals.

Festival	Month	Days	Example activities
Songkran			*visit temples*
Abu Dhabi F1			
Vilagarcia			
Lowell			

3 Every year the city of Lowell in the USA has a Southeast Asian Water Festival. This is a free cultural event and over 60,000 people from all over the world come to it. Look at the programme and complete the table in Exercise 2.

Lowell Water Festival August 18th–19th

River area	Stage 1	Stage 2
Friday evening **Parade** by river (traditional clothes) **Candle ceremony**	**Dance show** (Laos national flower dance and modern dance)	1_____ (Cambodian traditional then Malaysian pop)
Saturday morning **Save Water Now** (talk by Professor Rees) **Boat tour of river** (history of the river and canal)	**Fashion show** (designs from Asia) 2_____ (learn Asian styles)	**Thai boxing** (watch and learn) **Drum workshop** (learn to play and make drums)
Saturday afternoon **Traditional boat races**	3_____ (Thai, Burmese, Cambodian)	**Children's activities** (face painting, games)
Saturday evening **Short films from Thailand** (open air cinema)	**Barbecue and party** ($20 charge)	4_____ (Burmese)

4a **1.21** Listen to the Lowell Festival committee meeting about the programme. How many people speak at the meeting? What are their names?

4b Listen again to the conversation and complete the missing information 1–4 on the programme.

4c Listen again. Who makes these suggestions, Andy, Li or Cassie?

1 the music show on Friday evening *Cassie*
2 the dance workshop on Saturday afternoon
3 the international food market on Saturday afternoon
4 the drum concert on Saturday evening
5 something to eat
6 a burger

> **KEY LANGUAGE:**
> **making suggestions**

5 Complete these questions from the conversation.

1 *Does* anyone have any ideas for the last few spaces?
2 _____ about having a music show on Friday evening?
3 _____ about Saturday evening?
4 _____ would you like to have then, Li?
5 _____ don't we have a drum concert then?

6 Which of the questions in Exercise 5 ask for ideas, which ones make suggestions?

7 Look at Track 1.21 on page 147 and find two other ways to make suggestions. Complete the sentences below. What are the three different forms of the main verb?

1 *What about* having a music show on Friday evening?
2 _____ have the dance workshop on Saturday afternoon.
3 _____ _____ to have the international food market in the afternoon.
4 _____ _____ _____ have a drum concert then?

8 Complete these suggestions with the correct form of *go, play* or *visit*. Use each verb twice.

1 Why don't we *visit* a museum this weekend?
2 Let's _____ tennis this weekend.
3 What about _____ to the cinema this weekend?
4 I'd like _____ to the theatre this weekend.
5 What about _____ an art gallery this weekend?
6 I'd like _____ football this weekend.

pronunciation

9a **1.22** **Showing interest** Listen to the end of the conversation and answer the questions.

1 Does Andy think having the food market in the afternoon is a really good idea?
2 Does Andy think going for something to eat is a really good idea?
3 Does Cassie think having a burger is a really good idea?

9b **1.23** Listen to the word *OK*. Which intonation shows strong interest or enthusiasm and which shows weak interest or no enthusiasm, a) or b)?

Listen to and repeat the other examples of strong interest from the conversation.

10 **1.24** Listen to some more examples. Which intonation do you hear? Strong Interest (SI) or Weak Interest (WI)?

1 Great idea. *WI*   2 Yes.   3 Excellent.   4 OK.
5 Fantastic.   6 Great.

Now practise with a partner. Your partner says a word: which intonation do you hear? Then swap roles.

11 With your partner, make and respond to suggestions about this weekend. Use the language in Exercises 7 and 10.

Let's go to the cinema.
– Great idea!

> **TASK: making and responding**
> **to suggestions**

12a Look at the completed programme for the Lowell Festival. Choose the events you would like to go to or the things you would like to see. Choose one event for each time period.

12b In pairs or groups, decide and agree what to do at the festival. Make suggestions and reply to your partners' ideas. Use the Key language from the conversation and the practice exercises.

> **OTHER USEFUL PHRASES**
>
> | | |
> |---|---|
> | That sounds fun/good. | I don't want to do that. |
> | That sounds interesting. | That sounds boring. |
> | Good idea. | I'm not sure. |
> | So, on Saturday, it's … | In the evening, it's … |

STUDY SKILLS: classroom language

1 Classroom objects Work with a partner. Are these things in your classroom, or do you have them on your desk / in your bag?

a blackboard	a DVD player
a CD player	an English-English dictionary
a chair	a notebook
a computer	a pen / a pencil
a coursebook	a whiteboard

2a Classroom instructions Who usually says these sentences – the teacher, the student or both?

1 Open your books at page 28.
2 Work in pairs.
3 Do you understand?
4 Sorry, what do you mean?
5 Work on your own.
6 Check your ideas with your partner.
7 Can you repeat that, please?
8 What's the answer to number 1?
9 I don't know.
10 Close your books.

2b Sentences a–e have similar meanings to five of the sentences in Exercise 2a. Match them with the sentences.
a) Sorry, I don't understand.
b) I have no idea.
c) Look at page 28.
d) Can you say that again, please?
e) Work with a partner.

3a Questions about a word The questions below are common in a classroom. Complete the questions with the question words in the box.

How	~~What~~	Where	What	How	What	How

1 *What* does 'glacier' mean?
2 _____ part of speech is 'glacier'?
3 _____ do you spell 'glacier'?
4 _____ is the word stress in 'glacier'?
5 _____ do you pronounce it?
6 _____ do you say 'glacier' in Polish?
7 _____ is *lodowiec* in English?

3b `1.25` Match the questions from Exercise 3a with these answers. Then listen and check.
a) G-L-A-C-I-E-R.
b) It's on the first syllable.
c) In English, it's 'glacier'.
d) A large river of ice that moves down a mountain.
e) Lodowiec.
f) It's a noun.
g) /ˈɡlæsiə/

4 Asking about words Work with a partner. Ask for the English word, spelling and word stress for some pictures.

Student A: Look at pictures A–D on page 110 and ask your questions. Answer your partner's questions about pictures E–H.

Student B: Look at pictures E–H on page 115 and ask your questions. Answer your partner's questions about pictures A–D.

WRITING SKILLS: a description of a process

5a Look at the picture and find these things: the sun, the ground, mountains, clouds, the sea, rivers.

5b Now complete the sentences about the picture in Exercise 5a with the correct present simple form of these verbs.

| carry | change | ~~evaporate~~ |
| fall | form | heat | move |

1 The sun _____ the sea.
2 The water *evaporates*.
3 The water vapour _____ clouds.
4 The clouds _____ above the mountains.
5 The water vapour _____ into rain.
6 The rain _____ to the ground.
7 The rivers _____ the water to the sea.

6 Linkers Look at the phrases in the box. They show the order of different events. Complete this description of the water cycle with the phrases. Some can go in more than one gap.

| first of all, | next, | then | finally, | after that, |

¹_____ the sun heats the sea. ²_____ the water in the sea evaporates and it goes into the air. ³_____ the water vapour forms clouds. ⁴_____ the clouds move over the land and they move above the mountains. In the cold air, the water vapour changes into rain. ⁵_____ this rain falls to the ground and it goes into rivers. ⁶_____ the rivers carry the water to the sea and the cycle begins again.

7a **Pronouns *it* and *they*** Look at these three sentences. What do *it* and *they* mean?

1 … the water in the sea evaporates and *it* goes into the air. = *the water*.
2 … the clouds move over the land and *they* move above the mountains.
3 … this rain falls to the ground and *it* goes into rivers.

7b We can use the pronouns *it* and *they* to join two sentences or ideas. Look at the example, then join the pairs 1 and 2 below.

The rain falls to the ground. + ~~*The rain*~~ *goes into rivers.*
= *The rain falls to the ground **and it** goes into rivers.*

1 The water vapour goes into the air. + The water vapour forms clouds.
2 Animals go to the rivers. + Animals drink the water.

8a Choose the correct verb to describe stages in another water cycle, then check your ideas with a partner.

1 The sun *heats/~~melts~~* the sea.
2 The water *falls/evaporates*.
3 The water *becomes/changes* water vapour.
4 The water vapour *forms/moves* clouds.
5 The clouds *fall/move* above the ice.
6 The clouds *change/become* very cold.
7 The water vapour *moves/changes* into snow.
8 The snow *falls/becomes* to the ground.
9 The snow *changes/becomes* into ice.
10 The ice *heats/forms* icebergs.
11 The icebergs *evaporate/melt* and the water returns to the sea.

8b Now look at the picture of the water cycle in the Antarctic. Label the picture 1–11 with the stages of the cycle.

9 Now write a description of the water cycle in the Antarctic. Use sequencing phrases and pronouns.

GRAMMAR

1 Choose the correct verb in 1–14.

Where is the water?

A Jitbhai Chowdhury ¹*live/lives* in the village of Kushkal in India. There ²*is/are* almost no water here but Jitbhai ³*have/has* fruit trees and his cows ⁴*produce/produces* 25 litres of milk a day. So how ⁵*do/does* he ⁶*find/finds* water?

B A water pump ⁷*carry/carries* water from a lake under the ground up to Jitbhai's village. There ⁸*is/are* a lot of farmers like Jitbhai in his village, and in villages in other countries, including China and Argentina. About 10 percent of the water ⁹*is/are* from underground lakes. The farmers ¹⁰*needs/need* it to produce the food we ¹¹*buy/buys* every week from supermarkets.

A At the moment, water ¹²*isn't/aren't* a problem for Jitbhai (and the world) but we ¹³*need/needs* 11,000 litres of water to make one burger. Farmers ¹⁴*use/uses* 20,000 litres of water to produce a kilogram of coffee and 2,000 litres for one litre of milk. So what happens when there isn't any water under the ground?

2 Read paragraph A and write short answers to questions 1–5.

1 Is Jitbhai a farmer? *Yes, he is.*

2 Is Kushkal in China?

3 Does Jitbhai have fruit trees?

4 Are there cows on his farm?

5 Do his cows produce 50 litres of milk a day?

3a Read paragraphs B and C. Complete the question words.

1 Wh<u>y</u> does Jitbhai need a water pump?

2 Wh_ countries also take water from under the ground?

3 Wh_ do we buy food every week?

4 Wh_ do 2,000 litres of water make?

3b Now answer the questions in Exercise 3a.

4 Make questions. Match 1–10 with a–j.

1 Who do you   a) usually visit your city?

2 Are you a   b) 's your job?

3 Is there a university   c) student or do you work?

4 What do you   d) an airport?

5 What   e) your city?

6 Where exactly is   f) in the centre?

7 Do you live   g) study?

8 Does the city have   h) live with?

9 When do tourists   i) in your city?

10 Why do   j) they visit the city?

5a Marek, a Polish student, answers some of the questions. Match his answers a–h with questions from Exercise 4.

a) They want to see the old town in the centre. It has beautiful buildings.   <u>10</u>

b) Yes. There is. It's famous in Poland.

c) Gdańsk is in the north of Poland.

d) English and Art.

e) I'm a student.

f) With my mother and father in Gdańsk.

g) In the summer. The winter is very cold.

h) Yes, it does.

5b 1.26 Listen and check your answers.

6 Work with a partner. Ask and answer questions 1–10 in Exercise 4 for you and your cities.

VOCABULARY

7 Match the words in the box with gaps 1–10 in the factfile on page 31.

bookshops   bus tour   car parks
festival   park   market   museum
restaurants   tourist information   ~~zoo~~

UNITS 1–3

CHATTLESWORTH
in the summer.
We hope you enjoy your visit!

1 __zoo__
See animals from all over the world. Feed the dolphins at midday!

2 _____
There are over 30 in the centre, including Italian, Chinese, Indian, Thai.

3 _____
Chattlesworth is famous for books so visit Kings Street with its second-hand shops and street cafés.

4 _____
After lunch have a walk through the gardens and look at the fountains and flowers. Listen to the band. Opposite the town hall.

5 _____
Every Friday in the town square with local food and crafts for sale.

Music 6 _____
July 31st–August 2nd
Join us in the evenings in the park for outdoor music. Starts 8 p.m. Contact the 7 _____ centre for more details.

8 _____
Leaves the station every hour with stops around the town.
Also includes visit to 9 _____ and exhibition of local history.
10 _____
8 a.m.–4 p.m. $4.50
Free after 4 p.m.

8 In pairs or groups, look at the completed information in Exercise 7. You visit Chattlesworth on Friday 1st August. Make suggestions and decide what to do for the day.

KEY LANGUAGE

9 Work with a partner. Ask and answer these questions.
1 Do you often have lunch with friends?
2 Where do you go? Where is it?
3 What do you usually eat?

10 [1.27] Listen to a conversation at work. Answer questions 1–3 with a), b) or c).
1 What does Fabio ask Gill about?
   a) her job
   b) computers
   c) her new assistant
2 What does Fabio suggest?
   a) lunch with friends
   b) a coffee
   c) lunch together
3 Where is the café?
   a) near the office
   b) in the centre
   c) in the quiet part of the city

11a Find other ways to say the key language in bold. Match a–f with 1–6.
a) good   _4_
b) next to
c) when
d) Good idea!
e) Why don't we go
f) I'm not sure

FABIO: What's your job?
GILL: ¹I don't know exactly. I'm an assistant, with some computer work and filing, I think.
FABIO: Well, don't worry. ²What time do you have lunch?
GILL: At 12 o'clock.
FABIO: That's now! ³What about going together?
GILL: That sounds ⁴nice. Where do you usually eat?
FABIO: It depends. What do you want?
GILL: Something small. And a coffee.
FABIO: OK. I know a quiet café. Let's go there.
GILL: ⁵Great! Is it in the centre?
FABIO: Yes, it's ⁶on the right of the post office.
GILL: OK. Let's go.

11b Listen to the conversation again and check your answers.

LANGUAGE CHECK

12 What are the mistakes in sentences 1–10? Look at the pages to check.
                                            she is
1 Is she old? – Yes, she's.   (page 7)
2 There are lot of churches in the town.   (page 9)
3 Are there any museum in Tokyo?   (page 9)
4 My father is a accountant.   (page 14)
5 Jos and Marco fly planes. They're lawyers.   (page 14)
6 I go lunch at 2 p.m.   (page 18)
7 He uses often the Internet.   (page 25)
8 We eat every day fish.   (page 25)
9 I like to play tennis this weekend.   (page 27)
10 What means 'glacier'?   (page 28)

LOOK BACK

13 Find the exercises in Units 1–3 where you …
• learn 16 new adjectives. (U1)   2
• read an article about famous cities. (U1)
• say where places are. (U1)
• find out about two different jobs. (U2)
• listen to an interview with a student. (U2)
• write a CV. (U2)
• ask about routines and habits. (U3)
• make suggestions. (U3)
• describe a process. (U3)

4 Leisure time

4.1 SILVER SCREEN

All work and no play makes Jack a dull boy.
English proverb

VOCABULARY: types of film

1 Discuss these questions in small groups.

1 How often do you watch films?

2 Do you usually watch films at home or at the cinema? Which do you prefer? Why?

3 How often do you go to the cinema? Who do you go with?

2a Match the four film posters (A–D) with a type of film from the box.

> an action/adventure film   a romantic comedy
> an animation   a love story   a historical film
> a horror film   a musical   a comedy   a war film
> a western   a science fiction film   a thriller

2b Answer the questions about the types of film in Exercise 2a.

1 Can you think of an example of each type of film?

   Chicago *is a musical.*

2 Which types of film do you like? Why?

   I like historical films because I learn a lot about the past.

3 What types of film are on at the cinema in your town/city now?

READING

3 Read the *World Cinema* web page and tick the correct answers.

On this web page, there is information about:

1 a film from Ireland.

2 films in Iran.

3 the number of cinemas in Iran.

4 a film from Chile.

5 Hollywood films.

4 Match the words 1–5 with their meanings a–e.

1 actor

2 director

3 ordinary

4 private school

5 head teacher

a) This person controls a school.

b) It's normal, not different or unusual.

c) Students (or their parents) pay to go here.

d) You see this person in films or plays.

e) This person gives instructions to actors in a film.

WORLDCINEMA.COM

Are you tired of Hollywood blockbusters? Then this is the website for you!
We look at films from all over the world, from Ireland to Iraq, from Mali to Malaysia.

Blackboards

Country profile: Iran by Mahsa Nami

These days, Iranian films are quite popular, thanks to the work of three or four famous film directors, for example Abbas Kiarostami, Mohsen Makhmalbaf and his daughter, Samira. Iranian directors don't usually make thrillers or romantic comedies, but they make films about the lives of ordinary people, and life in the city or in the country. **Read more >>**

Machuca

This week's film: Machuca Director: Andrés Wood

This film is about two 11-year-old boys in Chile, in 1973. The two boys, Pedro Machuca and Gonzalo Infante (the excellent young actors Ariel Mateluna and Matías Quer), come from very different families. Gonzalo lives in a rich part of the capital city, Santiago, but he's unhappy at home and at school – a private school for rich children. The head teacher of the school opens it to children from the poor area … **Read more >>**

5 Read these sentences, and the web page again. Decide if they are true, false or if the text doesn't say (?).

1 People outside Iran don't like Iranian films. *?*
2 Mohsen Makhmalbaf is Samira's father.
3 Iranian directors make a lot of action films.
4 Gonzalo in *Machuca* lives in Chile, but we don't know where.
5 The rich area is near the poor area.
6 The main actors are very good.

GRAMMAR: articles

The articles are *a/an* and *the*. We usually use them like this:

a) no article with plural nouns, to talk about people or things in general.
Iranian films are popular.

b) *a/an* with a singular noun, and to talk about a person's job.
a rich part of the city

c) *the* with singular or plural nouns, to talk about a known or specific person or thing.
two 11-year-old boys in Chile … The *two boys*
the head teacher of the school

GRAMMAR TIP

Use *an*, not *a*, when the noun begins with a vowel sound: *an actor, an idea*

➡ Language reference and extra practice, pages 128–129

6 Match these sentences with grammar rules a–c.

1 A film star is a famous actor. *b*
2 Thrillers are exciting.
3 Gonzalo Infante is an 11-year-old boy.
4 I like *Machuca*. The actors are excellent.
5 Ian hates war films.
6 The musical *Grease* is still very popular.

7 Complete the sentences with *a/an, the* or no article (write Ø).

1 He's _____ actor.
2 Do you like _____ westerns?
3 Is there _____ cinema near your house?
4 What's the difference between _____ comedy and _____ romantic comedy?
5 *Tokyo Story*, by Yasujiro Ozu, is _____ number one film of all time, people say.

SPEAKING

8a Ask and answer these questions with a partner. Give reasons for your answers.

1 What's your favourite film from your country?
2 What's your favourite film from another country?
3 Who's your favourite film star/actor?
4 Who's your favourite director?

8b Tell the class about your partner.

Julia's favourite director is Pedro Almodóvar because he makes very interesting films and …

■ VOCABULARY: leisure activities, sports

1a A lot of people do exercise in their free time. What do you do?

> play basketball   play football   play tennis
> go running   go swimming   go to a fitness club
> dance   ride a bike   ski   do aerobics   do yoga
> do something different (what?)

1b Compare your answers with a partner. Use these questions.

*Do you … ?   How often do you … ?   Where do you … ?
When do you … ?*

■ LISTENING

2a `1.28` Listen to interviews with two members of a health club. Can Lisa swim? Can Dan swim?

2b Listen again and complete the questionnaire with Lisa and Dan's answers.

EXCEL Health and Fitness Club
Fitness questionnaire

	Lisa	Dan
1 How often do you come to the club?		twice a week
2 Do you use the running machines?		yes
3 Do you work out in the gym?		
4 Do you use the swimming pool?		

2c Complete these sentences from the interviews. Then listen and check your answers.

1 INT: What weight <u>*can*</u> you lift?
2 LISA: I _____ usually lift a lot, but I _____ lift 35 kilos.
3 LISA: Well, erm, I _____ swim, so I don't use it.
4 DAN: Oh, yes, I _____. I can run that in about 30 minutes.
5 DAN: I _____ swim two kilometres, but I _____ swim five kilometres.

■ GRAMMAR: *can, can't*

3 Complete these sentences with *can* or *can't*.

1 Lisa isn't a fast runner: she _____ run ten kilometres in an hour.
2 Dan is a fast runner: he _____ run ten kilometres in 30 minutes.
3 Lisa doesn't use the pool: she _____ swim.
4 Dan is a good swimmer: he _____ swim five kilometres.

4a Look at the sentences in Exercises 2c and 3. Are these statements (1–4) true or false?

1 In an affirmative sentence, we put *can* before a main verb.
2 In a question with *can*, we use *do/does*.
3 In a negative sentence with *can*, we **do not use** *don't/doesn't*.
4 When we use *can* after *he / she / it*, we add *s* to the main verb.

   ➡ Language reference and extra practice, pages 128–129

4b Tick the correct sentences and correct the mistakes in the others.

1 She can rides a horse.
2 They can to swim.
3 Can you ride a horse?
4 I can swim.
5 We don't can ski.
6 Lisa cans lift 35 kilos.
7 Do you can ride a bike?

pronunciation

5a `1.29` **Weak or strong vowel** Listen to six sentences. We can pronounce *can* with the schwa /ə/ or the strong vowel /æ/. Which sentence has the strong vowel? Practise the sentences.

5b `1.30` How do we pronounce the vowel sound in *can't*? Listen, then practise the interviews from Exercise 2a with a partner.

6 What can you do? Work with a partner. Ask and answer questions about these activities.

> drive a car   play a musical instrument
> lift 50 kilos   swim   sing an English song
> speak three languages   ride a horse

EXCEL Health and Fitness Club

Membership and opening hours

Full-time membership costs £100 per month.

Part-time membership costs £75 per month.

Opening hours

Full-time: Tues - Sun 06.30 – 22.30

Part-time: Tues – Sun 10.00 – 15.30
                                    19.30 – 22.30

Facilities and services

Gym
The gym has modern equipment, including running, cycling and rowing machines. On your first visit, a trainer teaches you about the equipment and designs an exercise plan for you.

Swimming pool
Our pool is 20 metres long and five metres wide.

Clubroom
In the clubroom there is a small café. You can buy sandwiches, fruit and drinks here. We show important sports events on the large-screen TV. Only full-time members can use the clubroom.

Classes
You can get a timetable for the classes from the reception desk. We offer the following classes: yoga, aerobics, cycling and dance.

Health and beauty centre
The health and beauty centre is for men and women. Our sunbeds are very popular. There is also a modern sauna. Part-time members cannot use the health and beauty centre.

READING

7a Read the health club leaflet and find the information below. You have two minutes!

1 the day the club is closed

2 the three machines in the gym

3 the size of the swimming pool

4 the food they sell in the café

5 the classes the club offers

7b Read the leaflet again. Answer these questions.

1 How do you learn to use the running machines?

2 Where do you go for information about class times?

3 What are the four differences between full and part-time membership?

8 Look at the leaflet and underline four sentences using _can_ or _cannot_ (_can't_) .

GRAMMAR TIP

The verb _can_ also means something is possible:
You **can** buy sandwiches, fruit and drinks here.

9 Complete the sentences 1–4 with the phrases in the box. More than one phrase can go in some gaps.

> borrow books   find information
> learn about the past   use a running machine

1 You can _____ from a library.

2 You can _____ in a fitness centre.

3 You can _____ on the Internet.

4 You can _____ in a museum.

SPEAKING

10 Choose a place from the list below. Think of three or four things you can/can't do in this place and tell a partner, but don't say the place. Can your partner guess it?

in the countryside   at home   in an Internet café
in a library   in the mountains   in a park
at the seaside   at a sports centre   in my town

You can read books. You can write. You can't buy books. – Is it a library?

PREPARATION

1 What do you do on holiday? Talk with a partner and use adverbs of frequency (see page 24).

eat in restaurants	play sports	stay on a campsite
go for walks	read books	swim in the sea
go shopping	sit on the beach	try different food
go to cafés	stay in a hotel	visit museums
make new friends		

I often visit museums on holiday.

2 Put these holiday phrases in the correct columns.

a family room   a chalet   mountain biking
scuba diving   wind-surfing   a sea view
a hiking trip   a painting class   a kids' club
a concert   a museum visit   satellite TV
a dance show   a double room

Accommodation	Sports and activities	Evening entertainment
a family room		

3 Many people go to all-inclusive resorts for their holiday. At these places you have everything you need for a holiday. Look at the advert and answer the questions.

1 Would you like to visit a Sarong holiday resort?
2 Do you like all-inclusive holidays? Why / Why not?
3 Are there any all-inclusive resorts in your country?

Sarong Holiday Resorts
THAILAND

All inclusive ◆ All ages ◆ All for fun
Great restaurants … Water sports …
Babysitters … Evening entertainment …

4a `1.31` Sarah asks the travel agent for more information. Listen and tick the things she asks about.

the bedrooms   food   the weather   sports
evening entertainment   local transport
children's activities

Do you think Sarah wants to make a reservation?

4b Listen again and answer these questions.
1 Do all the rooms have sea views?
2 Where do children sleep?
3 Can you eat breakfast in all the restaurants?
4 What sports can you do at the resort?
5 When does the babysitter work?

> **KEY LANGUAGE:**
> **asking for information (2),**
> **saying *no* politely**

5 `1.32` Complete these sentences from the conversation. Listen and check.

1 – _____ you give me some information about the Sarong Holiday Resort?
 – Yes, certainly. What would you _____ to know?
2 – First of all, can you _____ me about the accommodation, please?
 – Yes, of course. All the rooms are double rooms.
3 – Are there any family rooms?
 – No, I'm afraid _____.
4 – _____ I play other sports, tennis, for example?
 – I'm sorry. I'm afraid you _____.
5 – _____ there a kids' club in the day?
 – No, I'm afraid there _____.

pronunciation

6a `1.33` **Linked sounds** Listen to the pronunciation of *I'm afraid*. Notice the linking between *I'm* and *afraid*.

No, I'm afraid not.   I'm afraid you can't.

I'm afraid there isn't.

When the first word ends with a consonant sound and the second word begins with a vowel sound, we often link the two sounds.

6b Listen again and repeat. Find other examples of this linking on Track 1.32.

7 Find some more linked consonant-vowel sounds in Track 1.31 on page 148, then practise them with a partner.

CLUB Mexico

Quality all-inclusive resort • Beautiful beaches
Excellent water sports facilities • Great nightlife
Kids' club • Hotel accommodation

Scottish Dream

Scotland's only all-inclusive holiday resort

+ Beautiful mountains and lakes
+ Fantastic sports facilities
+ Wonderful food
+ Learn a new skill
+ Cottage-style accommodation

TASK: exchanging basic information

8a Look at the holiday resort adverts above. Which one:

1 is in the mountains?
2 has activities for children?
3 can teach you something new?
4 is good for young, active people?
5 is by the sea?

8b What are the differences between the holiday resorts?

The Scottish Dream resort is in the mountains, but the Club Mexico resort is …

8c Read more about the two resorts.

Student A: Read the holiday brochure on page 111 and complete the 'Scottish Dream' column in the table.

Student B: Read the holiday brochure on page 116 and complete the 'Club Mexico' column in the table.

9 Work with a partner and role-play a dialogue between a customer and a travel agent.

Student A: You are the customer. You are interested in Club Mexico. Ask the travel agent about it and complete your table on page 111.

Student B: You are the travel agent. Answer the customer's questions about Club Mexico.

Swap roles. Do the role-play again.

Student A: Now you are the travel agent.

Student B: Now you are the customer. Ask the travel agent about Scottish Dream and complete your table on page 116.

OTHER USEFUL PHRASES

Is there … ? (a kids' club, wind-surfing, etc.)

Are there … ? (restaurants, museum trips, etc.)

Can you tell me about … ? (the accommodation, the sports, the entertainment)

Can you give me some information about … ? (the resort, the sports, the activities)

10a Which holiday do you prefer? Why?

10b Which holiday is good for Sarah and her family? Write a few sentences to say why each holiday is good or bad for her.

I think _____ is a good place for her holiday, because she can … There is …

I don't think _____ is a good place for her holiday, because she can't … There isn't …

STUDY SKILLS:
working with numbers

1 `1.34` **Large numbers** Match the numbers with the statistics, then listen and check.

| 192 | 6,000 | 7,000 |
| 20,100,000 | 60,500,000 |

1 This is the number of people in the UK.

2 This is the number of people in Australia.

3 This is the number of countries in the world.

4 This is the number of languages in the world.

5 This is the number of tigers in the world.

2a `1.35` **Listen to these numbers. Tick the numbers that use the word *and*.**

a) 100   d) 2,300   g) 5,600,000

b) 140   e) 2,345   h) 5,670,000

c) 2,000   f) 5,000,000

2b **Listen again and repeat the numbers.**

3 **Work with a partner to practise numbers.**

Student A: Look at page 110 and read the numbers to your partner. Then listen and write your partner's numbers.

Student B: Write the numbers your partner reads. Then look at page 115 and read the numbers to your partner.

4a **Fractions and percentages** **Match the words with the numbers.**

1 a half   a) 1/4

2 a third   b) 1/5

3 a quarter   c) 1/2

4 a fifth   d) 1/3

4b **Now match the fractions in Exercise 4a with these percentages.**

1 twenty percent (20%) = _____

2 fifty percent (50%) = _____

3 thirty-three point three percent (33.3%) = _____

4 twenty-five percent (25%) = _____

4c **Write the numbers as percentages.**

1 100 out of 1,000 = _____

2 50 out of 150 = _____

3 12 out of 24 = _____

4 50 out of 250 = _____

5 30 out of 200 = _____

6 75 out of 500 = _____

WRITING SKILLS:
a description of a table or bar graph

Figure 1

Young people in England: Hours of sport a week

	Boys	Girls
Do not play	5%	5%
1 hour a week	5%	15%
5 hours a week	40%	50%
10 hours a week	25%	20%
15 hours a week	25%	10%

Adapted from *Sport England: A survey of young people and PE teachers. Source: Mori*

5 **Look at the table (Figure 1) and complete these sentences.**

1 Five percent of _____ and _____ do not play sport.

2 Two-fifths of _____ play sport for _____ a week.

3 Fifteen _____ of girls play sport for one hour a week.

4 A fifth of _____ play sport for _____ a week.

5 A _____ of boys play sport for ten hours a week.

6 Ten per cent of _____ play sport for _____ a week.

6 **Now work with a partner to exchange information and complete another table.**

Student A: Look at page 110. Tell your partner the information in your table, then listen and complete the table.

Student B: Look at page 115. Listen and complete your table, then tell your partner the information in the table.

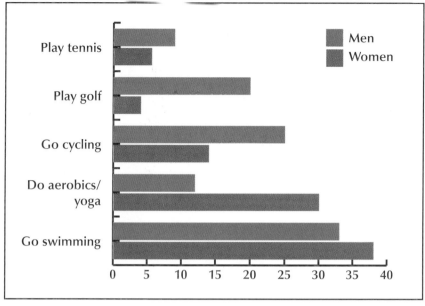

Figure 2
Adults in England: The sports they play

Adapted from Sport England: Participation in sport in England 2002.
Source: The General Household Survey 2002

7 Look at the bar graph (Figure 2) and complete these sentences.

Men

1 Over _____% of men go swimming.

2 Exactly _____% go cycling.

Women

3 Nearly _____% of women go swimming.

4 About _____% go cycling.

Tip: when we know the subject, we do not need to repeat *of men* or *of women*.

8 Approximation What do these expressions mean? Choose the correct answer.

1 over 50% = a) 49% b) 50% c) 51%

2 nearly 80% = a) 78% b) 80% c) 85%

3 exactly 60% = a) 59% b) 60% c) 61%

4 about 70% = a) 70.4% b) 70% c) 75%

9 Use the graph in Figure 2 to complete these sentences with the words in the box.

over (x1)   exactly (x2)   nearly (x2)   about (x1)

Men

1 _____ 10% of men do aerobics or yoga.

2 _____ 20% play golf.

3 _____ 10% play tennis.

Women

4 _____ 30% of women do aerobics or yoga.

5 _____ 5% play golf.

6 _____ 5% play tennis.

10a Figure 3 shows popular cultural events for adults in Britain. Complete the table with the percentage of people that go to each type of event, using the numbers in the box. Guess! Compare with a partner, then check on page 121.

63   13   16   6   25   24   61   25

Figure 3
Adults in England: Leisure and cultural events

Go to the cinema	___%
Go to the theatre	___%
Go to art exhibitions	___%
Go to the ballet and opera	___%
Go to classical music concerts	___%
Go to modern dance events	___%
Go to sports events	___%
Go to pop and rock concerts	___%

10b Write sentences to describe the table. Use the language from Exercises 7 and 8.

Nearly two-thirds of people go to sports events.

11a Ask ten different students about four or five of the leisure activities in Exercise 10. Write their answers.

Do you ever go to the cinema?

Do you ever go ... ?

11b Write sentences to describe the information that you get.

Over 50% of the students go to the cinema.

5 Transsport

In this unit

Grammar
- comparative and superlative adjectives

Vocabulary
- transport and travel

Scenario
- At a ticket agency

Study skills
- planning your written work

Writing skills
- a description of a transport system

5.1 SPEED

A

B

C

The only way to be sure of catching a train is to miss the one before it.
G.K. Chesterton, 1874–1936, British writer

VOCABULARY: transport

1a Look at the means of transport in the box. Match them with the verbs below.

| bike boat bus car lorry motorbike plane ship taxi (underground) train tram |

1 to travel/go by ... *bike, boat, ...*

2 to drive ... *a bus, a car, ...*

3 to ride ...

4 to fly ...

1b Which means of transport do you use? Which do you like / don't you like?

I usually travel by bus because buses are cheap.
I don't like motorbikes because they're noisy.

READING

2 Match the means of transport 1–5 with the photos A–E.

1 high-speed train 2 sports car 3 passenger ship
4 superjumbo 5 Maglev train

3 Match the means of transport in Exercise 2 with these speeds, then read the article and check your guesses.

a) 66kph *3* b) 300kph c) 325kph
d) 430kph e) 900kph

Q & A

Every month, *Transport Today* answers your questions.

Q How fast can I travel? What are the top speeds I can go – by sea, on land or in the sky?
James, Liverpool

5 **A** You're obviously in a hurry, James!

Let's start with travelling on land. Modern cars can go very fast – an Italian Lamborghini Murcielago has a top speed of about 325 kilometres per hour, but there's a speed limit on the majority of motorways, so you can
10 only drive at around 120kph.

Trains are usually faster than cars. The French high-speed train (TGV) goes at 300kph with passengers, but the Maglev train is even faster, with a top speed of 430kph. This new type of train travels just
15 above the ground, not on it. There are only one or two in use at the moment.

Of course, planes are faster than cars or trains. The new superjumbo (Airbus A380) travels at about 900kph – fast, but slower than the older Boeing 747
20 jumbo. This flies at 927kph.

But, James, life isn't all about speed. Ships are a nice, easy way of travelling. They're slow – even a fast passenger ship reaches only 66kph – but they're more comfortable and more relaxing than other means of transport. Isn't that important sometimes too?

---

4 **Which information below can you find in the article?**

1 We can drive at 120kph on motorways in Italy. ✗

2 The name of the French high-speed train is the TGV.

3 There is a Maglev train in Shanghai.

4 The superjumbo can fly non-stop from London to Sydney.

5 Both the jumbo and the superjumbo can go at over 850kph.

6 Travelling by sea is slow.

GRAMMAR: comparative adjectives

We use comparatives to compare one person or thing with another person or thing:

*Planes are **faster than** trains or cars.*

5 **Complete the table with adjectives from the article.**

Adjective	Comparative	
slow	1 _____	
fast	2 _____	
3 _____	nicer	
4 _____	easier	than
5 _____	more modern	
relaxing	6 _____	
comfortable	7 _____	

GRAMMAR TIP

A few common comparatives are irregular:
good → *better* – *bad* → *worse*

Note: for more spelling changes in comparative adjectives, see page 130.

➡ Language reference and extra practice, pages 130–131

D

E

6 **Use the comparative form of the adjective in brackets to complete the sentences.**

1 Plane travel is _____ than car travel. (safe)

2 The Suez Canal is _____ than the Panama Canal. (long)

3 Buses are _____ in London than in São Paulo. (expensive)

4 Lorries are _____ in the USA than in the UK. (big)

5 Chicago O'Hare Airport is _____ than Paris Charles de Gaulle Airport. (busy)

pronunciation

7a **1.36** **Vowel sound** Listen to the sentences in Exercise 6. What is the vowel sound in *than*?

7b **Work with a partner. Make comparisons with these prompts. Be careful with *than*.**

1 trains / planes / cheap

2 planes / motorbikes / noisy

3 motorbikes / ships / exciting

4 bikes / cars / safe

5 trams / buses / common

SPEAKING

8 **Work with a partner. You want to buy a new car. Look at the information below and compare the cars. Use adjectives from the box. Which car do you want?**

big	cheap	comfortable	expensive
fast	good	nice	safe	slow	small

The Clio is faster than the Polo.

Renault Clio   Volkswagen Polo

	Renault Clio	Volkswagen Polo
Top speed	182kph	171kph
Price	£9,950	£9,555
Size	3.9m x 2.0m	3.9m x 1.9m
Comfort	☆☆☆✫	☆☆☆
Safety	☆☆☆☆	☆☆☆

READING

1 Do you have these means of transport in your town or city? Do you use them?

bikes   boats   buses   cars   trams
metro / underground trains   trains

2a Read the article about urban transport in one minute. Which of the means of transport in Exercise 1 does the article mention?

2b Match photos A–E with the different cities in the article.

3 Read the article again. What facts do these numbers refer to?

3.2 million	468	720
4,300	3.2 billion	

1 the number of passengers a year on the Moscow metro

2 the length in kilometres of the St Petersburg tram system

3 the number of stations on the New York City metro system

4 the number of buses in New York

5 the number of passengers a day at Shinjuku Station

4 Read these sentences. Are they true or false?

1 London is smaller than Moscow.

2 New York's transport system is smaller than some others.

3 People do not know about the buses in London.

4 London's underground trains are cheap.

5 There are many passengers in Tokyo's metro stations.

Big, bigger, biggest
– urban transport around the world

Great cities need good transport systems. Which cities have the best systems?

➠ Moscow needs a good transport system because it is the largest city in Europe. The metro is the busiest system in the
5 world (3.2 billion passengers per year) and the stations are perhaps the most beautiful. Another Russian city, St Petersburg, is called a 'City of Trams' because it has the world's largest tram system – over 720km long.

➠ New York is a city that is famous for size – the population
10 is larger, the buildings are taller and the sandwiches are bigger than in many other cities. It has the world's largest metro system (with 468 stations), the world's largest station (Grand Central) and the biggest bus system in the world (more than 4,300 buses).

➠ London has perhaps the most famous buses in the world –
15 the red double-deckers. It also has a good metro or underground system, and it is the oldest in the world. Unfortunately, it is also the most expensive in the world.

➠ Many people think that public transport in Tokyo is the best in the world. It is certainly very busy and always crowded. In fact,
20 the busiest train station in the world is Shinjuku Station, Central Tokyo, with 3.2 million passengers a day.

GRAMMAR: superlative adjectives

5a Look at sentences 1–3 and match them with a–c below. Do we use superlative adjectives to compare one thing with another thing, or with several things in a group?

1 New York has the world's largest station.

2 London Underground is the oldest metro system in the world.

3 London Underground is the most expensive metro system in the world.

a) It's older than all the others.

b) It's more expensive than all the others.

c) It's larger than all the others.

5b Find more superlatives in the article and complete the table.

Adjective	Superlative
old	the [1]_____
large	the [2]_____
big	the [3]_____
busy	the [4]_____
famous	the [5]_____ _____
beautiful	the [6]_____ _____
good	the [7]_____
bad	the worst

➡ Language reference and extra practice, pages 130–131

6a Use the table to complete the sentences about three metro systems.

Metro system	New York	London	Tokyo
Length (km)	368	415	292
Ticket price ($)	1.50	2.50	1.35
Age (first trains)	1904	1863	1927

Length (*long/short*)

The metro system in New York is [1]*longer* than the metro in Tokyo, but the London Underground is [2]_____ system of the three.

The metro system in New York is [3]_____ than the metro in London, but the Tokyo metro is [4]_____ system of the three.

6b Write similar pairs of sentences for the other information in the table.

Price (*expensive/cheap*)

Age (*old/modern*)

7 Write the superlative form of the adjectives below, and then ask and answer questions with a partner about your country or city.

fast   comfortable   dangerous   slow   safe   exciting   busy

What's the fastest means of transport in Milan?

LISTENING

8a **1.37** Listen to three people talking about how they get around their cities. Underline the correct answers.

Person	City	Transport to college/work	Journey to college/work
1 Mei	Beijing / Nanjing	motorbike / bus / metro / bike	30 minutes / 13 minutes
2 Fuad	Khartoum / Cairo	car / bus / metro	1 hour / 1 hour 30 minutes
3 Sandra	Amsterdam / Anderlecht	tram / boat / bike / motorbike	20 minutes / 12 minutes

8b Listen again. Which city/cities does each sentence describe? Check your answers with the audioscript for Track 1.37.

1 The metro system is small.   *Cairo* and _____

2 The buses are busy.   _____ and _____

3 Bikes are popular.   _____ and _____

4 The metro is a nice way to travel.   _____

5 Some people travel by boat.   _____

SPEAKING

9 Work in groups to answer the questions.

• How do you go to work, college, university?

• How long does your journey take?

• Can you use different means of transport?

• What's the best way to get around your town/city?

WRITING

10 Write a paragraph about travelling around your town/city. Use Track 1.37 on page 149 to help you.

The best way to get around Paris is the metro, because …

IBA

International Budget Air

Low-cost airline of the year

20 percent cheaper than other airlines. How do we do it?

■ We have limited in-flight service:

– Free snacks, extra charge for meals and drinks

– In-flight radio, extra charge for video films

■ We fly twice a week to each destination.

Top Air

We give you **more** than other airlines

- Full meal and drinks service
- In-flight films and video games
- In-flight head massage service (extra charge)
- Bigger seats and more leg room
- We fly three times a week to all our destinations.

TA

A OZ Air

Everything you want from an international airline

● Daily flights to all destinations

● Standard in-flight service

Hot and cold meals   Snacks

Full drinks service   In-flight films

PREPARATION

1 Make these sentences true for you and compare with a partner.

1 I *often / don't often / never* travel by plane.

2 I *always / sometimes / never* watch the films on flights.

3 I *usually / sometimes / never* sleep during a flight.

4 I *always / often / never* take a book with me when I fly.

5 I *usually / don't usually / never* take a lot of hand luggage.

2 Match sentences 1–5 with the one with a similar meaning from a–e.

1 You board the plane at 17.00.

2 The plane departs at 17.00.

3 The arrival time is 17.00.

4 The price of the ticket is €500.

5 The flight takes ten hours.

a) The plane leaves at five o'clock.

b) The ticket costs €500.

c) The flight is ten hours long.

d) You get on the plane at five o'clock.

e) The plane lands at 5 p.m.

3 `1.38` Complete the sentences with the words in the box. Listen and check your answers.

> aisle   business   departures   window
> flight   in-flight   return   standard

1 Check the _____ board and see when the flight leaves.

2 I'd like a _____ ticket to Rio, please.

3 I usually travel in _____ class, but sometimes my company pays and then I fly _____ class.

4 This airline has really good _____ service. The _____ attendants are really helpful.

5 I always ask for a _____ seat. I love the view of the clouds.

6 I always ask for an _____ seat because I've got long legs!

pronunciation

4a `1.38` Stress in compound nouns
Listen to Track 1.38 again and circle the word with the strongest stress in each compound.

1 (departures) board

2 return ticket

3 standard class, business class

4 in-flight service, flight attendants

5 window seat

6 aisle seat

4b Practise the six sentences with a partner. Check your partner's pronunciation.

5 Read the different airline adverts above and answer the questions.

1 Which airline is the cheapest?

2 Which airline has the best in-flight service?

3 Which airline has the most frequent flights?

6 `1.39` Sasha wants to fly to New York from Australia. He phones a travel agent and asks for information about different flights. Listen and complete the table.

	Oz Air	Top Air
Departs	8 a.m.	
Arrives		5 p.m.
Length	14 hours	
Price		
In-flight service	good / ~~very good~~ / excellent	good / very good / excellent

KEY LANGUAGE: buying a ticket

7 `1.39` Complete these questions and write answers for the two airlines. Then listen again and check your ideas.

1 When _____ it leave?
2 When _____ it arrive?
3 How _____ does it take?
4 How _____ does it cost?
5 _____ it a good airline?

8a `1.40` Which flight does Sasha decide to book, do you think? Listen to the rest of the conversation and check.

8b Listen again and complete the booking form.

Full name: ¹ Sasha Andrei Kaplinski

From: ² Sydney   To: ³ New York

Airline: ⁴ _____

Departure date: ⁵ _____   Return date: ⁶ _____

Class: ⁷ _____   Seat: ⁸ _____

Payment method: ⁹ _____

9a Write the travel agent's questions for 1 and 4–9 on the booking form. Then read Track 1.40 on page 149 and check your ideas.

1 *Can I have …*
4 *Which airline would you like …*

9b Practise the conversation with a partner. Remember the compound noun pronunciation.

TASK: booking a travel ticket

10 Work with a partner and role-play a phone call between a business person and a travel agent.

Student A: You are Jo, the business person. You live in Sydney, Australia. Read your email (below) to your travel agent and underline the important information. Then, phone the travel agent, take notes of the information, choose the best flight and make a booking.

Student B: You are Chris, the travel agent. Read the email below from a frequent customer. Look at the timetable and price information on page 116 and follow the instructions.

From... | Jo Staveley
To... | Chris Braund
Subject: | Moscow flight – urgent

Hi Chris,
I need another flight – the third one this year! I'd like a return ticket to Moscow, departing next Sunday (to arrive Monday) and returning one week later. I need to arrive in Moscow by midday their time.
The return time is not important, but I don't want to leave Moscow very early in the morning. Of course, the cheaper the better! Can you find a suitable flight for me?
I think the flight is very long – what in-flight services do they offer?

Speak to you soon.
Best wishes,
Jo

OTHER USEFUL PHRASES

Customer
Can you tell me about … ?   How much does … ?
When does … ?   I'd like to …
How long does … ?

Travel agent
Would you like … ?
How would you like to pay?

STUDY SKILLS:
planning your written work

1a Stages in writing Look at these stages in doing a piece of writing. Number them in the order you do them.

a) Do a draft. ☐

b) Join ideas together. ☐

c) Read and understand the question or task. ☐

d) Do a final copy. ☐

e) Make changes and add new ideas to your draft. ☐

f) Think of ideas and write them down. ☐

g) Put ideas in the best order. ☐

1b Now compare your order with a partner. Is it the same or different?

1c Do you usually do all these things when you write? Which things do you miss out? Why?

2 Organising information Look at these sentences about transport in Italy. Organise them under these headings:

Air   General information   Rail
Road   Sea

1 People drive on the right.

2 Modern, comfortable trains run from one big city to another.

3 The speed limit is 50kph in towns.

4 There are about nine important airports.

5 Italy has a very good transport system.

6 The Fréjus tunnel for cars and lorries runs for 13 kilometres under the Alps between France and Italy.

7 There are flights between most cities.

8 There are underground railways, or metros, in Rome and Milan.

9 Italy has about six major ports.

10 It has one of the best motorway systems in Europe.

11 The name of the airport in Rome is Leonardo da Vinci.

12 The biggest sea port is Genoa.

13 There are excellent links both within Italy and with other countries.

3 Mind maps Use mind maps to organise information in a visual way. This helps you remember the information. Use the mind map below to record the information about Italy from Exercise 2.

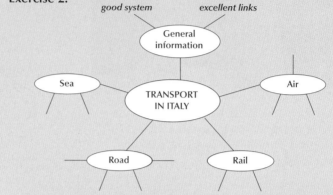

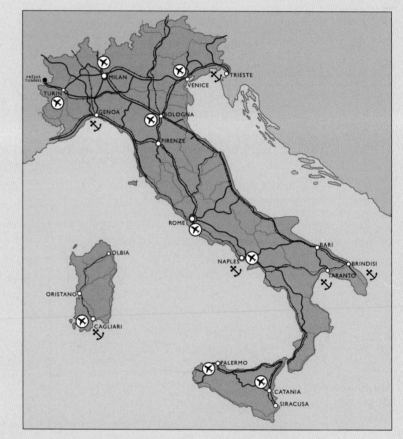

4a Work with a partner. Discuss these questions about transport in your town/city/area, your country or another country that you both know well.

1 Is the transport system good?

2 What is the most popular way to travel?

3 How many big ports / airports / railway stations are there? Which is the biggest?

4 Which means of transport is the most expensive?

5 Are motorways free?

6 What is the speed limit on roads?

4b Now make a mind map with the information from Exercise 4a.

WRITING SKILLS: a description of a transport system

5 Paragraphs What is a paragraph? Look at these statements from students. Which are correct?

1 'You use paragraphs when you speak or write.'

2 'A paragraph is a group of sentences.'

3 'It's about one topic.'

4 'It's usually part of a long piece of writing.'

5 'It starts on a new line.'

6 'You use it when you jump from a plane.'

6 Read the text *Transport in India* quickly and match the paragraphs with these headings.

- Rail transport
- Road transport
- Introduction to the topic

7a Topic sentences The topic sentence of a paragraph tells us the topic of the paragraph. It is usually the first sentence in the paragraph. Underline the topic sentences in paragraphs 2 and 3 of the text.

7b This paragraph comes after paragraph 3 in the text. Read it, then choose the best topic sentence.

> 4 _____ There are a lot of boats and ships on big rivers like the River Ganges. These boats carry people, animals, food and goods. Some people live on boats and catch fish to eat.

a) Calcutta is in India.

b) Indians make long journeys by boat.

c) In some parts of India river transport is important.

d) Rivers in India are often dirty.

8 Ordering ideas Look at these ideas about air transport in India. What is the best order for them?

a) There are over 200 airports.

b) Mumbai is the biggest international airport.

c) Air transport is more important now than in the past.

9 Linkers We use *but* when we add different or surprising information to a sentence. Underline the examples of *but* in paragraph 3 of the text.

10 Each sentence below has two *buts*. Take one out each time to make a correct sentence.

1 Flights in India are expensive but they're cheaper but at night.

2 In Mexico, buses are cheap but long journeys can take but more than 24 hours.

3 On Italian motorways, but the speed limit is 130kph but it's 50kph in towns.

11 Write three paragraphs about transport in your country/ city/area. Use your notes from Exercise 4 and the text *Transport in India* to help you.

Transport in India

1 India is a very large country with a population of over one billion people. There are very long distances between places. Different kinds of transport move people hundreds of kilometres every day.

2 The most popular kind of transport in India is the railway system. It carries more than ten million people every day. The longest train journey is 3,733 kilometres and it goes from Jammu in the north to Kanya Kumari in the south. It takes 89 hours.

3 In India, there are over 3,300,000 kilometres of roads, but there are a lot of problems with road transport. The roads are very narrow and they often aren't very near the villages. Also, a lot of people are poor and cannot buy cars. Buses are very popular, but they are often very crowded.

6 Food

In this unit

Grammar
■ countable and uncountable nouns
■ *some* and *any*
■ *much, many, a lot of*
■ *how much? how many?*

Vocabulary
■ food and drink

Scenario
■ At a conference

Study skills
■ correcting your writing

Writing skills
■ a restaurant review

6.1 SUPER FOOD

*Three things are needed for a good life –
good friends, good food and good song.*
Jason Zebehazy

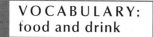

VOCABULARY: food and drink

1a Look at the photo. Which of the following can you see?

bananas bread broccoli carrots
garlic green tea milk noodles
nuts olive oil red peppers
oranges rice salmon sardines
strawberries

1b Look at the food in Exercise 1a. Find:

1 two things you can drink
2 two kinds of fish
3 four vegetables
4 three kinds of fruit
5 three things you often eat
6 two things you never (or almost never) eat or drink.

READING

2 *Super food* is food that is very good for your health. Read the magazine article. Which super food do you eat?

Super Food – Do you eat it?

Eat the right food and you can be healthier. But what is the best food?

Berries, such as blueberries and <u>strawberries</u>, are the number one fruit. They're good for your heart and for
5 your memory. They also fight <u>illnesses</u> such as cancer. For vitamin C, eat an <u>orange</u> every day.
Some vegetables are super food. Broccoli is a good example. It's high in vitamin C and it fights cancer.
<u>Carrots</u> are rich in vitamin A and this is good for your
10 skin. Eat *garlic* often because it's a natural medicine. It's important to eat a lot of <u>nuts</u> because they are good for your memory. *Oily fish*, such as salmon and sardines, is very good for your heart. <u>Olive oil</u> is also good for it.
15 Lastly, are there any super drinks? Well, green tea is certainly one. A nice cup of green tea after your meal is good for your health and it can protect you from illnesses. Finally, don't forget to drink a lot of <u>water</u>. It doesn't have any <u>vitamins</u>, it doesn't give you any
20 energy, but it's very important for you.
Next time you go shopping, check your basket for these types of food. Eat some super food and live longer.

3 Read the article again and complete the sentences with the correct food. You can use each kind of food more than once.

1 Oranges, _____ and _____ have a lot of vitamins.

2 Berries and _____ are good for your brain.

3 Berries, _____ and _____ are good for your heart.

4 _____, _____, _____ and _____ fight illnesses.

4 Choose the correct nouns from the box to answer the questions.

berries carrots garlic health vitamin A heart medicine olive oil super drink

1 In line 4, what does *They* mean? *berries*

2 In line 9, what does *this* mean? _____

3 In line 10, what does *it* mean? _____

4 In line 14, what does *it* mean? _____

5 In line 16, what does *one* mean? _____

> **GRAMMAR: countable and uncountable nouns; *some* and *any***

5a Nouns can be countable or uncountable. Look at the example nouns in bold and write *countable* or *uncountable* above the grammar rules in the table.

Countable

Berries are the number one fruit.

Some **vegetables** are super food.

Are there any super **drinks**?

A **cup** of green tea is good for your health.

Uncountable

Broccoli is high in vitamin C.

It doesn't give any **energy**.

Eat some super **food** and live longer.

¹_____ nouns …	²_____ nouns …
can have *a/an* in front of them. have a plural form.	do not have *a/an* in front of them. do not have a plural form. only use singular verbs.
can have *some* or *any* in front of the plural.	can have *some* or *any* in front of them.

➡ Language reference and extra practice, pages 132–133

5b Read the sentences in Exercise 5a. Complete these grammar rules with *some* or *any*.

1 We use _____ in affirmative sentences.

2 We use _____ in negative sentences.

3 We (usually) use _____ in questions.

6 Look at the underlined words in the magazine article. Which are countable and which are uncountable?

strawberries – countable

7 Complete the sentences with the correct form of the noun and the verb in brackets.

1 *Milk is* very important for babies.   (milk + *to be*)

2 A _____ more vitamins than an orange.
  (red pepper + *to have*)

3 _____ good for your health.   (fruit + *to be*)

4 Some _____ vitamin C.   (vegetable + *to have*)

5 Some _____ bad for your health.   (food + *to be*)

6 _____ any vitamins.   (water + *not to have*)

> **GRAMMAR TIP**
>
> Some nouns can be countable and uncountable, with different meanings:
>
> a tomato
>
> some tomatoes
>
> some tomato

> **SPEAKING**

8 Work with a partner. Find differences in your pictures of food.

Student A: Look at the picture on page 111.

Student B: Look at the picture on page 116.

9 Discuss the four questions in groups. Use the food from Exercise 1 and from the list below.

cakes and biscuits   chicken   chocolate
coffee   crisps   fast food   ice cream
meat   pasta   pizza   potatoes

1 What food do you usually/sometimes eat for breakfast? (lunch? dinner?)

2 What kinds of food and drink do you really like/ dislike?

3 What healthy/unhealthy food do you eat?

4 Who has the healthiest diet?

SPEAKING

1 Read these problems. Are any of them true for your country? In which countries/regions are these problems common?

1 People are often hungry.
2 People waste a lot of food.
3 There are more and more overweight children.
4 Some people do not eat healthy food.
5 Some children work to get food for their family.

2 Look at the photo in the leaflet. Don't read the text. Make guesses about the boy's life. Think about school, family, work, food, home.

I think he lives in Africa.
I don't think his family has a car.
Perhaps his father is a farmer.
I think he lives in Africa.
I don't think he has a car.
Perhaps his father is a farmer.

READING

3 Read the leaflet quickly and check your ideas about Fikru's life. Is his life better now than in the past?

4 Complete the text in the leaflet with *some* or *any*.

5 Answer these questions.

1 How old is Fikru?
2 How big is his family?
3 Where do they live?
4 What is his father's job?
5 Why don't they have a lot of food?
6 What happens when it doesn't rain for a long time?
7 What does Save the Children do in North Ethiopia?
8 What do the children have now?
9 What are Fikru's plans for the future?

Save the Children

The British charity *Save the Children* works in the Highlands of Ethiopia

Fikru is 15 and lives with his parents, brother and five sisters in the north of Ethiopia. Families in Ethiopia do not have much food because there is not much rain, so farmers such as Fikru's father cannot grow many vegetables. Fikru says, 'Some years, we don't have ¹_____ rain at all. Life is terrible then. We have a lot of land, but we don't have ²_____ food and our animals die. When there is ³_____ rain we can live here, but life is never easy. Fortunately, now we get ⁴_____ help from Save the Children.'

Save the Children runs a development project in this region. The project gives ⁵_____ money to families every month (15 euros). 'We don't get much money but it's better than nothing. The money is for us, the children,' says Fikru. 'Now, I've got ⁶_____ books for school and my brother's got a bicycle so he can cycle to the town. Of course, we can't buy a lot of different things and we can't get a lot of food – we haven't got ⁷_____ supermarkets here.' Now, the children can think about their future. 'I've got many plans. I want to go to university. I want to learn and help my country.'

www.savethechildren.org.uk

GRAMMAR: *much, many, a lot of*

6 Look at the leaflet and underline the examples of *much*, *many* and *a lot of*. Then complete the grammar rules. Use the examples in the leaflet to help you.

1 We use _____ and _____ with countable nouns.
2 We use _____ and _____ with uncountable nouns.
3 We can use _____ and _____ in both affirmative and negative sentences. (But *many* is quite formal in affirmative sentences; we don't use it very often.)
4 We usually use _____ in negative sentences, not in affirmative sentences.

➡ Language reference and extra practice, pages 132–133

GRAMMAR TIP

We use *have got* in British spoken English, as well as *have*:
I've got some books. =
I have some books.
He **hasn't got** a bicycle. =
He *doesn't have* a bicycle.

7a Complete the sentences with *much, many* or *a lot of*. Make two different sentences if you can.

1 Fikru's father hasn't got _____ money.

2 His sisters haven't got _____ clothes.

3 At the moment, they've got _____ food because there's _____ rain.

4 They've got some animals but they don't produce _____ meat.

5 Most people here haven't got _____ food.

7b You can use *much, many* and *a lot of* in questions. Complete the questions and answers below then ask a partner the questions.

1 Have you got *many* books?
Yes, I have. I read a lot. / No, I haven't.

2 Do you eat _____ chocolate?

3 Have you got _____ CDs and DVDs?

4 Do you drink _____ water every day?

5 Do you have _____ free time every day?

6 Do you eat _____ vegetables?

LISTENING

8 Fikru doesn't have much food, but in many countries, such as Britain and the USA, there are a lot of overweight children. Why?

9a [1.41] In Scotland, there are now fitness clubs for children. Listen to an interview with David, 14. What topics does he talk about?

his home   his family   exercise   education   the TV   food
the Internet

9b Listen again and complete the fitness club interview form below.

Name: David Midgely
Size of family: 1_____
Parents' jobs: 2_____ and 3_____
Amount of exercise: a little at school
Sports: 4_____   Hours of TV: 5_____
Number of computer games: 6_____
Fruit per day: 1 apple   Vegetables per day: 7_____
Burgers per week: 8_____   Pizzas per week: 1
Types of snack: 9_____, sweets and 10_____
Reason for joining club: 11_____

10 What are the differences between David's and Fikru's lives?
David has got one sister, but Fikru …

11 [1.42] Complete these questions from the interview. Then listen and check.

1 _____ _____ exercise do you do?

2 _____ _____ TV do you watch?

3 _____ _____ computer games have you got?

4 _____ _____ fruit do you eat?

5 _____ _____ vegetables do you have each day?

6 _____ _____ pizzas or burgers do you eat?

WRITING AND SPEAKING

12a Write five questions with *how much / how many*. Use these ideas.

drink: cups of coffee / cups of tea
eat: chocolate / fruit / burgers
do: exercise / sport
spend: money on food / time on a train / time asleep / time on the phone / time in the library
watch: TV / videos and DVDs / films
read: newspapers
waste: food

12b Now ask a partner the questions and make notes of the answers. Write a paragraph about your partner's habits.

Salim drinks perhaps nine or ten cups of coffee a day. He spends about three hours in the library on Saturdays …

Food
– culture on a plate

**International Conference,
City University, Toronto, Canada**

Countries and regions are famous for
different foods, but …

▶ How does national food make
national identities?

▶ Why is rice more famous than
couscous?

▶ Why is pizza more popular in the
USA than in Italy?

▶ Is fast food the end of national
food?

▶ What is international food?

Discuss these questions and more at
Food – culture on a plate.

100 places available

Speakers include:

**Dr Mohammed Aziz
(University of Cairo)**

**Prof. Jacques Rivette
(The Sorbonne, Paris)**

PREPARATION

1 Match the kinds of food (1–10) with
the different countries (a–j).

1 sushi	a) Italy
2 pasta	b) China
3 noodles	c) India
4 burgers	d) England
5 curry	e) Russia
6 roast beef	f) Japan
7 lamb kebab	g) Morocco
8 couscous	h) Turkey
9 caviar	i) the USA
10 chilli con carne	j) Mexico

2 Discuss these questions with a
partner.

1 Do you eat food from other countries?
Do you like it? Do you ever cook it?

2 Do you ever go to conferences (or
other occasions with a lot of people)? Is
the food usually good?

---

3 Read the flyer *Food – culture on a plate* and choose the best
answers.

1 What is the flyer for?
a) an event at a university
b) a business event

2 What is the subject of the event?
a) museums about food
b) countries, people and food

3 Who is the event for?
a) students and lecturers from Canada
b) students and lecturers from all over the world

4 **1.43** Tariq is a conference organiser. He phones a catering
company and orders the food for the conference. Listen and
write his order in the 'Tariq' column on the order form on
page 53.

KEY LANGUAGE:
requests and offers

5 Listen again and complete these sentences from the
conversation.

1 Could we _____ 50 chicken salads, please?

2 _____ we have 50 cheese salads, then?

3 For dessert, we'd _____ 100 ice creams and 50 apple pies.

4 Would you _____ some water or fruit juice?

5 _____ we have … some small bottles of apple juice?

6 _____ you like some coffee?

6 Look at the sentences in Exercise 5 and answer the questions.

1 Which sentences are requests and which are offers?

2 Which is more polite, *could* or *can*?

3 What is the contraction of *We would like*?

4 Do we use *some* or *any* in offers and requests?

7 **1.44** Put the words in the right order to make offers and
requests. Then listen and check. Which are offers and which are
requests?

1 send Could some me coffee you ?

2 I'd 50 kebabs please like lamb

3 Can water we bottles have 40 please of ?

4 like Would you bread some ?

5 chicken like salads please We'd some

pronunciation

8a **1.45** Intonation Listen to the two requests below. Which
one is more polite?

1 Could you send me some coffee?

2 Could you send me some tea?

8b It is very important to have polite intonation. Listen and
repeat the offers and requests from Track 1.44.

Event Catering Company Best food, best service		
Order form	**Quantity**	
	Tariq	You
First course		
Tomato and cheese salad		
Noodle soup		
Tomato soup		
Main course		
Cheese salad		
Chicken salad (Chinese style with noodles)		
Beef curry (with rice)		
Lamb kebab (with rice and vegetables)		
Vegetarian curry (with rice)		
Vegetarian pizza (tomato, mushroom)		
Burger meal (chips, onion rings)		
Sushi meal (fish and vegetarian)		
Desserts		
Chocolate ice cream		
Apple pie		
Fruit salad		
Drinks		
Sparkling water		
Still water		
Lemonade		
Orange juice		
Apple juice		

sushi

pasta

curry

roast beef

lamb kebab

couscous

chilli

9 Which of these are replies to offers and which are replies to requests?

1 That's no problem.
2 Yes, please.
3 Sure, no problem.
4 No, thank you.

5 No thanks.
6 Certainly.
7 I'm sorry, I'm afraid we haven't got any of those at the moment.

10a Work with a partner. Make the requests and offers from Exercise 7. Only reply when your partner is polite.

10b Look at Track 1.43 on page 150 and practise the conversation with your partner.

TASK: talking about numbers and quantities

11a You need to order the food for the lunch at the Food conference (Exercise 3). There are 100 people at the conference. Choose the food and complete the 'You' column on the order form.

11b Now work with a partner and role-play the dialogue between the conference organiser and the supplier.

Student A: You are the conference organiser. Phone Event Catering, the supplier, and make your order.

Student B: You work for Event Catering, the supplier. Look at your supply list on page 117. Take the order from the conference organiser. Can you supply everything?

Swap roles. Do the role-play again.

Student A: Now you work for Event Catering. Use your supply list on page 112 and take the order.

Student B: Now you are the conference organiser.

STUDY SKILLS: correcting your writing

1a Making mistakes Read these statements. Do you agree with them? Write *yes, not sure* or *no*.

1 We all make mistakes when we learn a new language.

2 I don't like making mistakes in front of other students.

3 We can learn to correct our mistakes.

4 It's easier to correct mistakes in writing than in speaking.

1b Learners often make mistakes in grammar, vocabulary and spelling. Which kind do you make the most, do you think?

2 Grammar Correct the mistakes in the underlined words.

1 There *is* about ten eggs in the fridge.

2 Does he *likes* chocolate?

3 The *more* important thing in life is health.

4 They haven't got *many* money.

3 Vocabulary The underlined words in the sentences below are incorrect. Replace them with the correct words from the box. You don't need all the words.

difficult	easy	fat	fish	meat
vegetables	waste	wear		

1 Broccoli and cabbage are kinds of *fruit*.

2 People in rich countries *watch* a lot of food.

3 A lot of children in rich countries are *fit* and this is a big problem.

4 Life is never *early* for children in Ethiopia.

4 Spelling Choose the correct spelling in each sentence below. Then check in your dictionary.

1 I *ofen/often/oftan* eat a banana for lunch.

2 Olive oil is good for your *hart/heart/haert*.

3 Blueberries are good for your *brain/brane/brian*.

4 Are there any *glassess/glasess/glasses* on the table?

5 Anh is a student from Vietnam. Her teacher uses a correction code for her work. Correct the mistakes in this piece of work.

Gr = grammar

WW = wrong word (vocabulary)

Sp = spelling

                         Gr

Food in Vietnam <u>are</u> healthy. It's important for food to look

Sp   Sp

<u>beatiful</u>, too. We sit at a low <u>tabel</u> and eat with chopsticks.

                Gr

Most people <u>eats</u> rice three or four times every day.

                           Sp

Everywhere in Vietnam is near the <u>see</u> or a river, so we eat a lot

                    Gr WW

of fish. The fish markets <u>has</u> <u>difficult</u> kinds of fish. We often eat

                         Gr

fish and meat together. We don't eat <u>many</u> cheese or milk.

CORFU

OK, you like Greek food, but you're tired of the same old restaurants. Corfu can help. It's a new Greek restaurant in the city centre.

The place is clean and bright. There are interesting pictures on the blue and white walls. The tables are big and the chairs are comfortable.

The starters are excellent, and for your main course, try one of the meat dishes – they're all fantastic.

Corfu is popular with local people, business people, students and tourists. After 8 p.m., it's always busy and noisy, but the service is fast and the waiters are friendly.

And the best thing? It's cheap! Two people can eat here for about £25. I think it's a fantastic new restaurant, so get down to Corfu now for a great Greek experience!

WRITING SKILLS: a restaurant review

6 Discuss these questions with a partner.

1 How often do you go to restaurants?
2 What kind of restaurants do you like?
3 What's your favourite restaurant?
4 Which restaurant on these pages would you like to go to? Why?

7 Read the review of the restaurant Corfu. Is it positive or negative? Would you like to eat here? Why / Why not?

8 The writer describes these things in the review. Number them in the order you read them.

a) other customers ☐
b) the food (good? bad?) ☐
c) the name of the restaurant ☐ 1
d) the service/waiters ☐
e) the kind of food (nationality?) ☐
f) a description of the restaurant ☐
g) the location ☐
h) the writer's opinion ☐
i) the price of the meal ☐

9 A good review needs a good beginning. Look at these beginnings. Which are the most interesting?

1 There are 18 French restaurants in the city. Well … 19 now!
2 This review is about a new French restaurant in the city.
3 Can a new French restaurant be better than our old favourite *Les Quatre Saisons*?
4 I love French food and I eat it every week.
5 Where's the best French restaurant in the world? In Paris? Or right here, in our city?

10 Look at this sentence from the review. How do we write things in a list?

Corfu is popular with local people, business people, students and tourists.

11 Commas in lists Put commas in the correct places in these sentences.

1 I love chips chocolate pizza and ice cream.
2 My favourite cities are Venice Kyoto Edinburgh and Sydney.
3 My favourite subjects are History French and English.
4 I like films ballet pop music and art exhibitions.
5 Our town needs a new shopping centre a bus station a car park a cinema and a swimming pool.

12 Write a review of a restaurant in your town/ city. Check your work for grammar, vocabulary and spelling mistakes. Check another student's work, too!

GRAMMAR

1 Read four DVD reviews (A–D) and complete the exercises.

A Write the missing articles in gaps 1–5.

The Family Dinner

¹_____ French family (mother, father, son and daughter) sit round their table for dinner. ²_____ son wants to be ³_____ actor but his father doesn't agree. ⁴_____ mother wants ⁵_____ husband for her daughter but the girl has other ideas.

In Jules Binoche's new film about family life, there's a laugh a minute. ★ ★ ★ ★

B Write *can* or *can't* in gaps 6–8.

Space Station Zero

A space station on Mars is silent. NASA ⁶_____ contact its people. Only one man ⁷_____ find out the reason. *Richard Steagler* returns as super-astronaut Red Turner. But ⁸_____ he arrive in time? And who or what is on the planet?

Slow but excellent. ★ ★ ★

C Write comparative or superlative adjectives. Use the adjectives in brackets.

Live Long 2

It's a slow, hot afternoon for Detective Crowley. Then, she gets a phone call. One of the ⁹_____ (*rich*) actresses in Hollywood needs her help. Two hours later Crowley finds the actress … dead. The detective's evening becomes ¹⁰_____ (*busy*) and then the night is the ¹¹_____ (*bad*) time of her life.

Live Long 2 has the same team as *Live Long* but it's a ¹²_____ (*good*) film. Exciting. ★ ★ ★ ★ ★

D Choose the correct word.

Life in the Fast Lane

There aren't very ¹³*many / much* good reasons to watch this film. Yes, it has ¹⁴*much / some* beautiful people, but it has ¹⁵*any / a* bad story, and how ¹⁶*a lot of / much* time does a film need for fast cars and explosions?

OK if you have a boring Saturday night. ★ ★

2a What types of films are reviews A–D about? Choose from the box.

| action   comedy   science fiction   thriller |

2b Which film would you like to watch? Why? Tell a partner.

VOCABULARY

3 Write the words in the job advertisement.

| CV   drive   ride   speak
tennis   weights   yoga |

Sports instructor
required

A large health and fitness club needs sports instructors and fitness trainers for clients.

The right person can:

◆ teach ¹_____ and aerobics classes.
◆ play ²_____.
◆ ³_____ a horse.
◆ help clients to use ⁴_____ and the fitness machines.
◆ ⁵_____ a car (all our trainers visit clients at home).
◆ ⁶_____ another language (we have many international clients).

Send us your ⁷_____ today!

4a [1.46] Listen to two interviews for the job at the health and fitness club. Make notes in the table.

	Interview 1	Interview 2
1 What can they do?		
2 What can't they do?		

4b Who is the best person for the job? Why? Ask a partner.

5 Work with a partner. Practise this conversation.

Student A: You work for the health and fitness club. Ask Student B questions: *Do you … ? Can you … ?*

Student B: You want the job in the advert. Answer Student A's questions: *Yes, I do … No, I don't … Yes, I can … No, I can't …*

6 Complete the crossword. Use the clues 1–15.

Across →

2 These are good for your memory.

5 It's a type of holiday accommodation.

6 Would you like _____ or coffee?

8 Metro trains and _____ trains are the same.

11 *I'm sorry* and *I'm afraid* are polite ways to say this.

12 Peppers can be this colour.

14 bad, worse, _____

15 You can make it from olives.

Down ↓

1 The flight takes two hours and the plane _____ in Seville at 5 p.m.

3 not business class

4 What do you usually _____ for dinner?

5 What _____ is Paris in? (France)

7 You can _____ by bike, boat, car and taxi.

9 _____, better, best

10 New York is a very big _____.

13 Let's _____ something different this weekend.

7 Find five new words in Units 4–6. Write a clue for each word. Read the five clues to a partner. Does your partner know the word?

KEY LANGUAGE

8 **1.47** A man wants a train ticket to Seattle. Listen to the conversation. Are these sentences true or false?

1 There's a train in the morning.

2 There's a train in the afternoon.

3 The first train is the cheapest.

4 The man buys a first-class ticket.

9a Number the conversation in the right order.

a) Hello. Could you give me some information about trains to Seattle? ☐ 1

b) The first train is 34 dollars. The other trains are 40. ☐

c) Is there a train in the afternoon? ☐

d) I'd like two tickets for the first train, please. First class, please. ☐

e) First of all, when do they leave? ☐

f) Yes, certainly. What would you like to know? ☐

g) OK. How much does a ticket cost? ☐

h) The first train is at ten in the morning and the next train is at 12. ☐

i) I'm afraid there isn't. There's a train in the evening. ☐

j) That has only standard class seats, I'm afraid. ☐ 10

9b Listen again and check your answers.

10 Practise similar conversations in pairs.

Student A: Look at the information on page 114.

Student B: Look at the information on page 119.

LANGUAGE CHECK

11 Delete the extra word in sentences 2–10. Look at the pages to check.

1 The two boys in *Machuca* live in ~~the~~ Chile. (page 33)

2 Films from India are the popular today. (page 33)

3 Can you do ride a horse? (page 34)

4 You borrow books from a library shop. (page 35)

5 Planes are the faster than trains or cars. (page 41)

6 Boats are the nicest way than to travel. (page 43)

7 A broccoli is high in vitamins. (page 49)

8 She doesn't have got a bicycle. (page 50)

9 We haven't got a lot of much money. (page 50)

10 I'd like to 20 bottles of water, please. (page 53)

LOOK BACK

12 Find the exercises in Units 4–6 where you …

• talk about your favourite film. (U4)

• say what you can do. (U4)

• ask for information. (U4)

• read about speed. (U5)

• listen to people talking about cities. (U5)

• sell a flight. (U5)

• find out about healthy food. (U6)

• make a request. (U6)

• write about a restaurant. (U6)

Shopping

7.1 CONSUMER HABITS

Grammar
- present continuous
- present continuous and present simple

Vocabulary
- shops and shopping
- American English words

Scenario
- At a meeting

Study skills
- giving a short, informal talk

Writing skills
- an informal email

What kind of shopper are you?

There are many different types of shopper. These four people are shopping on Oxford Street, London – one of the busiest shopping areas in the world.

José The _____ shopper

Shopping habits: 'I really don't like shopping. I don't spend a lot of time in the shops and I choose things very fast.'
Today: 'At the moment, I'm looking for a new suit. There's a good dark brown suit in this shop. It's expensive but I can pay for it.'

Hiromi The _____ shopper

Shopping habits: 'I go shopping every weekend. I usually buy clothes or things for my house. I love big department stores.'
Today: 'Right now, I'm carrying five new things – a coat, a shirt, a cookery book, a pair of shoes and a belt. Time to go home!'

Vince The _____ shopper

Shopping habits: 'I come to Oxford Street about once a month but I don't usually spend a lot. I just like to look at the different things in the shops.'
Today: 'I'm not looking for anything special. Right now, I'm waiting for my friend. She's trying on a pair of jeans.'

Ulrike The _____ shopper

Shopping habits: 'I always check the prices in different shops. I always look for the lowest price.'
Today: 'Today, I'm looking for a digital camera. I'm thinking about buying this one, but I'm not sure – it's a little expensive.'

The main thing today is – shopping.
Arthur Miller, 1915–2005, US dramatist

SPEAKING

1 **Discuss these questions.**

1 Do you like shopping?

2 How often do you buy these things?

books clothes   DVDs   food
furniture   make-up   music CDs
stationery

3 What other things do you regularly buy?

READING

2 **Read the magazine article and match each person in the photos above with a type of shopper. Which type are you?**

the window shopper   the speed shopper

the frequent shopper   the careful shopper

3 **Read the article again. Are these sentences true or false?**

1 José cannot buy the suit because it is expensive.

2 In her bags, Hiromi has got three things to wear.

3 Ulrike is interested in the digital camera in the shop.

4 Vince wants to buy a pair of trousers.

VOCABULARY:
shops and shopping (1)

4a Match the verbs with the correct objects.

to buy   to check   to pay for
to spend   to spend   to try on

1 a new shirt by credit card
2 the prices in different shops
3 time in a shop
4 50 pounds on DVDs
5 a new computer on the Internet
6 a pair of jeans before you buy them

4b Complete the questions with a verb from Exercise 4a. Then ask a partner the questions.

1 How much time do you _____ in clothes shops?
2 Do you _____ prices in different shops before you buy something?
3 Do you always _____ clothes before you buy them?
4 Do you often _____ things by credit card?
5 Do you _____ things on the Internet?
6 Do you _____ a lot of money on clothes and music?

GRAMMAR:
present continuous (1)

5a Look at these sentences from the article and answer the questions.

a) Right now, I'm carrying five new things.

b) I always check the prices in different shops.

1 Which sentence describes things that happen again and again? What do we call this tense?

2 Which sentence describes an action that is happening now?

5b Find more examples of the present continuous in the article.

5c Complete the table.

	Subject	*to be*	Verb + *-ing*
+	I	[1]_____ (am)	
	you / we / they	're ([2]_____)	
	he / she / it	's ([3]_____)	looking at it.
−	I	[4]_____ (am not)	
	you / we / they	aren't (are not)	
	[5]___ / ___ / ___	isn't ([6]_____)	

➡ Language reference and extra practice, pages 134–135

6 [2.2] Complete these mobile phone conversations. Use the present continuous of the verbs in brackets. Listen and check your answers.

1 I can't talk now, I _____ _____ _____ some trainers. (try on)
2 Call me back later. I _____ _____. (drive)
3 Can you see me? I _____ _____ at the corner, opposite the bank. (stand)
4 Can I call you back? The waiter _____ _____ for me to order. (wait)
5 We _____ just _____ at the bus station. See you in five minutes. (arrive)
6 I'm in the car park. I _____ _____ the food in the car. (put)

7 Complete this paragraph with the correct form, present simple or present continuous, of the verbs in brackets.

Tom The Christmas shopper
I [1]*don't* usually *come* (not come) to Oxford Street but today I [2]_____ (look for) some Christmas presents. That's why I [3]_____ (look at) these CDs – my Dad [4]_____ (listen) to music all the time. I [5]_____ (not live) in London, but it [6]_____ (be) always fun to visit Oxford Street and I [7]_____ (have) fun today. There's a lovely Christmas atmosphere in the city – that's why I [8]_____ (wear) this silly hat!

LISTENING AND WRITING

8 [2.3] Listen to three short conversations. Work with a partner and describe the situations. Use phrases from the list.

in a bookshop   in a café   in a cinema
in a clothes shop   in a shoe shop   to ask for
to buy   to order   to try on

1 *He's in a shoe shop. He's trying* _____
2 He _____
3 She _____

9 With your partner, write a similar conversation and practise it. Use Track 2.3 on page 150 to help you.

ASDA supermarket, present day

Grocery store, 1950s

VOCABULARY: shops and shopping (2)

1 Look at these words connected with shopping. Which ones have similar meanings?

customer   discount   hypermarket   product
Internet shopping   price   service   (to) shop
store   supermarket   online shopping

2 Discuss these questions with a partner.

1 How often do you go shopping? What do you usually buy?

2 Do you prefer supermarkets or smaller shops? Why?

3 What are the most famous supermarkets in your country?
Which do you like/dislike? Why?

READING

3 Read the article quickly. What is it about?

1 online shopping

2 a growing supermarket

3 town centres in Britain

4a Put these headings in the right place (A–D) in the article.

- Number and location of stores
- Products and services
- The effects of supermarkets
- A success story

4b Put these figures in the gaps (1–4).

30 percent   £1   15 million   1,000

5 Look at these sentences. Say if they are true, false or if the text doesn't say.

1 Tesco makes 65 euros a second.

2 Most Tesco stores are outside the UK.

3 The food business is growing very quickly.

4 A lot of small shops are not doing well.

5 Some British farmers are going out of business.

6 Some town centres have serious problems.

GRAMMAR TIP

We can use the present continuous to talk about a changing situation.
The food business is growing very quickly.

Business News

A _____
Tesco is the most successful supermarket in Britain. It takes 1_____ out of every eight pounds that British people spend, and makes about 65 pounds (100 euros) a second.

B _____
Tesco has over 2_____ stores in the UK and about 600 in countries in Central/Eastern Europe and East Asia. There are 100 Tesco hypermarkets and new stores are opening all the time.

C _____
Tesco has 3_____ of the UK food market but it sells more than just food. The non-food business is growing very quickly and Tesco now also sells clothes, DVDs, mobile phones, and 4_____ books a year. There are new services like online shopping and 150,000 people a week shop with Tesco.com.

D _____
Tesco and other large supermarkets are doing very well, but at the same time a lot of small independent shops are closing down. As a result, some town centres are dying.

LISTENING

6 Discuss these questions with a partner.

1 Do you use the Internet for shopping? Why / Why not? What do you buy?

2 What are the advantages and disadvantages of Internet shopping?

7a [2.4] Listen to this discussion. Put the topics in the order (1–5) you hear them.

a) what companies are doing to get business on the Internet ☐

b) the Internet and traditional shopping ☐

c) what people are buying ☐

d) how people are using the Internet to shop ☐

e) women and online shopping ☐

7b Now listen again and complete these notes.

Internet shopping

1 Most popular items: _____

2 Usual first item: _____

3 Useful: it's easy to compare _____

4 Convenient for: _____ with jobs and children

5 Offers from companies: big _____

6 Reason for using Internet: saves _____ and _____

GRAMMAR: present continuous (2)

8a Complete these questions, then check with Track 2.4 on page 151.

1 Is _____ becoming really popular?

2 _____ are they buying?

3 How are people _____ the Internet?

4 _____ women using the Internet for shopping?

8b Complete these grammar rules about the word order in present continuous questions. Use the words in the box.

after   question   subject   *to be*

1 Questions can start with the verb _____ or with a _____ word.

2 The verb *to be* usually comes before the _____ of the question.

3 The main verb + *-ing* comes _____ *to be* and the subject.

➡ Language reference and extra practice, pages 134–135

9 Complete these questions with the words in brackets. Then ask and answer the questions with a partner.

1 _____ a lot these days? (you / travel)
Yes, I am. I'm going to a lot of new places. / No, I'm not.

2 _____ a lot of English at the moment? (you / learn)

3 _____ much in the evenings? (you / go out)

4 What books _____ at the moment? (people / read)

5 What films _____ at the moment? (people / watch)

SPEAKING

10a Put the words in the right order to make questions about shopping in your country. Add two more questions if you can.

1 people's shopping habits   changing   are   How   ?

2 young people   What   buying   these days   are   ?

3 big   How much money   making   are   supermarkets   ?

4 doing   What   to get   are stores   business   ?

5 in   What changes   town centres   happening   are   ?

6 the Internet   people   How   using   are   ?

10b Discuss the questions in pairs or small groups, and then tell the class about your three most interesting ideas.

In … , big hypermarkets are becoming more popular.

More people are using them and small shops are closing down.

PREPARATION

1 Read about Charleston, a city in the USA. Would you like to visit it, or live there?

2 The words on the left (1–6) are American English. Find them in the text, then match them with the British English words on the right (a–f).

1	shopping mall	a) car park
2	store	b) petrol
3	gas	c) shopping centre
4	downtown	d) shop
5	highway	e) town centre
6	parking lot	f) motorway / main road

3 Look at the photos A–D and match them with these sentences. Can you say anything else about these types of shopping place?

1 In this place there are many stalls (open-air shops).

2 This is the traditional place for shopping.

3 This place has very large car parks and large, often famous stores.

4 There are often motels and petrol stations here.

4 Brad and Zara want to start a small bookshop in Charleston. They want to sell books about film, TV and music. Read the information in Exercise 5 about downtown Charleston and answer the questions.

1 What are the advantages of this area for their shop?

2 What are the disadvantages?

3 Do you think it is a good place for the shop?

5 [2.5] Listen to Brad and Zara talking about their plans for the shop. Tick the advantages and disadvantages of downtown that they discuss.

1 It's a nice place. People like to come here.

2 There are interesting local shops: some cafés, an art shop, a music shop.

3 The area is safe – there's not much crime.

4 There aren't any bookshops in the area.

5 It's near the bus station.

6 The rent is high ($500 a month).

7 Many people go to the shopping mall outside the town.

KEY LANGUAGE: giving advantages and disadvantages

6a Listen again and complete the sentences.

BRAD: So, what advantages does downtown ¹_____?

ZARA: Well, ²_____ of all, I ³_____ it's a nice place for people to visit.

BRAD: OK. Are there any ⁴_____ advantages?

ZARA: Yes, ⁵_____ advantage is that the area is safe.

BRAD: Right. What ⁶_____ the disadvantages?

ZARA: I think there are two ⁷_____ disadvantages.

ZARA: One ⁸_____ is that the rent is high …

ZARA: … and the ⁹_____ is that a lot of people go to the shopping mall outside the town.

ZARA: This ¹⁰_____ that sometimes there aren't very many customers downtown.

Charleston
CITY GUIDE

Reasons to come

Historical Charleston is a beautiful town in the south of the USA. It's a seaside town and it has many old buildings. The best way to see the town is on foot. Walk around and enjoy the lovely buildings and secret gardens. Life is relaxed here.

Eating and nightlife

Many restaurants serve the local food – especially the rice dish Jambalaya. Charleston has a history of Dixieland Jazz, so there are a lot of music bars. The Dock Street Theater is the oldest theater in America, dating back to 1736.

6b Match the sentences in Exercise 6a with the descriptions below.

1 asking about advantages/disadvantages

_____ _____ _____

2 giving advantages/disadvantages

_____ _____ _____ _____ _____

3 explaining why something is a disadvantage

_____

pronunciation

7a [2.6] Stressed words In sentences we stress some words more than others. Listen to Zara's sentences from Exercise 6a and notice the stressed words.

1 Well, <u>first</u> of all, I think it's a <u>nice</u> <u>place</u> for people to <u>visit</u>.

2 Yes, <u>another</u> advantage is that the area is <u>safe</u>.

3 <u>I</u> think there are <u>two</u> main disadvantages.

4 <u>One</u> disadvantage is that the <u>rent</u> is <u>high</u> …

5 … and the <u>other</u> is that a <u>lot</u> of people go to the <u>shopping</u> mall <u>outside</u> the town.

6 <u>This</u> means that <u>sometimes</u> there aren't very many <u>customers</u> <u>downtown</u>.

7b Listen again and repeat.

8 Look at Track 2.5 on page 151. Practise the conversation with a partner. Be careful with the stress.

Places to shop

Downtown Charleston is a lovely shopping area with many stores and cafés. There's also the City market, which sells many unusual things. In the north, there's the popular Northwoods shopping mall, with a variety of stores and a huge parking lot. There are many small highway shopping areas outside the town, where you can do your shopping and fill your car with gas at the same time.

TASK: describing places

9a Work in groups of three. You are helping Brad and Zara with the bookshop plans. You are looking at information about different shopping areas.

Student A: Read about the market on page 111 and make notes.

Student B: Read about the highway shopping area on page 117 and make notes.

Student C: Read about the shopping mall on page 120 and make notes.

Shopping Area	Advantages	Disadvantages
the market		
the highway shopping area		
the shopping mall		

9b Tell your group your information. Make notes about their information in the table.

9c Discuss the information in your group, using the Key language and the Other useful phrases. Decide which is the best shopping area for the bookshop.

OTHER USEFUL PHRASES

There are two main advantages … The first/second is …

The shopping mall is more expensive than the …

This means that …

I think the market is better because …

WRITING

10 Write a short paragraph to explain your choice of the best shopping area for the bookshop.

1a Preparing a talk Make a list of things we do when we prepare a talk. Match 1–6 with a–f.

1 Put your ideas

2 Check the pronunciation

3 Find out

4 Practise

5 Prepare some pictures or tables

6 Make some

a) the talk.

b) notes to help you remember things in the talk.

c) to make your points clearer.

d) in the best order.

e) of difficult words.

f) some interesting information.

1b Work with a partner and discuss the best order to do the six stages in Exercise 1a.

2 2.7 Listen to a student giving a short talk about Harrods. What does the student talk about? Tick the topics.

1 the building   4 places to eat

2 the area   5 opening times

3 what you can buy   6 Internet shopping

3 Making notes Some people write down every word of their talk. Others make notes. Complete the notes for the talk with these words.

every	building	food	department	floors

Harrods

huge ¹_____ store – London

beautiful ²_____ (at night)

open ³_____ day

7 ⁴_____

can find everything – give examples

also ⁵_____ halls + cafés/ restaurants (25) + doctor/bank

4 Listen again and complete the sentences from the talk.

a) *In this short talk, I'd like to _____ _____ about* my favourite store – Harrods …

b) *It's _____ for* its fantastic food halls …

c) *One of the _____ _____ things* is that there's even a doctor …

d) *To _____,* I think Harrods is the best department store in the world!

5 Giving the talk These things can be problems when someone gives a talk. Can you think of any other problems?

The speaker …

• looks down at the floor

• looks at just one or two people

• speaks very fast

• wears old or dirty clothes

• talks for too long.

6 Give a talk on Harrods to a partner. Use your notes from Exercise 3 and the completed phrases in *italics* in Exercise 4. Then listen to your partner's talk.

7 Prepare and give a short talk of about one minute on *My favourite shop* or *The best / worst / most unusual shop in my town/city.* Before you start, look at the stages in Exercise 1 again.

WRITING SKILLS: an informal email

8 Discuss these questions with a partner.

1 Do you ever shop for books? What kind of books do you buy?

2 Are they for you, or presents for someone else?

3 Where do you buy them – in a bookshop, in a supermarket or on the Internet?

9 Read these emails. What is the relationship between Miranda, Nick and Paula, do you think?

From... m.jones@ola.com
To... n.jones@tbnet.co.uk
Subject: Paula's present

Hello Nick

How's life? Just a quick message because I'm very busy today. I'd like to buy Paula a book for her birthday. Can you give me any ideas?

Thanks a lot.

Love
Miranda

From... n.jones@tbnet.co.uk
To... m.jones@ola.com
Subject: Paula's present

Hi Miranda

I'm fine, thank you. Paula likes historical novels and love stories, but also thrillers. She doesn't like war or science fiction books.

She's reading a lot of foreign novels these days – but in English, of course! We want to go to South America or Japan next year, so maybe you can get her something about those parts of the world. Is this any help?

See you soon.

Nick

10 Miranda finds these books on a website. Which book is best for Paula? Would you like to read any of these books?

Of Love and Shadows
by Isabel Allende

A great love story about two young people in a country in South America.

My Name is Red
by Orhan Pamuk

An excellent novel about Istanbul in the 1590s.
A thriller, but also a story about love and art.

Black Rain
by Masuji Ibuse

A sad, funny and beautiful book about Hiroshima, Japan, in 1945.

11 Look at the emails in Exercise 9 and complete the three lists below with the phrases in the box.

Bye for now   Dear ...   How are things?   Love
Hi   How are you?   Take care   Hope you're OK

Greeting: *Hello, ...*

Opening phrase: *How's life? ...*

Ending: *See you soon, ...*

12 **Linkers** The words *because* and *so* are linking words – they join two ideas. Find the examples in the emails, then put *because* or *so* in these sentences.

1 Books are expensive in my country _____ I don't buy many.

2 I like *Bridget Jones's Diary* _____ it's funny and true.

3 I love long books _____ I read a lot of Russian novels.

4 I don't read many books _____ I haven't got much free time.

13a You want to buy a music CD or film DVD for someone in your class for their birthday present. Write an email to a partner, asking for ideas.

13b Reply to your partner's email. Use the emails in Exercise 9 as models.

History and culture

Grammar
- past simple of *to be*
- *could, couldn't*

Vocabulary
- buildings
- cultures and civilisations
- verbs and prepositions

Scenario
- At a museum

Study skills
- learning new words

Writing skills
- a description of an object

History never stops ... Trying to stop it is like trying to stop geography.
Augusto Monterroso, 1921–2003, Guatemalan writer

VOCABULARY: buildings

1a Work with a partner. Which of these things can you see in the picture?

> courtyard   door   entrance   furniture
> garden   gate   ladder   painting
> roof   room   wall   window

1b How are these buildings different from your home and street?

READING

2a Guess the answers to these questions. Then read paragraph A of the text about Çatal Hüyük and check your guesses.

1 This city is in modern-day ...
   a) Iraq   b) Pakistan   c) Turkey.

2 The picture shows the place in about ...
   a) 10000 BC   b) 6000 BC   c) 2000 BC.

2b Now read paragraphs B and C quickly. Which paragraph, A, B or C, has information about these things?

1 location *A*   3 size of population
2 houses   4 people

ÇATAL HÜYÜK

A Çatal Hüyük (now in Anatolia, Turkey) was one of the world's first cities. In fact, many people think it is the oldest city. It was an important and busy place for 2,000 years, from about 7000 BC to 5000 BC. Compared with today's cities, it wasn't big; in 6250 BC, there were only about 6,000 people there.

B The people were, we believe, kind and peaceful. Many of the people were farmers, but the city was also a centre of trade and ideas. Çatal Hüyük was rich and well organised, but life was very short: an average age of 34 years for men and 29 for women. Women were important in this city: many were in high positions and there were a lot of special goddesses.

C There weren't any streets in the city; most of the houses were around a central courtyard. There weren't any doors in the houses. There was an entrance to each house through a hole in the roof and down a ladder. Inside, there were paintings of animals and people on some of the walls.

3 Use the words in the box to complete this summary of the text.

farming   good   population   place   unusual

Çatal Hüyük was an important [1]_____ about 8,000 years ago, when the [2]_____ was about 6,000. It was one of the first [3]_____ communities and also important for trade. Life was [4]_____ for the people here, but it was also short. The people's homes were [5]_____, but comfortable.

GRAMMAR: past simple of *to be*

We use the past simple to talk about events and situations that are finished.

4a Look at the three sentences from the text, then underline more examples of the past simple of *to be* in the text.

Çatal Hüyük **was** rich and well organised.
The people **were** peaceful.
There **weren't** any streets.

4b Complete the table with past simple forms of *to be*.

Affirmative (+)	Negative (–)	Question (?)
I was he / she / it [1]_____ you were we were they [2]_____	I wasn't he / she / it [4]_____ you weren't we [5]_____ they [6]_____	was I? was he / she / it? [8]_____ you? were we? were they?
there [3]_____ there were	there wasn't there [7]_____	[9]_____ there? were there?

Note: in more formal English, *wasn't* ➔ *was not* and *weren't* ➔ *were not*.
➡ Language reference and extra practice, pages 136–137

5 Complete these sentences with *was, wasn't, were* or *weren't*.

1 The people of Çatal Hüyük _____ peaceful.
2 Roman roads are famous – the Romans _____ very good at building them.
3 'Who _____ Cleopatra?' – 'The queen of Egypt.'
4 _____ there any important cities in your country in AD 1000?
5 I _____ good at history at school – it was my worst subject!
6 There _____ a horrible history teacher at my school. Now, what _____ his name?
7 'You _____ in the lecture on early cities. Where _____ you?' – 'We _____ in the café!'

6a ▪2.8▪ Vowel sounds Listen to *was* and *were* in these sentences. What is the vowel sound?

1 The city was lovely.
2 There were gardens everywhere.

6b ▪2.9▪ Listen to some sentences. Then listen again and repeat.

7a Look at these past time phrases. Put them in order, starting with the most recent.

1,000 years ago   last month last week   last year   six weeks ago yesterday   the day before yesterday two hours ago

Two hours ago, …

7b Put the words in the right order to make questions, then ask a partner. Use time phrases in your answer.

1 holiday When your last was ?
2 last school exam your was When ?
3 When your visit to a museum was last ?

SPEAKING and WRITING

8a What do you know about the Mayan, Inca and Aztec civilisations?

Aztec art

8b Work with a partner to find out more about these civilisations.

Student A: Look at the information on page 112.

Student B: Look at the information on page 117.

9 Now choose one of the civilisations and write a few sentences about it.

The Mayan civilisation was in Mexico, Guatemala, Honduras and Belize. It was important …

READING

1 Which of these changes are true for your country? Can you think of any other changes?

1 Families are smaller now than they were 50 years ago.

2 People work shorter hours than in the past.

3 Nowadays, many people cook food from other countries.

4 Religion is more important now than in the past.

5 United States' culture (films, food, music) is popular.

6 These days, people usually go abroad on holiday.

2a Read the article about changes quickly. Which countries or cultures does the reporter write about?

2b Complete the headings in the article with these words. There is one word that you do not need.

> climate   economics   government   technology

3 Read the article again. Who thinks the changes are positive and who thinks they are negative? Write P (positive) or N (negative).

1 Han Li   2 Bo Li   3 Farida   4 Tootega

4 Who says these things? Match the sentences with the names.

1 'Be a good boy and play with your sister.'

2 'Go to Toronto, son. There's no work here.'

3 'I need to buy some petrol.'

4 'On hot days, I just stay in the house.'

5 'I like school. I want to study medicine at university.'

a) Tootega

b) Bo Li

c) Farida's daughter

d) Farida

e) Han Li

All change!

Countries and cultures change for many different reasons. Our reporter, **Sarah Stephens**, talks to people about changes in their countries.

1 Changes because of _____

The Chinese economy is one of the fastest-growing economies in the world. Han Li's life is completely different from her grandparents' life. 'They couldn't travel to other countries, but I can. I can drive a car, but my grandfather could only ride a bicycle.' Bo Li, Han's grandfather, smiles and says, 'We can afford to buy an air conditioner. Before, we couldn't relax in the house during the hot summer.'

2 Changes because of the _____

Under the old government of Afghanistan, there were many strict laws. For example, people couldn't listen to music or watch TV. Farida, a mother of two children, says, 'Life is much better now. Boys and girls can play together, and I can go out on my own. But, best of all, teenage girls can go to school.'

3 Changes because of the _____

The Inuits of Northern Canada are losing their old way of life because the environment is changing. 'The ice is disappearing now, so we can't get food in the old way,' says Tootega. 'When I was young, I could travel on the ice for days and find seals. Now, there is almost no ice. Our children can't learn the old skills and they are leaving our villages to find work in the cities. It makes me sad.'

GRAMMAR: *could, couldn't*

5a Complete these sentences from the article with the correct verb. Which sentences are about the present and which are about the past?

1 I can _____ a car.

2 I could _____ on the ice for days.

3 They couldn't _____ to other countries.

4 Our children can't _____ the old skills.

5b Find more examples of *could* and *couldn't* in the article. Which form of the main verb do we use after *could/couldn't*?

a) *to* + infinitive   b) present simple

c) infinitive without *to*

➡ Language reference and extra practice, pages 136–137

6 Complete the sentences with *can, can't, could* or *couldn't.*

1 He _____ find seals on the ice when he was young.

2 We _____ take photos at the museum yesterday – you can't take cameras with you.

3 We _____ fly to other countries today. Our grandparents _____ fly.

4 I _____ run far now, but I _____ run ten kilometres when I was younger.

7 Ask a partner what he/she could do at the ages of five, ten and 15. Use these ideas.

cook   drive   ride a bicycle   write
speak a little English   swim   use a computer

When you were five, could you ride a bicycle?

– Yes, I could. / No, I couldn't.

LISTENING

8 **2.10** Listen to a short presentation by two students about technology and cultural changes.

1 What is the title of their talk?

2 Which four inventions do they talk about?

9a **2.11** Listen again to Marjorie's part of the talk. Tick the things that she says.

1 People can travel longer distances.

2 People can live and work in different places.

3 Travelling is more comfortable.

4 Modern transport is not safe sometimes.

5 Modern transport is bad for the environment.

9b **2.12** Listen again to Nathan's part of the talk and answer the questions.

1 What can we do because of television and the Internet?

2 What is the negative point about these things?

3 Do you agree with him?

**VOCABULARY:
verbs + prepositions**

10a Listen to the whole presentation again for these verbs, and underline the object you hear. Check your ideas with Track 2.10 on page 151.

1 to focus on *a topic / technology / an idea*

2 to go on *a business trip / a tour / holiday*

3 to read about *places / subjects / people*

4 to move onto *the next point / another topic / the next type of technology*

5 to stay in *one place / our house / a group*

6 to chat to *friends / people / colleagues*

7 to talk to *strangers / someone / your teacher*

10b Complete the sentences with a verb and preposition from Exercise 10a.

1 This essay _____ _____ religion and cultural changes.

2 I'm _____ _____ the Mayan civilisation.

3 Before I _____ _____ the next point, I want to say …

4 Do you _____ _____ strangers on the Internet?

5 We usually _____ _____ holiday in August.

6 We _____ _____ the garden all day in summer.

7 I _____ _____ my friends on the phone every day.

SPEAKING

11 Work with a partner. Compare your way of life now with your grandparents' way of life when they were young. Think of four positive differences and four negative differences. Compare your ideas with another pair of students.

I can travel by plane to other countries but my grandparents could only use trains.

PREPARATION

1 Work with a partner and answer these questions.

1 What country/city is this museum in? (The museum in the photos.)

2 What can you see inside?

2 Match the sentences 1–8 with the notices a–i. There is one notice you don't need.

1 You can't go in or out this way.   _D_

2 You can leave your coats and bags here.

3 You can't make a lot of noise here.

4 You can't put your hand on this.

5 You can go through here in your wheelchair.

6 You can leave the museum through this door.

7 You can use this to go upstairs.

8 You can't use a camera here.

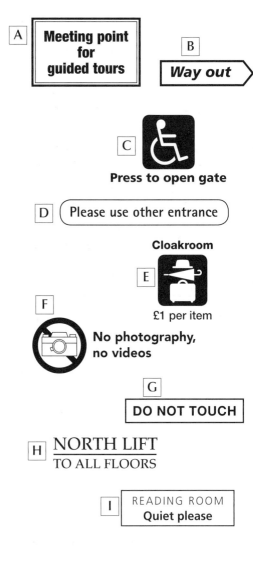

A
Meeting point for guided tours

B
Way out

C
Press to open gate

D
Please use other entrance

Cloakroom
E
£1 per item

F
No photography, no videos

G
DO NOT TOUCH

H
NORTH LIFT
TO ALL FLOORS

I
READING ROOM
Quiet please

3 [2.13] Richard and Jessica work at a museum. Listen to their conversations with six visitors to the museum. Match each conversation with one of these topics.

a) how much something costs

b) getting a map

c) how old something is

d) when something starts

e) taking a photograph

f) where something is   _1_

British Museum: Khorsabad Palace Reliefs

4 Listen again and answer these questions.

1 Where is the cloakroom?

2 How much does a long tour cost?

3 When does the film start?

4 How old is the statue?

5 How many maps does the Italian woman take?

6 Where can you take a photograph?

KEY LANGUAGE: polite requests

5 Put the lines of conversation 1 (below) in the right order. Check your answers with Track 2.13 on page 152.

a) Yes, madam. How can I help you? ☐

b) You're welcome. ☐

c) Could you tell me where the cloakroom is, please? ☐

d) Thank you. ☐

e) Certainly, madam. Can you see those stairs over there? ☐

f) Excuse me. 1

g) Yes, I can. ☐

h) Well, go down those stairs and then turn left. The cloakroom is next to the toilets. ☐

6a Complete the table with requests from the conversations in Exercise 3.

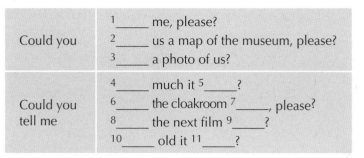

Could you	1_____ me, please?
	2_____ us a map of the museum, please?
	3_____ a photo of us?
Could you tell me	4_____ much it 5_____?
	6_____ the cloakroom 7_____, please?
	8_____ the next film 9_____?
	10_____ old it 11_____?

6b How can you respond to the requests in Exercise 6a? (Look at page 53, Exercise 9 and the Other useful phrases box on page 71.)

Certainly, …

7 `2.14` **Linked sounds** Listen to three requests. How do we pronounce *could you?* What happens where the words join?

8 `2.15` Put the words in the right order to make requests. Listen and check.

1 Could open you please the door ?

2 my coat you Could take please ?

3 me Could tell you when closes the museum ?

4 Could me what you tell this means please ?

5 where Could tell you me is the shop ?

9 Now make the requests and respond to them with a partner. Remember to use polite intonation.

TASK: finding out important information

10 Work with a partner and make short conversations in a museum.

Student A: You work at the British Museum. Use the information on this page to answer questions from a visitor.

Student B: You are a visitor to the museum. Look at page 117 and ask your partner questions.

Swap roles. Do the role-play again.

Student A: Now you are the visitor. Look at page 112.

Student B: Now you work at the museum.

OTHER USEFUL PHRASES

I'd like to do …	Yes, sir/madam.
Please.	Certainly.
I'm interested in …	That's no problem.
How can I help?	Sure, no problem.
Let me see …	Not at all.
(Yes,) of course.	I'm afraid not.
What would you like?	I'm afraid I can't do that.

THE BRITISH MUSEUM

The Great Court

Tickets

Entrance to the museum is free but there is a charge for some special exhibitions.

Forgotten Empire: The world of ancient Persia £10 (£6 Student and senior citizen)

Michelangelo Drawings: Closer to the Master £10 (£9 Senior citizen)

Main rooms

Britain and Europe	Upper floor (first floor)
Egyptian Mummies	Upper floor
Asia	Main floor
Greece and Rome	Main floor
Africa	Lower floor

Library – The Reading Room

The Reading Room is open to the general public.	10.00 – 17.30

Shops

The souvenir shop is on the west side of Great Court.	10.00 – 18.00
The bookshop is on the north side of Great Court.	10.00 – 18.00
The children's shop is on the east side of Great Court.	10.00 – 18.00

Food

The restaurant sells hot meals and afternoon teas.	12.00 – 20.00
The Great Court café sells sandwiches, cakes and drinks.	10.00 – 18.00

Front entrance

1 Managing new vocabulary How do you record and learn new vocabulary? Are these sentences true for you?

1 I have a special vocabulary notebook.

2 I read my vocabulary notes every day.

3 I learn ten new words every day.

4 I test my memory of new words every week.

5 I make grammar and pronunciation notes about

new words, e.g. *beautiful (adj)*.

6 I write translations for words.

7 I write English definitions for words, e.g. *wonderful – very good*.

2 Working with vocabulary The best way to learn new vocabulary is to do things with the words. Try these exercises. Use your dictionary. After each exercise, check your ideas with a partner.

a **Put words into groups by their meaning** Sort these words into two groups: materials and shapes.

circle   leather   metal   plastic   rectangle square   wood

Can you add more words to these two groups?

b **Do some word building.** Look at these dictionary extracts. *Circle* is the noun, what is the adjective?

---

cir·cle /ˈsɜːkəl $ ˈsɝːkəl/ *noun*
1 a round flat shape like the letter O, or a group of people or things arranged in this shape: *Draw a circle on this piece of paper* | *We sat in a circle round the table.* ⇨ *see picture at* POOR[1]

---

cir·cuit /ˈsɜːkɪt $ ˈsɝːkɪt/ *noun* 1 a track where people race cars, bicycles etc: *The racing cars go three times round the circuit.* 2 the complete circle that an electric current flows around: *an electrical circuit*
cir·cu·lar[1] /ˈsɜːkələ $ ˈsɝːkjələ/ *adjective* shaped like a circle: *a circular table.*

---

from Longman Wordwise Dictionary

• **What are the adjectives for these nouns? Use your dictionary.**

rectangle   square   wood

• **Complete the table with these words.**

long   widen   width   lengthen   weight

Noun	Verb	Adjective
1	2	wide
length	3	4
5	weigh	

c **Make mind maps.** Add more words to this mind map. Can you add more than four?

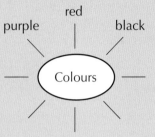

d **Find opposites for words.** Match the opposite pairs in this group of adjectives.

heavy   light   long   narrow   short   wide

e **Use the words** Make sentences with the new words.

circular – A coin is *circular*.

plastic – I use *plastic* bags from the supermarket.

3 Make sentences with five of the new words in this unit. Compare with a partner.

4 Which of these exercises do you like? Which do you think are more useful for you?

5 Look at the photos A–C. These three objects are for sale on an Internet auction site. Which sections can you find them in?

Antiques: Asia , Antiques: Games,
Collectables: North America

6a Match the description with one of photos A–C.

Photograph album

[This item] is very ¹_____. It is a ²_____ photograph album from Japan – when you turn the pages, you hear a beautiful song! It is about 50 years old. It is ³_____ (45cm long, 20cm wide) and it is in good condition. The album has got ten pages. These pages are now ⁴_____ with age. On the front of the album there's a wonderful picture. It is of a ⁵_____ temple and Mount Fuji. Thanks for looking and good luck!

6b Put these words in the correct places in the description.

musical   red   rectangular   unusual   yellow

7 it, this, these In the first sentence of the description, the words *This item* refer to the name of the item – photograph album. What do the other highlighted words refer to? Compare your ideas with a partner.

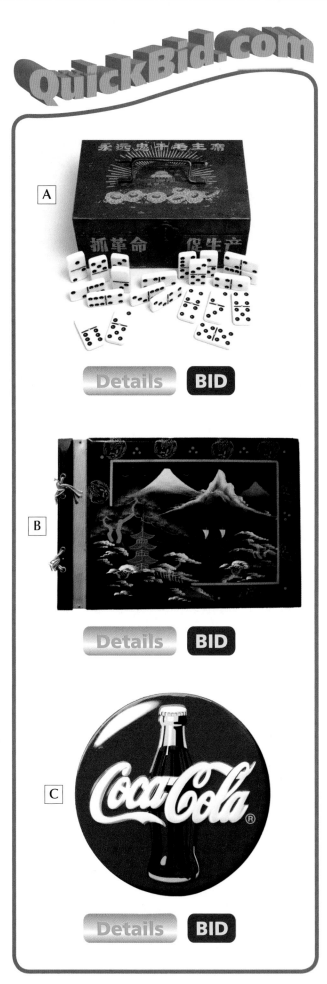

8 Match this description with one of the photos A–C. Use the words in the box to fill the gaps.

> it (x5)   these   they   this (x2)

Metal Coca-Cola® sign

¹_____ item is unusual. ²_____ is a Coca-Cola® sign from the 1950s. The metal sign is circular and ³_____ is 30cm wide. ⁴_____ weighs one kilogram. ⁵_____ is red and ⁶_____ has a great picture of the famous Coca-Cola® bottle. ⁷_____ picture is in good condition but there are some scratches on the side of the sign. ⁸_____ scratches are very small and ⁹_____ are not a problem. Hope you like it!

9a Complete the first sentence of the description of the object in photo A. Use the notes below.

Set of dominoes

This is a lovely item. It is a set of dominoes from ¹_____. It is ²_____ years old and it weighs ³_____ kilogram.

Item: Set of dominoes
Country: China   **Age:** 90 years
Weight of set: 1kg

Box:
Material: wood   **Colour:** red
Picture: some flowers   **Shape:** square
Width: 20cm
Condition: picture – excellent; box – good

Dominoes:
Number: 28   **Material:** plastic
Colour: white (black spots)
Shape: rectangular   **Length:** 4cm
Width: 2cm
Condition: very good

9b Work with a partner. One of you writes the description of the box. The other writes the description of the dominoes. Use the information above. Read your partner's work.
– The wooden box ...
– In the box, there are 28 ...

10 What were the final prices of these objects, do you think? Match a price with each object. Would you like to buy any of these objects?

> $45 $350 $75

9 Inventions

In this unit

9.1 MARVELLOUS MINDS

Grammar
- past simple, regular and irregular

Vocabulary
- inventions
- medical science

Scenario
- On the radio

Study skills
- taking notes while reading

Writing skills
- a short biography

| Alfred Nobel | Leonardo da Vinci | Levi Strauss |

Necessity is the mother of invention.
   Plato, 427BC–347BC, Greek philosopher

READING

1 What do you know about the three people in the photos? Discuss them with a partner.

2 Leonardo da Vinci was a famous inventor. Look at these inventions. Which are his ideas or inventions?

the bicycle   the car   the diving suit
the helicopter   high heels   the parachute
the radio   the robot   the telescope

Read the text *Leonardo da Vinci* quickly and check your ideas.

3 Read the text again. Are these sentences true or false?

1 When he was young, Leonardo was at a large school.

2 Leonardo was an engineering student.

3 A lot of modern inventions use his ideas.

4 The robot could only move its legs.

5 The car could only travel a short distance.

6 Leonardo's helicopter is the same as the modern ones.

7 Modern divers use Leonardo's diving glove.

4 Put the inventions in the text in order of importance. Compare with a partner.

GRAMMAR: past simple (affirmative)

When we talk about finished events and times in the past we use the past simple:

*In 1500 he **returned** to Florence.*

infinitive *return* ➔ past simple *returned*

5a Read the first paragraph of the text *(His life)* again and find other examples of the past simple. Complete the table below.

Infinitive	Past simple
return	returned

Note: we usually add *-ed* to the infinitive to form the past simple but sometimes there are spelling changes:

study ➔ *studied, travel* ➔ *travelled, live* ➔ *lived*

➡ Language reference and extra practice, pages 138–139

5b `2.16` Complete the sentences with your answers from Exercise 5a. Then listen and check.

1 Leonardo _____ his studies of art in 1468.

2 He _____ these studies in 1472.

3 He _____ money so he started work as an engineer.

4 Leonardo _____ as an engineer for 32 years.

5 He _____ in Milan from 1472 to 1500.

6 He _____ to Florence after 28 years in Milan.

LEONARDO DA VINCI

*Man of art. Man of ideas.
Man of inventions.*

His life

Leonardo da Vinci (1452–1519) lived in a small town in Italy with his grandparents. He studied at home and enjoyed music, singing and mathematics. At the age of 16, he wanted to study art, so he moved to the city of Florence for art classes. He finished his studies after four years. He then worked in Milan as an engineer and he started his life as an inventor. In 1500 he returned to Florence and in 1516 he travelled to France, where he stayed for the rest of his life.

His inventions

Leonardo da Vinci lived and worked before people used electricity and petrol for power, but he had the first ideas for many machines that we use today.

The robot
Leonardo built his robot in 1495. The robot stood up, sat down and held things in its arms.

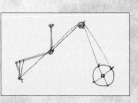

The car
A single passenger drove the car. It travelled 40 metres at a time.

The helicopter
Leonardo designed the first helicopter but he never made it. His design used a screw to lift the helicopter into the air. This is different from the modern design, but the general idea is similar.

The diving suit
Leonardo made the suit of leather and added long pipes to carry the air to the diver. He also invented special gloves for divers. Today, divers use them on their feet!

These are just some of Leonardo's hundreds of inventions. He also invented a parachute and even high heels!

6a `2.17` **Verb endings** The past simple ending *-ed* has three possible pronunciations. Listen to these examples and repeat them.

/ / *enjoyed*   / / *helped*   / / *needed*

6b Put the verbs from Exercise 5b in the correct column, then listen to Track 2.16 again, check and repeat the sentences.

GRAMMAR TIP

Some verbs in the past simple are irregular. We don't add *-ed* to the infinitive.

He **had** the first ideas.   (infinitive *have*)
He **built** his robot in 1495.   (infinitive *build*)

7 Read the rest of the text *(His inventions)* again and find the past simple forms of these verbs.

1 stand _____   3 hold _____   5 make _____

2 sit _____   4 drive _____

➡ Language reference and extra practice, pages 138–139

8 Complete the sentences with the past simple of the verbs in brackets. Is each verb regular or irregular? (See the irregular verb list on page 159.)

1 Last month, I _____ three films at the cinema. (see)
2 Last year, we _____ to Hawaii on holiday. (go)
3 He _____ Russia in 2006. (visit)
4 They _____ in a hotel by the sea last summer. (stay)
5 Yesterday, I _____ home at midnight. (get)
6 My father _____ mathematics at university. (study)
7 When I was a child, I _____ in a small town. (live)
8 I _____ to class by bus this morning. (come)

SPEAKING

9 Tell a partner about last weekend. What verbs do you need to use? Make a list.

Last weekend, I visited my grandparents on Saturday. I had lunch with them.

Last Sunday, I went skiing. I had a great time.

WRITING

10a Look at the information on page 121 about Alfred Nobel and Levi Strauss. Match the information with these inventors and then write a short text about them.

10b `2.18` Listen and compare your texts.

VOCABULARY: medical science

1 Choose the best words to complete the sentences. Use your dictionary.

1 *Science/Medicine* is the study and *trial/treatment* of illnesses.
2 *Teeth/Skin* and *bones/the heart* are hard parts of the body.
3 A *scientist/doctor* usually works in a *laboratory/waiting room*.
4 A scientist uses *tools/equipment* to do *examinations/experiments*.

READING

2 Look at the photos A–D and match them with paragraphs 1–4 in the text *Medical inventions*.

3 Complete the table with information from the text.

Medical inventions			
Name	Date	Country	Other information
scalpel	3000 BC	1	didn't change for ²_____ years
acupuncture needles	3	4	still popular in ⁵_____ and other countries
6	700 BC	7	didn't change until ⁸_____
9	10	Holland	people didn't want to look at ¹¹_____ things then

GRAMMAR: past simple (negative)

4 Underline the negative forms of the past simple in the text. (The first one is underlined.) Then complete the rule.

To make the negative of the past simple, we use: subject + _____ + _____ + infinitive without *to*.

Note: when we speak, and in informal writing, *did not* ➜ *didn't*.

➜ Language reference and extra practice, pages 138–139

5 Write true sentences with the past simple (affirmative or negative) of the verbs in brackets.

1 People _____ the scalpel for the first time around 3000 BC. (use)
2 The Japanese _____ acupuncture. (invent)
3 People _____ false teeth before 700 BC. (wear)
4 False teeth _____ between 700 BC and AD 1770. (change)
5 Zacharias Jansen _____ the first microscope. (make)
6 His microscope _____ objects ten times bigger than their real size. (show)

Medical inventions

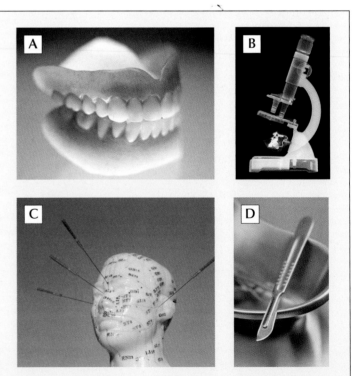

1 The scalpel is one of the oldest inventions in medicine. It is a small, light and very sharp knife. People used it for the first time around 3000 BC in the area of modern Iraq. The scalpel <u>did not change</u> very much for 4,000 years.

2 The Chinese invented acupuncture needles around 2000 BC. At first, they did not make needles from metal, but from stone. Today, people in China and other countries use acupuncture for many illnesses.

3 People in southern Italy invented the first false teeth about 700 BC. They used pieces of bone, or sometimes second-hand human teeth! After that, false teeth did not change for the next 2,500 years until, in 1770, a Frenchman called Alexis Duchateau first used porcelain, a hard, white material that we still sometimes use today.

4 Zacharias Jansen from Holland made the first microscope in about 1590. Through it, objects appeared nine times bigger than their real size, but it did not give a very clear picture. Jansen did not use his invention very much because people at that time did not want to look at small things!

LISTENING

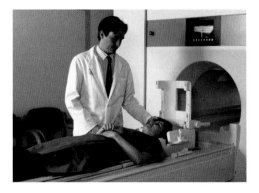

6a Look at this picture. What is this machine, do you think?

a) an MRI scanner   b) an X-ray machine
c) a microscope

6b `2.19` Listen to the first part of a radio interview and check your answer.

7a Do you think these sentences about the machine on Track 2.20 are true or false?

1 The machine looks inside you.
2 It can only take a picture of your head.
3 It's dangerous.
4 German scientists invented it.
5 Hospitals first used it in the 1980s.

7b `2.20` Now listen to the rest of the interview and check your answers to Exercise 7a.

8 Listen again and complete these sentences.

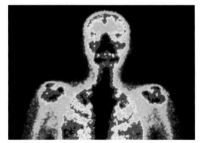

1 The scanner can show both the hard parts and the _soft parts_ of the body.
2 It can take a picture of the _____ body.
3 In the 1950s, Felix Bloch _____ the importance of NMR for looking inside the human body.
4 Raymond Damadian and his team built the first full-body MRI scanner in _____.
5 In _____, hospitals around the world bought their first MRI scanners.
6 The scanner isn't good for people who don't like _____ _____.

GRAMMAR: past simple (questions)

9 Look at the two questions below and choose the correct words in the statements 1–4.

Did Felix Bloch invent the MRI scanner?

When did they build the first scanner?

1 Past simple questions use the past form of _do/have_.
2 *Did* always comes <u>before/after</u> the subject of the question.
3 The main verb comes <u>before/after</u> the subject.
4 The main verb is in *the <u>infinitive (without to)</u> / the past simple (affirmative)*.

GRAMMAR TIP

Notice the short answers:
Did you see him there? – Yes, I did. / No, I didn't.
Did they arrive on time? – Yes, they did. / No, they didn't.

➡ Language reference and extra practice, pages 138–139

10 Put the words in the right order to make questions. Ask and answer the questions with a partner. Check your answers on page 121.

1 Thomas Edison   TV   Did   invent   ?
2 make   Europeans   the first paper   Did   ?
3 did   invent   Wilhelm Röntgen   What   ?
4 the Americans   When   on the moon   did   land   ?
5 Where   first arrive   did   in America   Christopher Columbus   ?

SPEAKING

11 Tell your partner about your first experiences. Use ideas from the list. Answer your partner's questions.

cook a meal   play a sport   move to a new house
eat foreign food   win something   hold a baby
organise a party   fly   travel alone   vote
go abroad

I first travelled alone when I was 18.

Then listen to your partner's experiences and ask questions.

Did you like it / enjoy it?

How did you feel?

What happened next?

PREPARATION

1 Match the things below with photos A–E on page 79. How often do you use them?

chewing gum   lipstick   Post-it® notes
tin cans   umbrellas

2a **2.21** Listen to the introduction to a radio programme and complete the following.

1 the title of the programme:
   The nation's _____ everyday _____
2 the phone number of the radio show:
   0810 _____

2b Listen again, then complete this description of the programme with the words in the box.

| choose   history   information |
| normal   opinion   texting |

This programme gives the ¹_____ of inventions that people use in their ²_____ lives. We learn some important ³_____ about the inventions. Each week, the presenter gives her ⁴_____ about the inventions and, after the programme, the listeners ⁵_____ their favourite invention by ⁶_____ a phone number.

3a How much do you know about the history of the umbrella? Are these sentences true or false? Guess.

1 People first used umbrellas in places like India, Egypt and China.
2 At first, only rich and important people used umbrellas.
3 The British made the first umbrella for the rain.
4 In Europe, for many years, only men used umbrellas. Women did not like them.
5 The first umbrella shop opened in London.

3b **2.22** Listen to the radio programme and check your ideas.

4 **2.23** The presenter next gives four reasons for voting for the umbrella. What do you think she says? Choose four reasons from this list, then listen and check.

1 It is one of the oldest everyday inventions.
2 It is a good simple design.
3 It has three different uses.
4 Umbrellas can be very colourful.
5 Umbrellas are not expensive.
6 They are easy to carry.

KEY LANGUAGE: giving reasons

5 **2.24** Look at the reasons below from the programme. Complete the sentences, then listen and check your ideas.

1 Well, the _____ important reason _____ that it's one of the oldest inventions in the world.
2 Secondly, the umbrella is a great invention _____ it's got several different uses.
3 Vote for the umbrella _____ umbrellas bring colour to our grey, rainy streets.
4 My _____ reason _____ that umbrellas are very cheap to make.

6 You can put many different things before the phrases *… reason is that …* and … *because* … Write the following words or phrases in the correct place below.

| a very good   they are popular   another |
| one   people buy umbrellas   the main |
| umbrellas are useful   buy an umbrella |

A very good	*They are popular*
_____	_____
_____ reason is (that) …	_____ because …
_____	_____

pronunciation

7a Stressed words Look at these phrases. Underline the words that are different in each phrase.

1 An important reason is that …
2 A good reason is that …
3 The second reason is that …
4 One reason is that …
5 Another reason is that …
6 The main reason is that …

7b **2.25** Listen to the phrases fom Exercise 7a. Which word has the most stress in each phrase?

7c Say the phrases with a partner. Is your sentence stress good?

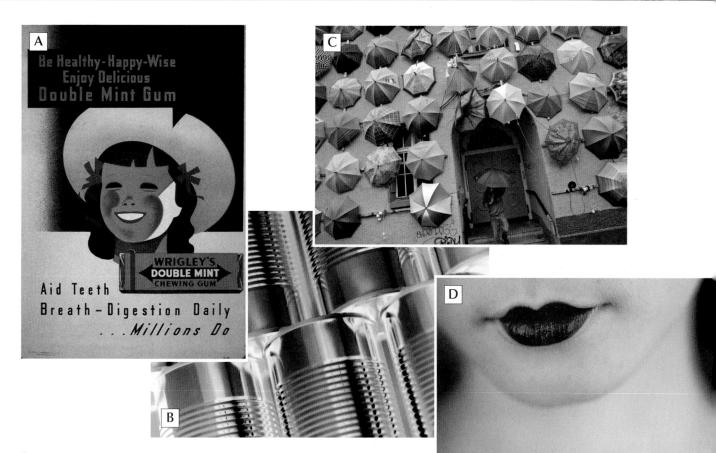

A
Be Healthy-Happy-Wise
Enjoy Delicious
Double Mint Gum
WRIGLEY'S
DOUBLE MINT
CHEWING GUM
Aid Teeth
Breath—Digestion Daily
...Millions Do

B

C

D

E

8 Ask and answer these questions with a partner. Use the phrases from Exercise 6.

1 Why are you learning English?

I'm learning English because I like the language.

The main reason is that I want a better job.

2 Why do people join clubs?

3 Why do people go to university?

4 Why do people play sport?

5 Why do people have pets?

6 Why do people go abroad on holiday?

> **TASK:** giving a short presentation

9a Work with a partner. You are the presenters of the radio show. Prepare a short talk about an everyday invention. Follow the instructions below.

Pair A: Look at page 113.
Pair B: Look at page 118.
Pair C: Look at page 120.
Pair D: Look at page 120.

Make sure you …

• give a short introduction to the invention – perhaps an interesting fact, or a description of the invention
• give three facts about the invention
• give some reasons for voting for this invention
• make a final comment.

Look at Tracks 2.22–2.23 on page 153 for an example.

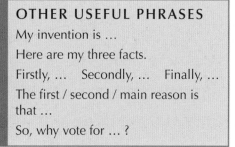

> **OTHER USEFUL PHRASES**
> My invention is …
> Here are my three facts.
> Firstly, …   Secondly, …   Finally, …
> The first / second / main reason is that …
> So, why vote for … ?

9b Now work in groups of four students. Each group has an A, B, C and D student. Give your talk to the other students in your group.

10 Vote for your favourite invention and say why you like it.

Winds from the East: Chinese inventions

The Chinese invented many things that we use today, long before they appeared in the West.

The Chinese invented paper in the 2nd century BC. Over a thousand years later, in the 12th century AD, Europeans first made paper. Another example is matches: the Chinese had matches in the 6th century, but Europeans did not use them until the 19th century. Paper money is another Chinese invention: Europeans first made it in Sweden in 1661, but the Chinese invented it 800 years earlier, in the 9th century.
Knowledge of other inventions came along the 'Silk Road', linking East and West, and more information came by sea. Sailors brought Chinese ideas to the

Marco Polo travelling by camel caravan, Catalan atlas, 1375

Arabian Gulf and northern Africa and, from there, they spread north to Europe. Travellers like Marco Polo (1254–1324) also brought stories of Chinese inventions back to Europe.

STUDY SKILLS: taking notes while reading

1 Discuss these questions with a partner.

1 When do you take notes?
2 How do you take notes?
3 Do you think you are good or bad at taking notes? Why?

2 Recording notes There are different ways of taking notes. There is no right or wrong way. Read the text above and complete the two different kinds of notes.

3 Note-taking style Study the notes and answer these questions.

1 Do we use words like *a, the* and *in* in notes?
2 What do these symbols mean?
a) → b) + c) " d) c.

4 Which kind of notes do you prefer, A (the mind map) or B? Why?

5 Look at the text about Leonardo da Vinci on page 75. Make notes on it. Compare your notes with a partner. Can you make your notes better?

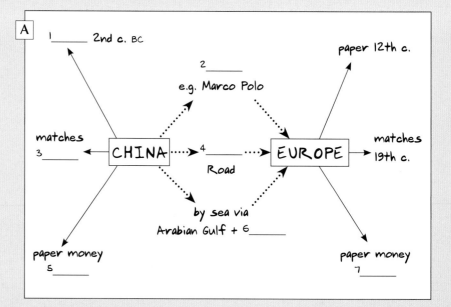

A

1_____ 2nd c. BC

paper 12th c.

2_____
e.g. Marco Polo

matches
3_____   CHINA ····▸ 4_____ ····▸ EUROPE   matches
                          Road   19th c.

by sea via
Arabian Gulf + 6_____

paper money
5_____

paper money
7_____

B

Chinese inventions

Chinese invented 1_____ 2nd c. BC   Europe 12th c.

   "   "   matches 2_____   "   19th c.

   "   "   paper money 9th c.   "   AD 1661

Ways to Europe

· 3_____ Road

· by sea, China → Arabian 4_____ + northern Africa → Europe

· 5_____, e.g. Marco Polo

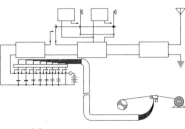

Detail from communications system

6 Discuss these questions with a partner.

1 Do you know the names of any women inventors?

2 Why are most inventors men, do you think?

7a Look at these events in the life of Hedy Lamarr and number them in the correct order.

Discuss your order with your partner.

a) She went to America. ☐

b) She acted in the European art film *Extase* and she became famous. ☐ ☐

c) She wrote a book about her life.

d) When she was a teenager, she went to acting school in Berlin. ☐

e) After four years, she left her husband and she went to London. ☐

f) She became a Hollywood star. ☐

g) She and George developed a radio communications system for submarines. ☐ ☐

h) As a child, she grew up in Vienna. ☐

i) She married Fritz Mandl, the first of her six husbands. ☐

j) She met George Antheil, a composer. 9

k) Hedy Lamarr was born in Vienna, Austria, in 1913. 1

7b 2.26 Listen and check your answers.

8 Linkers Look at Track 2.26 on page 153. Complete this table with the underlined linking words.

At the same time	Next
during	*later*

9 Read the text about Ada Lovelace and choose the best linking words.

Lady Ada Lovelace – the world's first woman in computers

Ada Byron was born in 1815 in Piccadilly, London. Her parents (the poet Lord Byron and Anne Milbanke) separated immediately [1]*then / later / after* her birth. Four months [2]*during / before / later*, Lord Byron left England forever. In 1828, at the age of 13, Ada produced a design for a flying machine. [3]*Before / Then / During*, in 1833, Ada met the mathematician and inventor Charles Babbage. Two years [4]*after that / next / then*, she married William King (later Lord Lovelace) and they had three children. [5]*During / After / Next* the birth of her third child, she began work with Charles Babbage. She developed the idea of using binary numbers (0, 1) and understood many ideas that we use in computer programming today. She died in 1852.

10 Use the information below to write a short biography.

Madam CJ Walker (Sarah Breedlove) – the first African-American woman millionaire

1867 – born Sarah Breedlove in Louisiana, USA

1874 – parents died / she went to work in cotton fields

1881 – married Moses McWilliam

1885 – only daughter Lelia born

1887 – husband died / she got a job washing clothes

1890s – lost some of her hair

1905 – developed new hair care products / changed her name to Madam CJ Walker

1908 – opened a training college in Pittsburgh

1910 – built a factory in Indianapolis

1916 – gave money to help African-Americans

1919 – died in New York State / richest African-American woman

Charles Babbage's Analytical Engine

Malta

Today, Malta is a popular holiday island in the Mediterranean Sea, but it ¹_____ (not/be) always an island: thousands of years ago, there ²_____ (be) a large desert between Europe and Africa, but at that time there ³_____ (be) no people there. Between 7000 and 5000 BC, people ⁴_____ (travel) across the sea from Sicily to Malta. They ⁵_____ (build) the famous temples on the island.

The Ħaġar Qim temple in Malta

The Phoenicians ⁶_____ (be) the other early visitors. They ⁷_____ (use) the island's natural harbours for their ships, and they also ⁸_____ (trade) with other countries around the Mediterranean from these harbours. During the Roman Empire, Rome also ⁹_____ (control) the island for seven centuries.

Like the Phoenicians, the Romans ¹⁰_____ (not/can) control the islands any more and they ¹¹_____ (leave). Malta ¹²_____ (have) many more visitors after that. The Arabs ¹³_____ (live) there for two centuries and ¹⁴_____ (give) the modern Maltese language many words. The Spanish, the French and the British all ¹⁵_____ (come) and ¹⁶_____ (leave) the island, and, finally, in 1964, Malta ¹⁷_____ (become) independent and ¹⁸_____ (can) make its own laws and protect its own people.

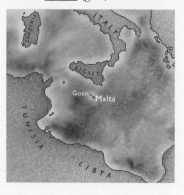

GRAMMAR

1 Write the verbs in the text in the past simple.

2 Complete the questions about Malta in the past simple.

1 Q: How did the first visitors_____?
   A: They travelled by boat.

2 Q: Who _____?
   A: The Phoenicians.

3 Q: Why _____?
   A: For their ships and because they could trade with other countries.

4 Q: How long _____?
   A: For seven centuries.

5 Q: What _____?
   A: Many words.

6 Q: When _____?
   A: In 1964.

3 Work with a partner. Ask and answer questions about the past.

Student A: Look at the information on page 114.

Student B: Look at the information on page 119.

4 Where do you normally buy food and clothes? How much do you usually spend on food shopping a week?

5 🔊 2.27 Listen to a conversation and choose the best answer.

1 Where is the woman?
a) in a supermarket   b) in a car park
c) in a manager's office

2 What does she want to buy?
a) food   b) clothes   c) food and clothes

3 How is the woman paying for her shopping today?
a) by credit card   b) with cash   c) by direct debit

4 How much does she usually spend?
a) £100   b) under £100   c) over £100

6a Choose the correct form of the verb in the conversation between a supermarket manager and a customer.

M: Hello. ¹*I'm / I'm being* the manager of this supermarket and today ²*we talk / we're talking* to some of our customers. ³*Do you have / Are you having* five minutes?

C: Yes, OK.

M: Great. What ⁴*do you buy / are you buying* today? Food or clothes?

C: Food and clothes. ⁵*I always buy / I'm always buying* food on Mondays and today ⁶*I also look for / I'm also looking for* some clothes for my children.

M: OK. And ⁷*do you usually pay / are you usually paying* by credit card?

C: Yes, I do but ⁸*I use / I'm using* cash today.

M: I see. And on average how much ⁹*do you spend / are you spending* here every week – under or over £100?

C: Oh, probably over £100.

6b Listen again and check your answers.

UNITS 7–9

VOCABULARY

7 Read the email from Camilla to her sister Susie in the UK. Choose the best word, a), b) or c), for gaps 1–9.

```
☑                                              _□×
✉Send  🖫 🖨 ✂ 🗎 📋 🔳 🔗 🕮 ❗ ↓ ▼ 🔳 Options... ❓ ▾
From...  Camilla Nichols
To...    Susie Nichols
Subject: Mum's birthday
```

Dear Susie
¹_____ are things? I'm emailing you from a petrol station. The petrol, or what Americans call ²_____, is really cheap here. I can fill the car for about $20 and drive across California! The ³_____ are like our motorways but a lot ⁴_____ and ten times longer. I'm driving a big American car – it's so big that yesterday, I couldn't drive it out of the parking ⁵_____ (that's car park for you!).
It's Mum's birthday next week. I think she'd like a ⁶_____ camera. Are they expensive? In the United States everything is so cheap compared with the UK. I found trainers for about £5 at a shop called The Big Shoe ⁷_____, so I bought two pairs. And I also got some gold ⁸_____ heels. I can't walk in them but they look wonderful!
⁹_____ for now.
Camilla

1 a) Hope   b) Hi   c) How

2 a) oil   b) gas   c) water

3 a) main streets   b) highways
   c) high roads

4 a) widen   b) width   c) wider

5 a) lot   b) market   c) car

6 a) electric   b) computer   c) digital

7 a) Store   b) Motel   c) Station

8 a) long   b) heavy   c) high

9 a) Bye   b) Care   c) Love

KEY LANGUAGE

8 Put the words in the right order to make sentences.

a) you   some   mobile   show   could   phones
   me   please   ?

b) problem   no   that's

c) can   you   help   I   ?

d) not   afraid   I'm

e) to see   would   like   phones   which   you   ?

f) has   advantages   main   two   it

9a Complete the conversation with the sentences in Exercise 8.

A: Hello, ¹_____
B: Yes. ²_____

A: Certainly. We have over 50 different designs.
   ³_____
B: I don't know. There are so many!
A: This one is popular.
B: Why?
A: Well, ⁴_____. The first advantage is the camera and the second is that you can listen to music on it.
B: Yes, but that means it's the most expensive. Sorry, but I'd like something cheaper.
A: ⁵_____. This model is half the price.
B: Does it play music?
A: No, ⁶_____, but it has a camera.

9b 🔳2.28 Read the conversation in Exercise 9a and listen to a similar conversation. There are five differences. Write the changes.

LANGUAGE CHECK

10 Write in the missing preposition in sentences 1–10. Use the prepositions in the box and look at the pages to check.

before	down	during	for
~~in~~	in	of	on	on	to

                                    in
1 I don't spend a lot of time ⋀ the shops.   (page 58)
2 How much did you pay these DVDs?   (page 59)
3 A lot of companies are doing business the Internet.   (page 61)
4 First all, it's an interesting place to visit.   (page 63)
5 We saw that film the day yesterday.   (page 67)
6 We usually go holiday to Spain.   (page 69)
7 Do you chat friends on the Internet?   (page 69)
8 You're on the third floor. So go those stairs to the second floor.   (page 70)
9 Leonardo started his studies 1468.   (page 75)
10 She married three different men her life.   (page 81)

LOOK BACK

11 Find the exercises in Units 7–9 where you ...

• discuss your shopping habits. (U7)
• learn American English. (U7)
• give a short talk. (U7)
• read about one of the world's first cities. (U8)
• compare your grandparents' way of life with yours. (U8)
• ask politely for something. (U8)
• find out about the first helicopter. (U9)
• say what you did last weekend. (U9)
• listen to a radio programme. (U9)

10 Money

In this unit

Grammar
- should, shouldn't
- have to, don't have to

Vocabulary
- money
- phrases connected with money

Scenario
- In my opinion

Study skills
- taking notes while listening

Writing skills
- a formal letter

10.1 KEEPING IT SAFE

Time is money.
Benjamin Franklin, 1706–1790, US politician and scientist

VOCABULARY: money

1a Look at the words and phrases in the box. Check any new words in your dictionary. Which two are *cash*?

| cashpoint | cheque | coin | credit card |
| note | PIN number | purse | wallet |

1b Make true sentences, using the words above. Compare with a partner.

1 I've got / I haven't got a lot of _____.
2 I don't often use _____.
3 There are a lot of _____ in my _____.
4 It's easy/difficult to remember my _____.
5 I always destroy old _____.
6 _____ is/are more useful to me than _____.

READING

2 Look at the poster below. Where can you see it?

> **Sheffield Metropolitan University**
> _____
> ## INTERNATIONAL STUDENTS!
>
> *Are you new to this city?*
> *Are you worried about:*
> * **keeping your money safe?**
> * **going out at night?**
> * **using tsaxis alone?**
> * **people stealing your mobile?**
>
> Come along to a talk by **Sue Cutler**, Sheffield Met International Student Welfare Officer
> **Staying safe: looking after yourself and your money**
> Wednesday 3 October
> Peak Building Lecture Theatre, 4 p.m.
> Tea and biscuits from 3.30 p.m.
> *Everyone welcome!*

3 Are these sentences about the talk true or false?

1 The talk is for all students of the University.

2 The talk is only about money.

3 Sue Cutler works for the University.

4 The talk is on Wednesday morning.

5 There is nothing to eat or drink there.

LISTENING

4 **2.29** Read these sentences, then listen to the first part of Sue's talk and choose the best summary.

1 The city is dangerous and it's important to be very careful with your money.

2 The city is safe, but it's important to be careful with your money.

3 The city is safe, so it's not important to be careful with your money.

5 **2.30** Now listen to the rest of Sue's talk and fill the gaps.

1 You should be careful in _____ places.

2 You should keep your _____ _____ safe.

3 You shouldn't keep your _____ in your back pocket.

4 You shouldn't carry a lot of _____.

5 You shouldn't take your money out in _____ _____ places.

6 Look at what these people say. Do they follow Sue's advice?

1 I can never remember my PIN numbers so I keep them on a piece of paper in my wallet.

2 I always carry my wallet in my inside jacket pocket.

3 I don't like cheques or credit cards so I always carry a lot of cash.

4 I sometimes check how much money I've got in my purse when I'm on the bus.

GRAMMAR: *should, shouldn't*

7 Look at the examples and explanations. Answer the two questions below.

Examples	Explanations
*You **should** be careful.*	It's the right thing to do.
*He **shouldn't** put his money in his back pocket.*	It isn't the right thing to do.
***Should I** wear a money belt?*	Is it the right thing to do?

➡ Language reference and extra practice, pages 140–141

1 Do we add -s to *should* after *he, she* and *it?*

2 Can you think of another verb with grammar like this?

8 Complete the sentences with *should* or *shouldn't* and the verb.

1 *Should I keep* this money? I found it in the street. (I/keep)

2 _____ to that restaurant on your birthday – the food is really bad. (you/go)

3 Max lost his wallet yesterday. – _____ more careful with his money. (he/be)

4 _____ a new camera. Her other camera is only six months old. (she/buy)

5 Someone stole my purse from my car. – _____ the police. (you/tell)

6 _____ all our money on a round-the-world trip or on a swimming pool in the garden? (we/spend)

9 Look at some more problems of international students in the UK. Give them advice with *should* and the ideas in the box.

> don't use your computer late at night
> go out in a group   join a sports club
> watch TV and practise listening

1 I don't know any British people.

2 I can't understand what British people say.

3 I don't feel safe in the city.

4 I send emails to my friends back home until 2 a.m., and then I can't sleep.

SPEAKING

10a Work with a partner. Think of some advice for Nadia.

> I'm a student in London. This is a very expensive city and I don't get a lot of money: my parents pay my university fees but they can't afford to give me any extra money. I have a part–time job in a restaurant, but it doesn't pay very much. I'm using my credit cards a lot and now I'm in debt. What should I do?
> *Nadia*

10b Look at page 121 and check your advice. Then give advice to the other people on that page.

WRITING

11 Work with a partner. Write a reply to one of the people on page 121.

VOCABULARY:
phrases connected with money

1 Complete the definitions with the phrases in the box.

> borrow money (from someone)
> charges you interest   earn money   get a loan
> lend money (to someone)   pay back

1 When you _____, you get money from your job.

2 When you _____, you get some money from someone and return it later.

3 When you _____ some money, you return the money that you borrowed before.

4 When you _____, you give someone some money and he/she returns it later.

5 When you _____, you borrow money, for example from a bank.

6 When a bank _____, you pay back more money than you borrowed.

READING

2 Look at the FAQs (Frequently Asked Questions) page for Credit Aid and answer these questions.

1 Who does Credit Aid help?

2 What does Credit Aid do?

Credit Aid

Helping the poor to change their lives

FAQs

Is Credit Aid the same as a bank?

No, it isn't. Many poor people want to start their own business in order to make their lives better, but banks don't lend money to these people because they don't have jobs or houses.

How do we help people?

We work in poor or developing countries. We lend money to poor men and women for their businesses. These micro-credit loans are very small. They are usually less than 250 dollars. We charge interest of only two percent.

How can someone borrow money from Credit Aid?

He/She ...
- has to be over 21 years old
- has to earn less than one dollar a day
- has to have a good business idea
- doesn't have to be in work
- doesn't have to own a house

3 Are the sentences about the text true or false?

1 A 20-year-old can get a loan.

2 A person without a job can get a loan.

3 A person without a house can get a loan.

4 A person without a business idea can get a loan.

5 A rich person can get a loan.

GRAMMAR: *have to, don't have to*

4 Match the sentences with the correct explanations.

1 She doesn't have to do it.

2 He has to do it.

3 We have to do it.

4 You don't have to do it.

a) It is necessary.

b) It isn't necessary.

GRAMMAR TIP

Notice the question form:

Does he / she have to ... ?
Do I / you / we / they have to ... ?

➡ Language reference and extra practice, pages 140–141

5 Complete the sentences with the correct form of *have to* (affirmative, negative or question form) and a verb from the box.

> check   give   keep   pay   pay   ~~show~~   use

1 When you open a bank account, you *have to show* some identification.

2 When you borrow money from a friend, you _____ interest.

3 In a foreign country, you _____ foreign currency because you can use a credit card.

4 The bank _____ your money safe.

5 _____ the bank manager _____ my loan application?

6 How much interest _____ I _____?

7 A bank manager _____ you a loan; he/she can choose.

6 What are the differences between these jobs? What do/don't the people have to do?

a doctor   a footballer   a musician   a pilot
a police officer   a student   a teacher

A teacher has to prepare lessons / doesn't have to wear a uniform.

People who borrow from us: *Jane*

I live in Rwanda and I'm a widow – my husband died in an accident. I live with my elderly mother and I've got two children. I have to look after all of them.

Two months ago I started my business – I opened a cinema! I borrowed 300 dollars from Credit Aid and I have to pay back six dollars every week for one year. I bought a TV, a video player and some chairs. My brother built the room and now I show a film every evening. The cinema is always full and I make 15 dollars every week. It's quite easy to run a cinema: I don't have to work in the daytime, but I have to choose good films!

Now my children can go to school because they don't have to work. I can afford better food and, because the cinema is only open in the evening, I can still look after my mother.

○ **Click here to find out about these people.**

READING

7a Micro-credit can change the life of a family. Work with a partner to find out about two women's stories.

Student A: Read about Jane (above) and answer the questions below.

Student B: Read about Maya on page 118 and answer the questions below. Do not look at the text above.

1 Where does she live?
2 Does she have a family?
3 What is her business?
4 When did she start it?
5 How much money did she borrow?
6 How much does she have to pay back every week?
7 What did she spend the money on?
8 How much money does she earn?
9 Is her life better now? Why?

7b Tell your partner about the woman in your text.

SPEAKING

8a Work with a partner. You and your partner work for Credit Aid. Read about four people and then, together, decide who can get a loan. Read carefully and note any important information for your discussion.

Student A: Look at the information on page 112.
Student B: Look at the information on page 118.

8b Discuss the four people and their ideas with your partner. You can only choose two ideas for loans. Who should you give the loans to?

PREPARATION

1 Do you agree or disagree with these quotes? How true are they – definitely true, partly true or not at all true?

1 'Money can buy you happiness.' *Anon*

2 'Time is more valuable than money.' *Jim Rohn*

3 'You can be young without money, but you can't be old without it.' *Tennessee Williams*

4 'Money makes the world go round.' *Kander and Ebb, from the musical* Cabaret

2a **2.31** A bank is doing a survey about money. Listen to an interview.

1 What is the relationship between David and Katie, do you think?

2 Which person is more careful with their money, David or Katie?

3 Which person are you most similar to?

2b Listen to the interview again. Are these sentences true or false?

1 David thinks that you can spend too much money with a credit card.

2 Katie likes to buy things immediately.

3 Katie never saves any money.

4 David says he is saving money for a holiday.

5 David thinks that borrowing money from friends is a very bad idea.

6 Katie thinks that it is a good idea to borrow a lot of money from friends.

7 Katie never gives money to charity.

8 David gives money to charity every month.

KEY LANGUAGE: asking for and giving opinions

3 **2.31** Complete the questions and answers from the interview. Listen and check.

1 – What's your opinion about _____ credit cards?
– Well, personally, I _____ that they're a bad idea.
– Well, in my _____, they're great.

2 – Do you _____ _____ saving money is important?
– Erm, yes, I suppose _____ _____, …
– Oh yes, _____.

3 – Do you think that borrowing money from friends is a _____ _____?
– Oh, no, not at _____.
– Well, I'm not _____.

4 – Do you agree that people _____ _____ money to charity?
– No, not at all. I _____ that the government should look after everyone.
– Well, yes, I _____.

pronunciation

4a **2.32** **Stressed words** Listen to part of the interview again and answer the questions 1–3.

1 Which word is stressed most in each question below? Mark the correct words.
'OK madam, and do you think that saving money is important?'
'And sir, do you think that saving money is important?'

2 Which question above means *Tell me about this topic?*

3 Which question above means *I want to know your opinion?*

4b Listen again and repeat the two questions.

5 Work with a partner. Ask and answer the questions in Exercise 3. Remember to change the stress when you say the question the second time.

Student A: Do you think that saving money is important?

Student B: Oh yes, definitely. And do <u>you</u> think that it's important?

Student A: No, not at all. I think that <u>you</u> should spend your money while you can!

6 In Exercise 3 there are three different types of question. In each pair of questions below, complete the second question so that it means the same as the first.

1a Do you think that saving money is important?

1b Do you agree that people should _____ _____?

2a Do you think that borrowing money from friends is a good idea?

2b What's your opinion _____ _____ _____ _____ _____?

3a Do you agree that people should give money to charity?

3b Do you think that _____ _____ _____ _____ _____ important?

4a Do you agree that students should have part-time jobs?

4b What's your opinion about students having _____ _____?

5a What's your opinion about children having credit cards?

5b Do you think that children _____ _____ _____ _____ a good idea?

TASK: expressing thoughts and opinions

7 Work with a partner and make a questionnaire about money. Choose from these ideas and the ideas in Exercise 6 and complete the questions in the questionnaire.

- give money to homeless people
- borrow money for a computer
- students pay for university
- directors earn a very high salary
- buy expensive clothes
- parents give children pocket money
- children work
- save money for retirement

Money Questionnaire

Section A — Notes

1 What's your opinion about _____? _____
2 What's your opinion about _____? _____

Section B (tick one)	Yes	No	Not sure / Don't know
3 Do you think that _____ important?	☐	☐	☐
4 Do you think that _____ a good idea?	☐	☐	☐
5 Do you agree that _____?	☐	☐	☐
6 Do you agree that _____?	☐	☐	☐

8a With your partner, make copies of your questionnaire and interview as many other students as you can. Keep good notes.

OTHER USEFUL PHRASES

I think that …	I don't know.
In my opinion, …	Yes, definitely.
Personally, I think …	Yes, I suppose it is.
I'm not sure.	No, not at all.

8b Share your notes with your partner.

Ten students think that we should save money for our retirement. Three students think that it isn't necessary …

9 Write a short paragraph about the results of your survey. You can use tables to show some of the information. Show your results to other students.

Fifteen students think that giving money to homeless people is important. Five students think that it isn't a good idea and ten students aren't sure.

STUDY SKILLS:
taking notes while listening

1 `2.33` Look at the mind map, listen to the first part of a talk by Sue at Sheffield Metropolitan University about British banks and fill the gaps a–f with one word.

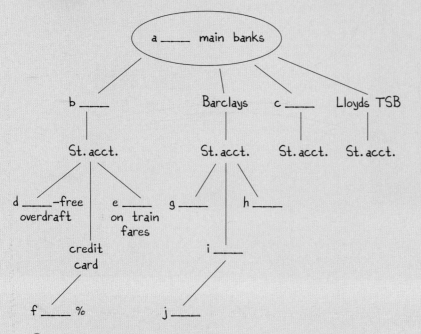

2a Introducing extra information Complete this section from the talk, using the notes in the mind map.

OK, so, first of all, the NatWest ¹_____ _____. This account offers an ²_____ _____. As well as this, you can get a ³_____ _____ and the interest rate for that is about ⁴_____ percent per year. Also, the bank offers discounts on ⁵_____ _____ in Britain.

2b Which words and phrases in Exercise 2a introduce extra information, i.e. they have a similar meaning to *and*?

3a `2.34` Listen to the second part of the talk, about Barclays, and fill the gaps g–j on the mind map. Compare your notes with a partner.

3b Listen again and complete the sentences below with the correct words.

1 _____ _____, this bank offers a credit card with …

2 With this account, students _____ get free …

4 You looked at three ways of adding information in Exercises 2 and 3. Where do we usually put these words and phrases? What is different about *also*?

5 `2.35` Listen to the third part of the talk and take notes in a mind map style. Compare your notes with a partner.

6 Use your notes to write a short paragraph about each of the last two student accounts. Use the words from Exercises 2 and 3 to introduce extra information. Compare with your partner and Tracks 2.33–2.35 on page 155.

7 Work with a partner. Exchange information about two other student accounts and take notes. Use the mind map style.

Student A: Look at page 113.

Student B: Look at page 119.

8 Which account, of all six in this lesson, is best for you?

WRITING SKILLS:
a formal letter

9 Read the letter from Manuela to her bank on page 91 and answer these questions.

1 What is Manuela's problem?
   a) The Bolivian bank charged the wrong amount of money.
   b) The English bank moved the money to the wrong bank account.
   c) The English bank charged more money than it promised.

2 What does Manuela want?
   a) She wants the bank to give her £10.
   b) She wants the bank to give her £25.
   c) She wants the bank to give her £1,000.

10 Match these parts of the letter with gaps 1–5.

a) Dear Sir/Madam

b) Manuela Rosa

c) I look forward to hearing from you.

d) 14 Hill Street
Bristol
BR3 6TH

e) Customer Services
National Bank of England
Pin Street
London
EC1 4GR

11 In formal letters, we do these things. Find examples in the letter.

1 We usually write both addresses (the person it is to/from).

2 We always write the date.

3 We don't usually use short forms and contractions.

4 We use polite and formal language.

5 We use a formal way to end the letter.

12 Linkers In formal writing, we often use *that* to link two clauses. (We don't usually use *that* in speech or informal writing.) Where can you put *that* in these sentences? Read the letter to check your ideas.

1 I noticed you charged me £25 for this service.

2 The bank assistant told me the charge was only £10.

3 I am afraid I am unhappy with this situation.

---

1 _____ 2 _____

3 February 2007

3 _____

<u>Re: International money transfer to account number 568392561</u>

I am writing about a problem with a recent international money transfer.

On 4th January, I went to the main branch of your bank in Bristol and I made a transfer of $1,000 from my Bolivian bank account to my English account.

When I checked my account statement, I noticed that you charged me £25 for this service. However, when I made the transfer, the bank assistant told me that the charge was only £10.

I am afraid that I am unhappy with this situation. Could you please refund this charge?

4 _____

Yours faithfully,

Manuela Rosa

5 _____

13 Put the words in the right order to make sentences.

1 was I it thought free that

2 charge said the he was £100 that

3 realised I was there mistake that a

4 you hope that can I me help

5 am I that unhappy happened this

14 Write a letter to the National Bank of England about one of the problems in the table below. Use Manuela's letter as your model.

Subject	Charge (bank assistant said)	Final charge
credit card application	no charge	£20
overdraft application	£15	£30
loan application	no charge (January special offer)	£50

11 Homes

In this unit

Grammar
- will, won't
- be going to

Vocabulary
- compound nouns
- green living
- homes

Scenario
- At an accommodation agency

Study skills
- examination skills

Writing skills
- an informal letter

11.1 MY HOME, MY CASTLE

Home is where the heart is.
English proverb

READING

1 Work with a partner and answer the questions.

1 Describe the area where you live.

2 Do you feel safe in your area / in your home?

3 Look at the photo in the article. What is this place, do you think?

2 Read the article *Separate Lives* quickly and choose the best answer.

The article tells us about gated communities:

a) in the future   b) now   c) now and in the future
d) in the future, now and in the past.

3 Read the article again. Which of these ideas are in it?

1 Gated communities existed a long time ago.

2 Gated communities will have a lot of facilities.

3 You can already find these communities in many places around the world.

4 They are expensive to live in.

5 There is no crime in them.

6 Some people are against gated communities.

4 Which paragraph (A–D) from the article is each sentence connected with?

1 People are nervous these days.

2 There will be cameras everywhere.

3 They say that people in the communities are too similar.

4 They will check people, bicycles and cars as they come in.

5 They are more common in the Americas and Africa than in Europe or Australia.

SEPARATE LIVES

5 Do you think that gated communities are a good idea?

VOCABULARY: compound nouns

6a Look at these compound nouns (noun + noun). Find three more compound nouns in the article.

security guards   play areas
business centres

6b Match nouns from A with nouns from B to make ten compound nouns. You can use some nouns more than once. Which of these things can you see in your area?

A
| car Internet police post |
| railway shopping sports |
| swimming tennis theme |

B
| café centre court office |
| park pool station |

car park, …

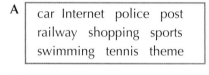

A   What kind of homes will we live in 20 or 30 years from now? Some people think that many of us will live in 'gated communities'. There will be high walls and fences around our houses and flats. Security guards will control the entrances. Inside, there will be parks and play areas for children, supermarkets, business centres and travel agencies, restaurants, gyms and golf courses.

B   These gated communities already exist in many countries. Some of them are like small towns, and in Brazil some even have their own schools. Of course, they aren't cheap places to live in: at Beverley Park, in Los Angeles, houses cost between 12 and 32 million dollars.

C   It's clear why people want to live in them. In Johannesburg, South Africa, 65 percent of residents feel unsafe in their homes at night. In many cities, public spaces like parks are sometimes dangerous. A gated community gives people a feeling of security and, after 9/11, people want to feel safe, especially in the USA.

D   But not everyone is happy about a future of gated communities, including some top police officers. They say that the people in the communities won't mix with people outside. Also, the gap between the rich and the poor will increase, and society will become more dangerous.

GRAMMAR: *will, won't*

7 Look at the first and last paragraphs of the article and answer the questions.

1 Do we usually use *will* and *won't* (*will not*) to talk about:
  a) what is generally true in the present?
  b) what happened in the past?
  c) what we know or think about the future?

2 Do we add *-s* to *will* after *he, she, it* or *there*?

3 Do you know any other verbs with grammar like this?
      ➡ Language reference and extra practice, pages 142–143

8 Complete the sentences with *will* or *won't* (*will not*) and a verb from the box.

| be   change   have   have to   live   meet |

1 Gated communities _____ high walls.
2 There _____ safe places where children can play.
3 People outside _____ people inside.
4 Poor people _____ in these communities.
5 People in these places _____ leave the community very often.
6 The communities _____ society in some ways.

9 Put the words in the right order to make questions. Then ask and answer the questions with a partner.

In the year 2100, …
1 families   be   will   smaller than   now   bigger or ?
2 any fish   there   will   in the sea   be ?
3 the Internet   use   people   will ?
4 people   all their life   will   keep   all their teeth ?
5 India   will   be   the most important country ?
6 will   love   in relationships   be   important ?

pronunciation

10 **2.36** Contractions Listen and complete the sentences. Then practise saying them.
1 I'll _____ rich.
2 You'll _____ three children.
3 She'll _____ a sports car.
4 He'll _____ alone.
5 It'll _____ them happy.
6 We'll _____ excellent English.
7 They'll _____ to Australia.

SPEAKING

11 Work with a partner. Discuss some ideas about your lives in the future.

Student A: Look at page 113 and follow the instructions.
Student B: Look at page 119 and follow the instructions.

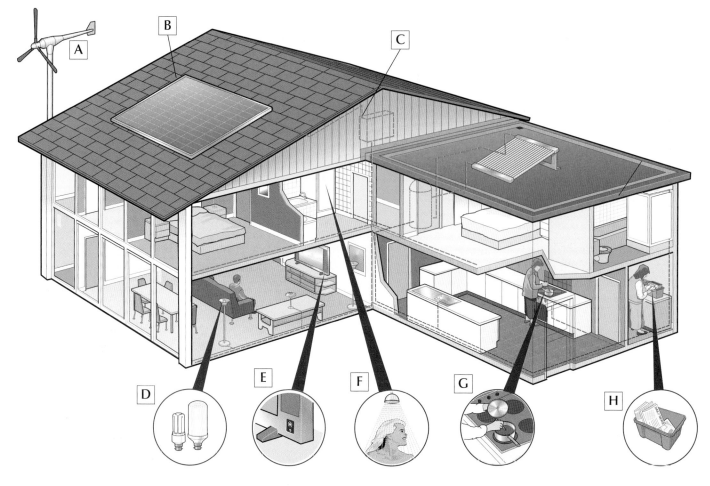

VOCABULARY: green living

1 Match sentences 1–8 with labels A–H on the picture.

1 Cook food in a saucepan with a lid. _G_

2 Have a shower, not a bath.

3 Use solar panels to make electricity from the sun.

4 Use a wind turbine to make electricity from the wind.

5 Save energy with low-energy light bulbs.

6 Use the on/off button to switch off your TV.

7 Recycle old newspapers.

8 Use green electricity, from wind or solar power.

READING

2 Read the questionnaire and do it with a partner. Who lives the greenest life at home? Check your score on page 121.

Aston Council

How green is your home? Do this questionnaire and find out!

A Personal energy use in the house
Count your points:
Always = 5   Usually = 4   Sometimes = 3
Occasionally = 2   Never = 0

1 I turn off lights when I leave a room.
2 I turn off my TV with the on/off button.
3 I have showers, not baths.
4 I turn off the tap when I brush my teeth.
5 I cover saucepans when I cook.
6 I recycle old paper.
7 I recycle cans and plastic.
8 I recycle glass.

B Green technology
Answer *Yes* or *No*. (*Yes* = 5 points, *No* = 0)

9 I buy green electricity.
10 My home has solar panels.
11 My home has a wind turbine.
12 My home has low-energy light bulbs.

LISTENING

3 `2.37` Listen to three interviews with people who did the questionnaire. Listen to their plans (1–3) and match the people with the descriptions below. Who is the greenest?

Here are some people who did our questionnaire and are going to make some changes. Click on the picture to listen.

Vicky
Lives alone in a small house.

Martin, single man
Shares a flat with a friend, Richard.

Simon and Rachel, married
Live together in large house with two young children.

Done

4 Are these sentences true or false?

1 Richard is greener than Martin.
2 Richard decided to recycle things in the future.
3 Simon and Rachel want a solar panel because it's cheaper.
4 Simon and Rachel never have showers.
5 Vicky does not want to change her life.
6 It will be difficult for Vicky to buy green electricity.

GRAMMAR: *be going to*

5 `2.37` Match the plans 1–5 with the people who made them. Then listen again and check.

Interviewer: What are you going to do?

1 I'm going to have showers.
2 He's going to cover his saucepans.
3 They're going to recycle their paper.
4 We aren't going to have showers.
5 I'm not going to do anything new.

Vicky
Simon and Rachel
Richard
Martin
Simon and Rachel's children

6a Look at the sentences in Exercise 5. Choose the correct words in the explanation.

We use be going to for <u>present habits</u> / <u>future plans and intentions</u>.

6b Now complete the table.

+	subject + am / 1_____ / are + going to + infinitive
–	subject + am / 2_____ / 3_____ + 4_____ + going to + infinitive
?	am / is / are + 5_____ + 6_____ + 7_____?

➡ Language reference and extra practice, pages 142–143

7 `2.38` Complete these plans with the correct form of *be going to* and the verbs in brackets. Listen and check your answers.

1 I _____ about green electricity. (find out)
2 She _____ a wind turbine because it's expensive. (not buy)
3 We _____ anything. We're already very green. (not change)
4 They _____ their TVs with the on/off button. (turn off)
5 _____ you _____ any changes? (make)
6 He _____ to work every day. (cycle)

SPEAKING

8a Look back at the questionnaire and make plans to improve your score. What can you do to use less energy? Work with a partner and explain your plans.

8b Work with your partner. How can you make your school/college greener? Make some plans, then compare them with other students.

9a Work in a group. You want to organise an end-of-course celebration for your class. Think about the details for the celebration.

• What exactly is it? A party? A day trip? A picnic?
• Location? Where do you want to hold it / go?
• Time and day?
• Guests? People from other classes?
• What do you need to organise? Food? Music?

9b Decide who is going to do what and then tell your class about your plans.

9c Listen to all the plans. Which plan is the best?

WRITING

10 Write a short description of your plans for your college principal.

PREPARATION

1 Put the words in the box into three groups: rooms, furniture, equipment.

> armchair bathroom bedroom bookcase
> chair cooker cupboard desk dining room
> dishwasher fridge-freezer kitchen living room
> sofa table wardrobe washing machine

2 Think about where you would like to live. Work with a partner. Put these things in order of importance, then compare your ideas.

The place should have:
• large bedrooms   • a garden
• a balcony   • a large kitchen
• modern furniture.

It should be:
• in a quiet road   • near public transport
• near a supermarket   • near restaurants
• in a central location.

3a Look at the adverts below for places to rent in Dublin, Ireland. Quickly find the answers to these questions.

1 Which places have gardens?
2 Which places are near public transport?
3 Which place has the lowest rent?

3b Read the adverts. Which flat would you like to rent?

A
Church St Lovely 2-bedroom flat. 4th floor (lift). Shared garden. Large kitchen – fridge-freezer, cooker. Very close to bus station. €200 per person per week.

B
Harbour Rd Modern 2-bedroom flat. Ground floor with garden. 2 bathrooms. Good local facilities – supermarket, restaurants. €150 per person per week.

C
Canal St Large 2-bedroom flat. Fourth floor. Living room. Dining room. Local buses. Car parking. €90 per person per week.

D
Museum Ave. Lovely old building. 2-bedroom flat. Ground floor. Small garden. Fully furnished. Central location. Near train station. €100 per person per week.

4a `2.39` Conor is a student in Dublin. He is looking for a flat so he phones an accommodation agency. Listen. Which two places in Exercise 3 does he ask about? Does he decide to rent one of them?

4b Listen again and complete Conor's notes.

Flat:	1	2
Number of bedrooms:	1_____	9_____ large bedrooms
Other rooms:	kitchen, living room, 2_____	small 10_____, dining room, living room, large 11_____
Floor:	3_____	12_____ – no lift
Garden:	4_____	no
Furniture/Equipment:		
kitchen:	5_____, 6_____	cooker, 13_____, washing machine
bedrooms:	no furniture	bed, 14_____, wardrobe
living room:	7_____	15_____
dining room:	no	16_____, chairs
Public transport:	no information	bus (17___ min. away)
Local facilities:	no information	no information
Rent:	8€_____ per person per week	18€____ per person per week

KEY LANGUAGE: checking understanding

5 `2.39` Listen again and complete these questions from the conversation. Check with the audioscript on page 155.

1 Could you _____ that, please?

2 _____, there's a cooker, a fridge-freezer and a washing machine. Is that _____?

3 I'm sorry, could you say that _____?

4 _____ that 15 or 50 minutes?

5 I'm sorry, _____ you say 19 or 90 euros?

pronunciation

6 `2.40` **Stressed words** When you check information, you stress the words you want to check. Listen to questions 4 and 5 from Exercise 5. Which words have the strongest stress? Mark them (•). Listen to the questions again and repeat them.

7a Complete the questions to check the bold information in A's sentences. Read your ideas to a partner. Remember the stress.

1 A: It's on the **fourth** floor.
　B: I'm sorry, was that the _fourth_ or the _fifth_ floor?

2 A: The rent is one hundred and **fifty** euros.
　B: Did you say one hundred and _____ or _____?

3 A: It's got a **living room**.
　B: Was that a _____ _____ or a _____ _____?

4 A: **There's** a sofa in the living room.
　B: Did you say _____ _____ or _____ _____ a sofa?

5 A: It **hasn't** got a balcony.
　B: Did you say it _____ or _____ got a balcony?

7b `2.41` Listen and check. Then look at the audioscript and practise the conversation with your partner.

TASK: asking for information about accommodation

8 Work with a partner to find out about flats.

Student A: You are a student in Ireland and you are looking for a flat to share with a friend. Phone the accommodation agency and find out about a flat. (Check when you are not sure about something.) Complete the form below.

Student B: You work in an accommodation agency. Look at page 119.

Swap roles. Do the role-play again.

Student A: Now you work in the accommodation agency. Look at page 113.

Student B: Phone the accommodation agency and complete the form below.

Flat (address):	_____
Number of	
bedrooms:	_____
Other rooms:	_____
Floor:	_____
Garden:	_____
Furniture/Equipment	
kitchen:	_____
bedrooms:	_____
living room:	_____
dining room:	_____
Public transport:	_____
Local facilities:	_____
Rent:	€_____ per person per week

OTHER USEFUL PHRASES

How can I help?	I'm looking for …
Let's see …	What floor is the flat on?
I'm afraid there isn't …	What furniture is there?
Would you like to see the flat?	What about the local area?
	How much is the rent?
	Thanks for your help.

9 You want to share a flat with your partner. Look at the information about the four flats in Exercise 3 and, with your partner, choose the best flat for you both to share.

STUDY SKILLS: examination skills

1 Discuss these questions with a partner.

1 Do you like examinations and tests? Why / Why not?

2 What was the last exam you did? When was it?

3 How did you feel before, during and after the exam?

2 **Do you know these words connected with exams? Check them in your dictionary.**

to pass an examination

to fail an examination   instructions

a practice test   to relax / relaxation

to revise / revision

3a **Before the exam** Look at these ideas about preparing for an exam. Which do you do? Which do you think are good ideas?

1 'I find out everything I can about the exam or test.'

2 'I make a revision plan.'

3 'I don't revise all day. I study in the morning and relax in the afternoon.'

4 'I revise with a group of my classmates.'

5 'I do a lot of practice tests. Every time you do a practice test, you get better.'

6 'I always start my revision a long time before the exam.'

7 'I usually study at the same time every day.'

8 'I always study in a quiet place.'

9 'I like to go to a party the night before the exam.'

10 'I drink a lot of coffee on the morning of the exam.'

3b Now discuss the ideas with a partner. Decide on two or three things that both of you will try in the future.

4 It is important to relax and take breaks when you are revising. Look at these relaxation techniques. Can you add four or five more to the list?

watching TV   walking   playing tennis   yoga

5 **During the exam** Look at these 'golden rules'. Fill the gaps with one of the words in the box.

watch   take   do   do   do   make   read   spend

1 _____ the instructions carefully.

2 _____ what the questions ask you to do.

3 Don't _____ a long time on one or two difficult questions. Come back to them later.

4 _____ sure that your writing is easy to read.

5 Don't _____ other students working.

6 Don't _____ the exam too quickly and make careless mistakes.

7 Don't _____ the exam too slowly, and not finish. Answer all the questions.

8 _____ time at the end of the exam (about ten minutes) to check your answers (information, grammar, spelling, etc.).

6 **After the exam** Which of these things do you do after an exam?

1 Think about which questions you answered well (or badly).

2 Think about how you used your time.

3 Think about how you can prepare better next time.

4 Worry about mistakes you made in the exam.

5 Continue to study hard.

WRITING SKILLS: an informal letter

7 Look at the photo on the right. What is happening? What is the reason, do you think?

8a Read Carla's letter quickly and check your answers. Do you do this in your country?

8b Read the letter again. Say if these sentences are true, false or if the letter doesn't say.

1 Carla is happy with her new flat.
2 Carla is living alone in her new flat.
3 You have to get a taxi from the station.
4 Erdem is going to go to the party.
5 The tube is a kind of bus.

9 Look at Carla's letter and the formal letter on page 91. What are the main differences between the two letters? (Think about the address, dates, the ending, etc.)

10 **Directions** Find words in the letter to complete these sentences.

1 Go _____ on for 300 metres.
2 My house is _____ the right.
3 _____ the number 329 bus to Enfield Town station.
4 _____ down the hill.
5 _____ right at the traffic lights.

11 **Linkers** We can use *when* to join sentences, and often use it for directions. Find the example of *when* in the letter, then match 1–3 with a–c.

1 When you get off the bus,
2 When you get in the taxi,
3 When you get to my house,

a) park your car in the next street on the left.
b) walk to the traffic lights.
c) ask the driver to take you to Wood Green.

12 Write a letter to a friend, inviting him or her to a party at your house (see the map on the right). Use the letter as a model to help you.

147 Wood Green Road
London N22 9DT

9/6/07

Dear Erdem

How are you? I'm in my new flat now, and I'm really enjoying it.

I'm going to have a housewarming party on Saturday 7th July, starting about 8 p.m. Can you come? A lot of our old friends will be here (I hope!) and I'm going to cook something very special! (It's a secret!)

My new address is above. It's really easy to get here. Take the tube* to Wood Green station. You can walk from there. When you come out of the station, turn right and go up the hill. Turn left at the traffic lights – then you're on my road. Go straight on for about 200 metres. The building is on the left.

Hope to see you on Saturday 7th.

Best wishes,
Carla

PS My new phone number is 020 8888 0563.

*That's what we call the underground.

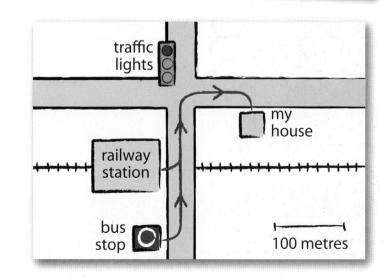

traffic lights

my house

railway station

bus stop

100 metres

12 Travel

12.1 CHILDREN OF THE WIND

The world is a book and those who do not travel only read a page.
Augustine, 354–430, scholar

LISTENING

1 Which country would you like to live in, apart from your own? Why?

2a `2.42` Listen to an interview with Kirsty, a student who has lived abroad. In general, is she happy or unhappy about her time abroad?

2b Listen again and complete Peter's form about Kirsty.

> **Experiences of living abroad**
>
> Name: *Kirsty Andrews*
>
> Countries: ¹____, *Oman and* ²____.
>
> Favourite country: ³____ Reason: ⁴____
>
> Languages: *A little* ⁵____.
>
> Work experience: *None.*
>
> Changes (in the person): *Knows more about differences between* ⁶____.
> *Doesn't think that her way is best.*
>
> Problems: *Seeing old* ⁷____.
>
> Future: *Wants to live in a* ⁸____ *country, and in* ⁹____ *America.*

GRAMMAR: present perfect

3 Look at these sentences. When exactly did Kirsty live abroad?

– *Have you ever lived abroad?*

– *Yes, I have. I've lived in a lot of countries.*

When we talk about an experience in the past, but we don't say when we did it, we use the present perfect.

4 Look at the audioscript for Track 2.42 and complete this table.

	Subject + *have*	Past participle
+	I ¹____ / we've / you've / they've he's / she's / it's	worked
−	I / we / you / they ²____ he / she / it hasn't	³____
?	⁴____ I / we / you / they ⁵____ he / she / it	(ever) worked?

➡ Language reference and extra practice, pages 144–145

GRAMMAR TIP

Regular past participles are the same as the past simple form of the verb (see page 144):

I worked – I have worked

Have your say …

Global nomads

Global nomads are people who have grown up abroad because of a parent's job. They've often had a good life, with large homes and nice holidays, and they're well-educated, international citizens of the 21st century. However, they often feel different from other people and can't stay in one place for a long time. Are you a global nomad? What's your experience?

By: Nina Rendquist (mail)   Posted on: 26/10/2006
I'm from Sweden but I left the country when I was six. I've lived in Saudi Arabia and the Philippines. I don't feel at home anywhere, but I think that I've done a lot. Because of my past, I'm good at learning new skills and at meeting people.

By: Maria (mail)   Posted on: 27/10/2006
Nina, I really understand you. I spent my childhood saying hello and goodbye. I'm from Argentina but my parents took us from one country to another: Malaysia, Nigeria, Russia. Now I'm living in Paris. I feel I'm a stranger everywhere, but I'm independent and strong. I've travelled, I've seen the world and I speak three languages.

By: Andy (mail)   Posted on: 29/10/2006
Like you, I'm proud to be a global nomad – I've lived in Kuwait, Venezuela and Kazakhstan. Sometimes I've felt lonely but I'm comfortable with people from all over the world. And I've become really close to my Mum and Dad – they're like my best friends.

5a Complete these sentences with the present perfect of the verb in brackets.

1 We _____ a lot of interesting places. (visit)
2 I _____ a lot in the last ten years. (change)
3 She _____ to people from a lot of countries. (talk)
4 He _____ films in different languages. (watch)
5 They _____ house several times. (move)

5b `2.43` Listen and check your answers. Then repeat the sentences.

5c Use the sentences in Exercise 5a to ask a partner questions.

– *Have you visited a lot of interesting places?*
– *Yes, I have. / No, I haven't.*

READING

6 Read the web page above. Why are these people writing? Choose the best reason.

1 to find new friends
2 to practise their English
3 to communicate with other people like themselves

7 Answer the questions and write *Nina, Maria* or *Andy*. You can use each name more than once.
Who …

1 has lived in the most countries?
2 has a good relationship with his/her parents?
3 has no problems meeting people?
4 doesn't feel comfortable anywhere?
5 is the most successful person, do you think?

8 According to the web page, what are the advantages and disadvantages of being a global nomad? Make two lists. Are there more advantages or more disadvantages?

> ## GRAMMAR TIP
>
> Many common verbs have irregular past participles:
> *to have* → *had*
> *to see* → *seen*

9a Find the past participles of these verbs in the web page.

to grow   to do   to feel   to become

9b Now use your dictionary or the verb list on page 159 to find the past participles of the verbs in Exercise 10.

➡ Language reference and extra practice, pages 144–145

SPEAKING

10 Work with a partner. Ask and answer questions using the ideas below. Then think of some other questions to ask your partner.

drive a sports car   eat Indian food   fly at night
live away from home   read a travel book
travel on a boat   visit another continent
work/study with someone from another country

Have you ever driven a sports car?
– *Yes, I have. / No, I haven't.*

VOCABULARY: adjective + noun

1 Look at the information about four travel books by Michael Palin. Match the books with photos A–D.

1 *Pole to Pole* is about a 141-day journey from the North Pole to the South Pole.

2 *Himalaya* is the story of a journey across the world's greatest mountains, from Afghanistan to China.

3 *Sahara* is about a journey across the desert that is the size of the USA and covers ten different countries.

4 *Full Circle* is the story of a 50,000km trip round the Pacific Ocean. The writer visited 17 countries on four continents.

2 These extracts come from the four books. Match each extract with one of the books.

A The air is still, and a watery sun gives the place a lonely feel. The temperature is minus 25 degrees C. They say this is warm.

C Everest Base Camp is nowhere near as romantic as it sounds. In high season, between June and August, this area is packed with mountaineers and trekkers. This year there were 32 separate expeditions.

3a Read the book extracts and find adjectives with these meanings.

Extract A **1** not moving   **2** sad and alone

Extract B **3** full of people   **4** with nothing in it

Extract D **5** light, not strong colour

6 not covered, nothing there

3b Match the adjectives in Exercise 3a with the best pair of nouns below.

1 _____ city/train   4 _____ person/life

2 _____ face/colour   5 _____ feet/wall

3 _____ room/bottle   6 _____ lake/water

B We are out of the crowded Asian Pacific area and into the great empty spaces of Australasia. In Java there are 850 people for every square kilometre of land; in Australia, just over two.

D Morocco has changed colour. The greens and golds of the north have become a line of pale yellow trees running beside the road. Beyond them, the land is brick-red and bare.

READING

4 Read the interview with Michael Palin and put the questions 1–6 in the right place (a–f).

1 Which countries have you visited?

2 How many books have you written?

3 What have you learned from your different trips?

4 What's the best place that you've visited?

5 When did you become a travel writer?

6 Have you eaten any unusual things?

Around the world with Palin
by Stuart McCarthy

Michael Palin has visited many countries and he has become one of our most popular travel writers. I asked him about his fascinating life.

a) _____
When I was 42, in 1988. I made a TV series – *Around the World in 80 Days* – and wrote a book about that trip, and so I started this great career.

b) _____
I've written six travel books – one for each TV series.

c) _____
Perhaps you should ask which countries I haven't visited! I've travelled from the North Pole to the South Pole, and across every continent. A very lucky man!

d) _____
Oh, definitely. I've eaten insects and a snake. I ate that when I was in China, in 1985. It tasted like chicken.

e) _____
Ah, my favourite place is in Peru – the river near Machu Picchu. It's the most wonderful, magical place I've ever been to in all my travels.

f) _____
The most important thing that I have learned is that people are warm, kind and fun all over the world, and that a smile really is universal.

5 Are these sentences true or false?

1 He wrote his first travel book after he made a TV travel series.

2 He has made six TV travel series.

3 He has never visited South America.

4 He ate insects in 1985.

5 His favourite place is in Africa.

6 He thinks there are friendly people everywhere.

GRAMMAR:
present perfect and past simple

6 Look at these sentences and answer the questions.

   a) *I made a TV series when I was 42.*
   b) *I've travelled across every continent.*
   c) *I've written six books.*
   d) *I wrote a book in 1988.*

1 Which sentences give the time when Michael Palin did something?

2 Which tense do we use when we give the time we did something?

3 Which tense can we use when we do not give the exact time we did something?

GRAMMAR TIP

I've been = I've gone and I've come back

➡ Language reference and extra practice, pages 144–145

7a Complete this personal travel history with the present perfect or the past simple.

I [1]*have visited* (visit) many different countries but I [2]_____ (not go) to South America and Africa – I hope to go there soon. I first [3]_____ (go) abroad in 1991. I went to France with my school and two years later I [4]_____ (visit) Spain – my favourite country. I also love Asia. I [5]_____ (work) in China and I [6]_____ (visit) Thailand and Japan. I [7]_____ (work) in China in 2003 – I [8]_____ (have) a wonderful time because it [9]_____ (be) so different from my country. Finally, last year I [10]_____ (study) at film school in New Zealand – that was great!

7b Write a short travel history, about yourself or someone you know.

SPEAKING

8a Work with a partner. Ask and answer questions about your experiences. Complete the tables at the back of the book.

Student A: Use the table on page 113.

Student B: Use the table on page 120.

Have you ever visited another country?
– Yes, I have. I've been to Britain.
When did you go there?
– Last year. I went with my family.
Did you have a good time?

8b Tell the class about your partner's experiences.

Mehmet has visited Britain. He went there last year with …

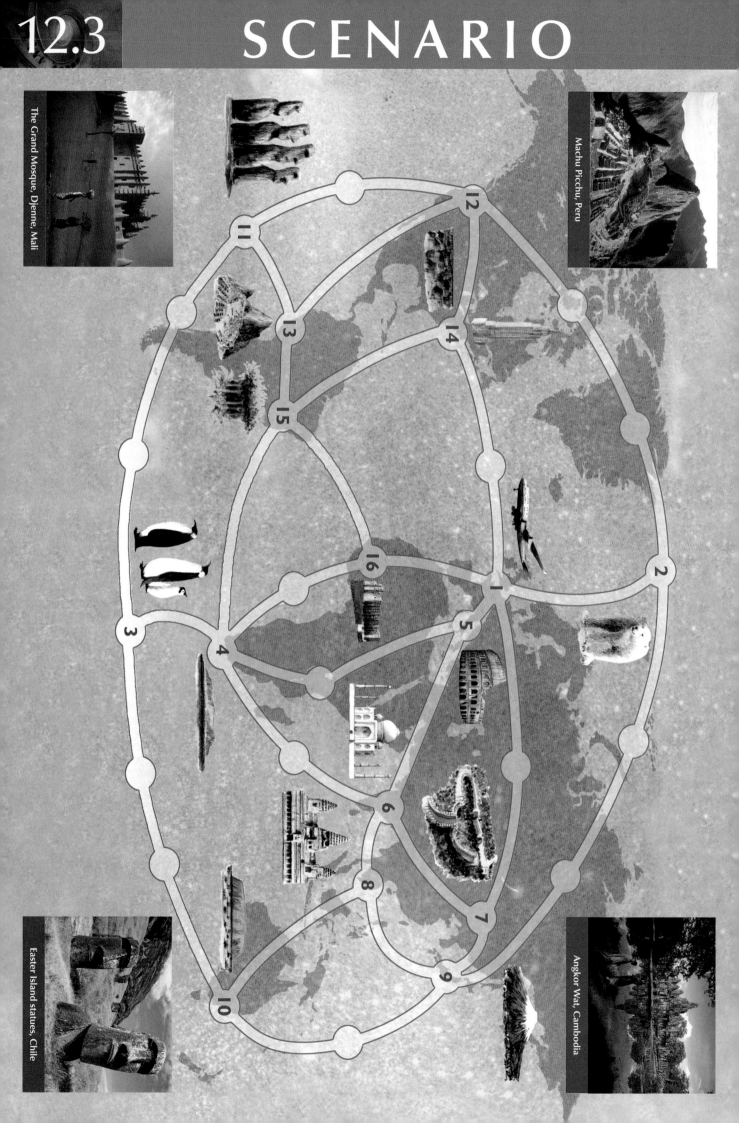

The Grand Mosque, Djenne, Mali

Machu Picchu, Peru

Easter Island statues, Chile

Angkor Wat, Cambodia

PREPARATION

1 Work with a partner and discuss these places. Have you ever been to any of them, or seen any of them? What do you know about them?

1 Heathrow Airport
2 the North Pole
3 the South Pole
4 Table Mountain
5 the Coliseum
6 the Taj Mahal
7 the Great Wall of China
8 Angkor Wat
9 Mount Fuji
10 Uluru (Ayers Rock)
11 Easter Island
12 the Grand Canyon
13 Machu Picchu
14 the Empire State Building
15 the Amazon Forest
16 the Djenne Mosque

2a `2.44` Listen to a woman talking about one of the places. Which place is it?

2b Listen again. What does she say about it? Make notes.

1 when she saw the building:
2 first view of it:
3 visits to it:
4 reasons for liking it:

2c Look at the Other useful phrases below. Which language does the woman use? Tick the words or phrases each time you hear them.

OTHER USEFUL PHRASES

then	so
let me see	also
what else?	in my opinion
I think	perhaps

3 Work with a partner and practise talking for one minute, then swap roles.

Student A: Talk about your last holiday for about one minute. Use the Other useful phrases.

Student B: Listen to your partner. What useful phrases does he/she use?

TASK: giving short talks

4a Choose six places from Exercise 1 that you would like to visit. You have to choose from at least three continents. Write the places and their numbers below.

_____	☐	_____	☐
_____	☐	_____	☐
_____	☐	_____	☐

4b Work with a partner to practise giving short talks. Play this game. In the game, you travel around the world and visit the six places from Exercise 4a. On your trip, you have to talk about different topics for 30 seconds. Read the rules.

Rules

- You need one or two dice and two counters.
- Everyone starts at Heathrow Airport (number 1 on the map).
- Throw your dice and move your counter the correct number of spaces. You can move in any direction.
- When you reach a tourist attraction (2–16), you have to stop and talk about a topic for 30 seconds. The topics for each place are below.
- When you land on one of the six places you chose in Exercise 4a, tick the box next to it.
- When you have visited all of your six places, you have to return to Heathrow and talk about the final topic. The winner is the first person to return to Heathrow Airport.

Topics for your talks

1 the journey that you have just made in the game
2 the coldest place that you have ever been to
3 the quietest place that you have ever been to
4 a famous person, dead or alive, that you admire
5 the hottest place that you have ever been to
6 the most beautiful building that you have ever seen
7 food from other countries that you have eaten
8 an old religious building that you have been to
9 a mountain that you have been to
10 a sport that you have played
11 some art (paintings/statues) that you have seen
12 an American film that you have seen
13 a different culture that you have learned about
14 the tallest building that you have seen
15 an animal that you have looked after or known
16 a national festival that you have been to

STUDY SKILLS: learning outside the classroom

1 Ways of practising English You can practise your English outside the classroom in many different ways. How often do you do these things outside the classroom?

- use the Internet in English
- watch DVDs/films in English
- use the coursebook CD-ROM
- revise your classwork
- listen to songs in English

2 Many students ask for learning advice on Internet message boards. Look at these questions. Can you give any advice?

1 How can I learn vocabulary?

2 How can I improve my listening?

3 Is it better to learn alone or with friends?

3 Match the e-teacher's advice with the questions in Exercise 2. Have you done any of these things?

A You should do things with the words. Make vocabulary cards and put them in your house so you can see them every day. Put vocabulary in groups and make sentences with them.

B I think you should do both: on your own, you can practise at your speed, but, with friends, you can practise speaking and test each other.

C The Internet is perfect because you can usually listen again and again. Also, listen to songs; you can usually get the song words from the Internet to help you.

4a 2.45 **Using technology to learn** Listen to a lecturer giving a talk about using technology to learn English. Which of these things does he talk about?

radio programmes   message boards
language-learning websites   TV   video clips

4b Listen again and take notes about his advice. Take your notes in the form of a mind map, using these headings. Then compare your notes with Track 2.45 on page 156.

- Writing practice
- Listening practice
- Language-learning sites

5 Look again at all the advice in this Study skills section. Which are the best ideas, do you think? Compare your answer with a partner.

6 2.46 Complete this quote with the words in the box. Listen to the end of the talk and check your ideas.

say do read see hear say see

The important thing is to do lots of different things:

'We remember 20 percent of what we read,

30 percent of what we hear,

40 percent of what we [1]_____,

50 percent of what we [2]_____,

60 percent of what we do and

90 percent of what we [3]_____, [4]_____, [5]_____, [6]_____ and [7]_____!'
(Flanagan 1997)

So, follow my advice and enjoy practising your English outside the classroom.

WRITING SKILLS: a postcard

7 Discuss these questions with a partner.

1 Do you ever send postcards? When, and who to?

2 How long do you keep postcards that other people send you? Where do you keep them?

8 Which of these topics do people usually write about on postcards?

education   famous buildings
food   health   hotels   activities
interesting places   jobs   leisure
money   TV   the weather

9 Which topics from Exercise 8 can you find in postcards A and B below?

10a Use the words in the box to complete postcard A.

amazing   dresses   lots
OK   really   temple

10b Match these sentences and phrases with gaps 1–6 in postcard B.

a) We're going to stay here for another week and then go to Lombok.

b) I hope you're well.

c) Love, Hannah

d) Hi Sarah

e) Do you remember Richard from the psychology course?

f) The weather has been lovely.

11 Write this address in the correct way on postcard B. Use postcard A as an example.

UK   49 Clifton Road   BS8 2HP   Sarah Gilbert   Bristol

12 Is Hannah enjoying her trip? Find words or phrases in the postcards that show this.

13 **Adjectives** These sentences come from two postcards. Who is having the worst holiday?

Osman	Mariam
1 The food isn't very good.	The food is disgusting.
2 The weather is very bad.	The weather is terrible.
3 The people aren't very nice.	The people are horrible.
4 The hotel is unpleasant.	The hotel is awful.

14 Imagine you are on holiday. Write a postcard to someone in your family or a friend. Tell them about the weather, food and your activities.

A

August 14th

Dear Mum and Dad,
I arrived here in Yogya last Monday. Everyone is ¹____ friendly and the palace is ²____! It's been very hot, but it's a bit cooler today. I've bought lots of beautiful ³____! Guess what? I bumped into a friend from university! Tomorrow we're going to see the famous ⁴____ at Borobudur.
Hope everything is ⁵____ at home.
See you soon. ⁶____ of love,
Hannah

Mr and Mrs G. White

87 Kirkstall Road

Leeds

LS5 1AN

UK

B

August 23rd

¹____,
I'm in Bali now. Everyone said it's beautiful and they're right. The Balinese people are very kind and always look happy. ²____ I've swum in the sea and I've seen some incredible sunsets from Kuta Beach. ³____ Well, we met in Yogya and now we're travelling together. He's really nice. Yesterday, we went up a mountain and went on a lovely boat trip around a lake. ⁴____
⁵____ Is the summer job OK?
Take care.
⁶____

GRAMMAR

1 Read the article about *Green cars*. Choose the correct verb 1–12 in the text.

Green cars

Green driving

New technology and small, modern cars ¹*helped / have helped* our roads and our environment but scientists say we ²*should / shouldn't* be even greener. So, what 'green' cars ³*do people / are people going to* drive in the near future and the not-so-near future? We ⁴*visited / have visited* the Geneva Motor show last week to find out.

Half electric–half petrol

The electric-petrol car isn't actually new. It ⁵*was / has been* on the road for a few years. For long distances you drive on petrol, but for short trips around town you ⁶*should / are going to* use the electric battery. It's currently the most popular green choice.

100% Electric

At the moment you ⁷*have had / have* to plug your electric car into the electricity every evening, but in the future you ⁸*won't / don't* need to do this. This is the cleanest way to drive but designers ⁹*have found / are going to find* one problem with electric cars – they're very quiet. These cars make no noise. Look out if you're walking!

Biofuel

Do you recycle your vegetable oil and animal products? You ¹⁰*should / have to* do this because one day these 'biofuels' ¹¹*are going to run / are running* our cars. Biofuel cars aren't on our roads now but many people believe they ¹²*should / will* be a better choice than electric cars in the future.

2 Read the article again. Are these statements true or false?

1 There are no green cars now but there will be in the future.

2 At the moment you can drive electric cars for days without stopping.

3 Green drivers like electric-petrol cars more than other types of green car.

4 Recycled vegetable oil and animal products are types of biofuels.

3 What do you think is the greenest type of transport? What type of transport will be the most popular in the future?

4 Complete the conversation with a–f.

a) Where did you　　　　d) Should I take

b) Do I have to　　　　e) What are you going to

c) Have you ever　　　　f) Will it

A: I want to go to India in November. ¹_____ been there?

B: Yes, I have. It's beautiful. ²_____ visit?

A: I'm not sure. ³_____ go?

B: I spent six months there. So I visited Delhi and Agra and then went north to Ladakh.

A: ⁴_____ be cold in November?

B: Maybe in the north, but the south is very hot.

A: What about money? ⁵_____ cash or credit cards?

B: It depends. In the cities you can use credit cards. But cash is useful. Have you got your visa?

A: ⁶_____ get a visa?

B: Yes, you do! It takes a few weeks, so apply to the Embassy soon …

5 Work with a partner. You want to visit the places below. Prepare six questions using phrases a–f in Exercise 4, then ask and answer the questions.

You want to visit:
• your partner's country
• a country he/she has visited
• your partner's favourite city.

VOCABULARY

6 Read the **creditnow.com** leaflet opposite and choose the correct word, a), b) or c), in 1–10 below.

1	a) cooker	b) desk	c) bookcase
2	a) bathroom	b) wardrobe	c) sofa
3	a) wallet	b) loan	c) cashpoint
4	a) money	b) note	c) purse
5	a) Lend	b) Give	c) Borrow
6	a) earn	b) charge	c) pay
7	a) pay back	b) keep	c) get
8	a) PIN number	b) card	c) book
9	a) discounts	b) accounts	c) salaries
10	a) charge	b) give	c) save

7 What are the main advantages of **creditnow.com**?

8 Work with a partner. What are the advantages and disadvantages of borrowing money from

• a bank　• a credit card　• your family
• your friends?

creditnow.com

NO INTEREST FOR 12 MONTHS

Let's have a special holiday this summer ...

We need a new ¹_____ for the kitchen ...

I saw a great ²_____ in the shop for our living room ...

Why are you waiting?
You can get a ³_____ from creditnow.com in six hours and your ⁴_____ will arrive the next day. ⁵_____ between £1,000 and £25,000 and we won't ⁶_____ you any interest for 12 months.

Special offer!
Visit our website today and you won't have to ⁷_____ anything for six months. So that's no interest and no repayments.

Also from creditnow.com
All our customers now also receive our gold credit ⁸_____. You can use this in all good department stores and in most hotels worldwide. This also gives you ⁹_____ on clothes, insurance and many other items. And you ¹⁰_____ even more money because you have no interest to pay for the first six months.

KEY LANGUAGE

9 `2.47` Listen to two phone conversations. Write in the missing information in the two advertisements.

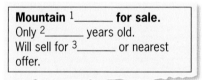

Mountain ¹_____ **for sale.**
Only ²_____ years old.
Will sell for ³_____ or nearest offer.

⁴_____ **player.**
Brand new. Never ⁵_____ _____.
Will sell for ⁶_____.

10a Match the two halves of the questions.

1 Sorry, did   a) I come and see it?
2 Would   b) you say two?
3 What else   c) did you say?
4 Could   d) repeat that?
5 Sorry, was   e) do you want to know about it?
6 Sorry, what   f) you like to see it?
7 Can you   g) that 15 or 50?

10b Listen again. Which questions do you hear in each phone conversation?

First conversation: _1b_, ___, ___, ___

Second conversation: ___, ___, ___

11 Complete this phone conversation with questions from Exercise 10a.

A: I'm interested in the sofa for sale in the paper.
B: Well, it's three years old.
A: ¹_____, please?
B: It's three years old. And it costs £15.
A: ²_____?
B: Fifteen pounds. ³_____?
A: I don't know. ⁴_____?
B: Of course. How about this afternoon?

12 Work with a partner. Practise similar conversations.

Student A: Look at the information on page 114.
Student B: Look at the information on page 119.

LANGUAGE CHECK

13 Delete the extra word in sentences 1–10. Look at the pages to check.

1 You should to keep your purse in
  your bag.   (page 85)

2 He did shouldn't pay for the coffee –
  it's included in the price of the meal.   (page 85)

3 You don't have not to show
  any identification.   (page 86)

4 In my opinion personally it's a
  good idea.   (page 88)

5 Will they to speak good English at the
  end of the course?   (page 93)

6 I'm be going to work for a credit
  company after university.   (page 95)

7 From the station, go straight right on
  to Wood Avenue, then turn left.   (page 99)

8 Have you ever have lived abroad?   (page 100)

9 She has talked to a lot of people about
  the plan last week.   (page 103)

10 I haven't never been to Australia.   (page 105)

LOOK BACK

14 Find the exercises in Units 10–12 where you …

• give advice. (U10)
• give your opinion about money. (U10)
• write a formal letter. (U10)
• talk about the year 2100. (U11)
• plan a party. (U11)
• give directions to your house. (U11)
• read about people who have grown up abroad. (U12)
• talk about places you've visited. (U12)
• write a postcard. (U12)

COMMUNICATION

INFORMATION FOR STUDENT A

Lesson 1.2 Exercise 7 (p. 9)

Look at the table below and ask your partner questions.

Is there a river in Bangkok? (– Yes, there is.)

Answer your partner's questions.

(In Amman, is there a river?) – No, there isn't.

	Bangkok, Thailand	Amman, Jordan	Auckland, New Zealand	Berlin, Germany
River		✗		✓
Canals	✓		✗	
Harbour		✗		✗
Beaches			✓	
Opera house	✗		✗	

Lesson 1.4 Exercise 4b (p. 12)

Spell these words to your partner.

1 beach **2** station **3** fountain **4** temple **5** exciting

Lesson 2.3 Exercise 9 (p. 19)

Use the information below to answer your partner's questions about the project manager job.

Project Manager

Company name: Fitness Fashion Sales
Location: 30 minutes outside the city centre
Transport: Local train station
Working hours: Monday to Friday. 8.30 a.m. to 6.30 p.m. Sometimes weekend work.
Salary: £1,500 per month

Work duties
You ...
- answer the phone
- send and write emails
- organise meetings
- visit other companies
- go on business trips abroad.

Qualifications/Skills
You need ...
- a university degree
- good computer skills
- very good communication skills.

Lesson 3.1 Exercise 7 (p. 23)

Write four questions with these words. Then ask your partner your questions and note the answers.

1 of our bodies What percentage water is ?
_____ percent

2 desert of the world What percentage is ?
_____ percent

3 do Why fresh water drink we not sea water ? _____

4 do water live without camels How long ? _____

Now choose the correct answers to your partner's questions and tell him/her.

about 95 percent   a tap   about 5 percent   only a few days

Lesson 3.4 Exercise 4 (p. 28)

Ask your partner questions about pictures A–D. Don't show him/her the pictures.
– *What's A in English?*
– *It's a ...*
– *How do you spell/pronounce it?*

A   B

C   D

Now answer your partner's questions about pictures E–H.

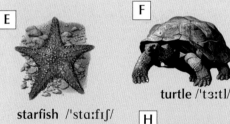

E   F

starfish /ˈstɑːfɪʃ/   turtle /ˈtɜːtl/

G   H

speedboat /ˈspiːdbəʊt/   lagoon /ləˈguːn/

Lesson 4.4 Exercise 3 (p. 38)

Read these numbers to your partner, then listen and write your partner's numbers.

19   190   3,240   22,587   4,732,000

Lesson 4.4 Exercise 6 (p. 38)

Adults in England: Frequency of sporting activity

	Men	Women
Never	_____%	17%
Once a month	50%	_____%
Once a week	_____%	26%
Three times a week	19%	_____%

110 COMMUNICATION ACTIVITIES

Lesson 9.3 E

<u>Tin cans</u>

Work with you
Follow these s

1 Think of an
*You can find th
world.*

2 Here are fou
sentences with
for your talk. T
teacher.

be   invent

a) 1796 / an E
cans

b) 40 years late

c) Now / squar

d) Britain / 20

3 Think of fou
Many early ex

4 Decide how
final comment

Lesson 10.4

Use the inform
presentation a
from Exercises
information.

Royal Bank of

1 interest-free

2 credit card –

3 discount on

Lesson 11.1

Read these ser
you in 2037? T
you think. The
and tick the b

1	I'll be in th
2	I'll own m
3	I'll speak f
4	I'll wear je
5	I won't lau
6	I'll be hap

Discuss the st
disagree abou

Lesson 4.3 Exercises 8–10 (p. 37)

Look at the brochure and complete the 'Scottish Dream' column in the table.

Scottish Dream Resort

Our resort is in the heart of the Scottish countryside.

First class facilities

You stay in a chalet – perfect for families. You have a kitchen and a living room with satellite TV. There are five restaurants in the resort – Scottish, Chinese, Indian, Italian and American food.

Be active with us

Explore the wonderful Scottish countryside and mountains with us. You can go hiking and mountain biking. You can play tennis and our golf course is a very popular facility.

Learn with us

There are visits to old castles and there are museum trips. Our visit to a salmon farm is popular with the adults. We offer classes in painting and Scottish music.

Relax with us

Our Fitness Centre has two indoor swimming pools. One swimming pool is for children and teenagers. In the evening there are music and dance shows in the two bars. There is no cinema. Our guests prefer to sleep and enjoy the next day.

Resort name	Scottish Dream	Club Mexico
	Yes/No + info	Yes/No + info
Accommodation		
Family rooms	yes – chalet	
TV		
Kitchen		
Sea view	no	
Sports		
Swimming		
Scuba diving	no	
Wind-surfing		
Hiking	yes	
Mountain biking		
Tennis		
Golf		
Fitness centre	yes	
Activities		
Day trips		
Classes		
Kids' club	yes	
Entertainment		
Restaurants	yes – 5	
Cinemas		
Shows	yes	

– Ask the travel agent questions about Club Mexico and complete the column.

– Answer the customer's questions about Scottish Dream.

Lesson 6.1 Exercise 8 (p. 49)

Look at the picture and ask and answer questions. Find differences between your picture and your partner's picture.

Is/Are there any … ?
There is/are some …
There isn't/aren't any …

Lesson 7.3 Exercise 9 (p. 63)

Read the information about your area and decide the advantages and disadvantages for the bookshop. Then complete the table on page 63.

The market

- The market is a tourist attraction.
- Many young people and students live in the local area.
- Parking lot for 100 cars.
- Near the bus station.
- 1,000 people visit every week, number is increasing all the time.
- Low rent: small store (without air conditioning), $350 a month; open-air stall, $200 a month.
- No bookstores.
- Musical instrument store and a CD stall.
- The market closes at 10 p.m.

Lesson 6.3

This is your su...
organiser's o...
the food.

Event Ca...
Best food,...
Order forn...

First course
Tomato and c...
Noodle soup
Tomato soup
Main course
Cheese salad
Chicken salad (Chinese style
Beef curry (wit...
Lamb kebab (with rice and
Vegetarian cur...
Vegetarian piz... (tomato, mush...
Burger meal (chips, onion r...
Sushi meal (fish and vege...
Desserts
Chocolate ice...
Apple pie
Fruit salad
Drinks
Sparkling wate...
Still water
Lemonade
Orange juice
Apple juice

Lesson 8.1

Look at the in...
questions to 1...

Where was M...
What were th...
When was Az...

	Lo... civ...
Mayan	mo... Me... Ho... Be...
Inca	mo... ___ ___
Aztec	mo... ___

Review Units 4–6 Exercise 10 (p. 57)

You work at a train station. Give information about trains to Dallas.

Trains to Dallas:

Time	10.00	11.00	20.00
Price	$45	$38	$45

Review Units 7–9 Exercise 3 (p. 82)

Find out information about the island of Mallorca in the Mediterranean Sea. Ask questions starting:

– When were … ?

– Why did … ?

– What did … ?

Answer your partner's questions with the words in bold.

The first people were on the island _____. They lived **in holes in the mountains**. Later, the Greeks used Mallorca _____. It was part of the Roman Empire **for 500 years** and the Romans built _____. Finally, Mallorca became part of Spain **in 1479**.

Review Units 10–12 Exercise 12 (p. 109)

You want to sell your dining table. Your partner phones about it. Answer his/her questions.

Dining room table
for sale!
———
Only three years old.
———
Only £13.
———
For six people.

Now, you want to buy a computer desk. Your partner is selling one. You are interested in it. Phone him/her and find out:

– the age.

– the price.

– does it also have a chair?

Do you want to buy it?

INFORMATION FOR STUDENT B

Lesson 1.2 Exercise 7 (p. 9)

Look at the table below and ask your partner questions.

In Amman, is there a river? (– No, there isn't.)

Answer your partner's questions.

(Is there a river in Bangkok?) – Yes, there is.

	Bangkok, Thailand	Amman, Jordan	Auckland, New Zealand	Berlin, Germany
River	✓		✗	
Canals		✗		✓
Harbour	✗		✓	
Beaches	✗	✗		✗
Opera house		✗		✓

Lesson 1.3 Exercise 10 (p. 11)

Use the map below to answer your partner's questions about the city. Say where the places are.

Yes, there is. It's between / opposite / next to the … / in …

No, there isn't.

On your map there are six places with no name. Ask your partner questions about the places, then write the names of the places on the map.

Is there a … ?

bookshop bus station canal cinema harbour library market swimming pool

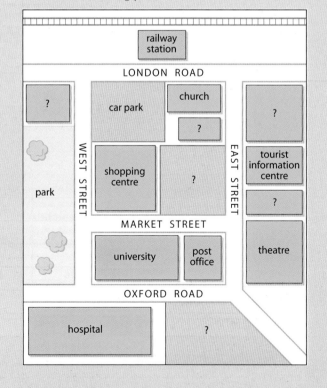

Lesson 1.4 Exercise 4b (p. 12)

Spell these words to your partner.

1 expensive 2 canal 3 university
4 cinema 5 lovely

Lesson 2.3 Exercise 9 (p. 19)

Use the information below to answer your partner's questions about the administration officer job.

Administration Officer

Company name: Language Leader English Academy

Location: 1 hour from the city centre

Transport: Bus stop opposite the academy.
Car park.

Working hours: Monday to Friday.
10.30 a.m. to 5.30 p.m.

Salary: £1,200 per month

Work duties

You ...

• answer the phone
• do the filing and photocopying
• organise student events and parties
• help students with problems
• go on day trips with the students.

Qualifications/Skills

You need ...

• a school certificate
• good computer skills
• good communication skills
• basic English.

Lesson 3.1 Exercise 7 (p. 23)

Write four questions with these words. Then ask your partner your questions and note the answers.

1 live in deserts What percentage world's people
  of the ? _____ percent

2 is in the seas and oceans of the world's water
  What percentage ? _____ percent

3 How long without live people water do ?
  _____

4 in your house water Where come from does ?
  _____

Now choose the correct answers to your partner's questions and tell him/her.

because sea water has a lot of salt

about 70 percent two or three weeks about 25 percent

Lesson 3.4 Exercise 4 (p. 28)

Answer your partner's questions about pictures A–D.

penguin /ˈpeŋgwɪn/   crocodile /ˈkrɒkədaɪl/

submarine /sʌbməˈriːn/

umbrella /ʌmˈbrelə/

Now ask your partner questions about pictures E–H. Don't show him/her the pictures.

– *What's E in English?*
– *It's a ...*
– *How do you spell/pronounce it?*

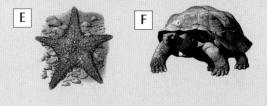

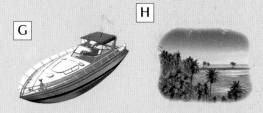

Lesson 4.4 Exercise 3 (p. 38)

Listen and write your partner's numbers then read these numbers to your partner.

13 130 8,743 34,984 8,456,00

Lesson 4.4 Exercise 6 (p. 38)

Adults in England: Frequency of sporting activity

	Men	Women
Never	4%	_____%
Once a month	_____%	46%
Once a week	27%	_____%
Three times a week	_____%	11%

Lesson 4.3 Exercises 8–10 (p. 37)

Look at the brochure and complete the 'Club Mexico' column in the table.

CLUB
Mexico

Our resort is on the beautiful east coast of Mexico.

Enjoy your stay
All our rooms are double rooms with sea views and TVs.

Enjoy the sea
We have excellent water sports facilities. You can go scuba diving, sailing, wind-surfing and canoeing. For beginners, we offer classes in all these sports. There is a swimming pool and the sea is perfect for swimming.

Enjoy the evening
There are four restaurants and two cinemas at the resort. Enjoy a meal with your friends and family – choose from Asian, American, Mediterranean and African food – and then see a film!

Enjoy your family time
We have a kids' club. There are fun activities for children all day long – the parents can come too. Every day there is a day trip on a boat – visit wonderful beaches and local villages.

– Answer the customer's questions about Club Mexico.
– Ask the travel agent questions about Scottish Dream and complete the column.

Resort	Club Mexico	Scottish Dream
	Yes/No + info	Yes/No + info
Accommodation		
Family rooms	yes	
TV	yes	
Kitchen	no	
Sea view	yes	
Sports		
Swimming	yes	
Scuba diving	yes	
Wind-surfing	yes	
Hiking	yes	
Mountain biking		
Tennis	no	
Golf	No	
Fitness centre	no	
Activities		
Day trips	yes	
Classes	yes	
Kids' club	y	
Entertainment		
Restaurants	yes	
Cinemas	yes	
Shows	no	

Lesson 6.1 Exercise 8 (p. 49)

Look at the picture and ask and answer questions. Find differences between your picture and your partner's picture.

Is/Are there any … ?

There is/are some …

There isn't/aren't any …

Lesson 5.3 Exercise 10 (p. 45)

You are Chris, the travel agent. Look at the timetable and price information below and choose the two best flights for your customer. Then, give your customer the flight details. Which flight does your customer want? Take his/her booking.

Airline	OA	IBA	TA
Dep Sydney	Sun 8.30 p.m.	Sun 1.00 p.m.	Sun 7.30 p.m.
Arr Moscow	Mon 11.30 a.m.	Mon 1.00 p.m.	Mon 12.00 p.m.
Dep Moscow	Mon 6.30 a.m.	Mon 9.00 a.m.	Mon 11.00 a.m.
Arr Sydney	Tues 1.30 p.m.	Tues 3.00 p.m.	Tues 7.00 p.m.
Flight time	22 hours	19 hours	24 hours
Ticket prices			
Business class	AU$1,000	Not available	AU$1,500
Standard class	AU$700	AU$500	AU$900
Service	****	**	*****
	(meals, drinks, films, snacks)	(snacks, radio)	(as OA + video games and head massage)

Lesson 6.3 Exercise 11b (p. 53)

This is your supply list. Take the conference organiser's order and tell him/her if you can supply the food.

Event Catering Company Best food, best service		
Order form	**Quantity available**	**Quantity ordered**
First course		
Tomato and cheese salad	50	
Noodle soup	50 cans	
Tomato soup	50 cans	
Main course		
Cheese salad	100	
Chicken salad (Chinese style with noodles)	30	
Beef curry (with rice)	200	
Lamb kebab (with rice and vegetables)	60	
Vegetarian curry (with rice)	40	
Vegetarian pizza (tomato, mushroom)	100	
Burger meal (chips, onion rings)	50	
Sushi meal (fish and vegetarian)	50	
Desserts		
Chocolate ice cream	40	
Apple pie	40	
Fruit salad	40	
Drinks		
Sparkling water	100	
Still water	50	
Lemonade	100	
Orange juice	50	
Apple juice	50	

Lesson 8.1 Exercise 10 (p. 67)

Look at the information below. Ask your partner questions to fill the gaps.

Where was Mayan civilisation?

When was Inca civilisation important?

What were the Aztec people good at?

Lesson 7.3 Exercise 9 (p. 63)

Read the information about your area and decide the advantages and disadvantages for the bookshop. Then complete the table on page 63.

The highway shopping area

- Busiest road in Charleston – 1,000 cars drive past every hour.
- Three fast food restaurants, a supermarket, a motel, a music CD store.
- No bookstores.
- Parking lot for 50 cars + private parking for store (five cars).
- Bus stop opposite the store.
- Large stores with air conditioning.
- Low rent: $300 a month.
- Main customers: families and business people.
- Not very safe at night – high crime.

Lesson 8.3 Exercise 10 (p. 71)

Have six short conversations with your partner and find the following information.

1 the cost of a student ticket for the *Forgotten Empire* exhibition

2 where the Egyptian Mummies are

3 the Reading Room's opening time

4 where the bookshop is and its closing time

5 what food the restaurant sells and its opening and closing times

6 Ask the assistant to look after your children because you want to go to the toilet.

	Location of civilisation	Main period of civilisation	Capital city	Abilities/Skills of people	End of civilisation
Mayan	modern-day _____, _____, _____ and _____	between _____ and AD 250	_____	writing, mathematics, studying the stars and building large cities of stone	in about _____
Inca	modern-day Peru, Ecuador, Bolivia and Chile	from _____ to AD 1525	Cuzco, in Peru	building _____, building _____	in AD 1532
Aztec	modern-day Mexico	from about _____ to AD 1500	under modern-day Mexico City	_____	in _____

Lesson 9.3 Exercise 9a (p. 79)

Chewing gum
Work with your partner and prepare your talk. Follow these steps.

1 Think of an idea to use in your introduction.
Teenagers love this invention.

2 Here are four facts about your invention. Make sentences with the verbs in the box. Choose three for your talk. Then check your sentences with your teacher.

> add be make produce spend

a) Chewing gum / very old. People / gum from trees / 5,000 years ago
b) 1914 / Mr William Wrigley / mint to chewing gum
c) Now / Wrigley's / 90 percent of the world's chewing gum
d) Americans / 2 billion dollars / chewing gum / every year

3 Think of four reasons to vote for your invention.
Sugar-free gum is good for your teeth.

4 Decide how to end your talk. Can you make a final comment about the invention?

Lesson 10.2 Exercise 7 (p. 87)

Read about Maya and answer the questions on page 87.

Lesson 10.2 Exercise 8 (p. 87)

Read about two people, take notes and prepare to tell your partner about them. Use full sentences.
Cara is 25. She's a single mother with two children, three and …

Cara from Vietnam
Personal information

25 – single mother – two children (aged 3 and 4).

What is her business idea?
A flower stall at the station.

What does she have to do?
Buy a market stall – $50.
Buy first flowers – $20.
Pay for a babysitter (for the first month) – $20.

Amira from Indonesia
Personal information

28 – married, four children (aged 8, 6, 4, 2).

What is her business idea?
Home and business cleaning service.

What does she have to do?
Buy cleaning equipment (bucket, brush, etc.) – $20.
Buy a bicycle – $50.
Pay for advertising (posters, local newspaper) – $30.

People who borrow from us: *Maya*

I live in the Philippines. I'm a widow – my husband died in the war. I've got three teenage children and I have to pay for their school. We haven't got a house, so we live with my sister.

I started my business six months ago – it's a laundry business. I wash the clothes of the local taxi drivers! They're all single men, they're very busy and they have to look smart for work. I borrowed 100 dollars from Credit Aid and I have to pay back two dollars a week. I spent the money on two irons, two sinks and a lot of soap! I have to work very hard every day but now I've got an assistant – my sister! We make about 50 dollars a week, and I save three dollars each week. Now I don't have to worry about the school fees, and perhaps my children can go to university in the future.

I'm using the money to build a house for my family. It's only a small house but we need it very much.

Lesson 10.4 Exercise 7 (p. 90)

Use the information below to prepare a short presentation about this account. Use the language from Exercises 2 and 3 to introduce extra information.

Halifax Bank student account

1 interest-free overdraft

2 earn interest on your money (2%)

3 no credit card

4 discount on travel insurance (10%)

Lesson 11.1 Exercise 11 (p. 93)

Read these sentences. Will these things be true for you in 2037? Tick the box that best describes what you think. Then ask your partner what he/she thinks and tick the box.

	You			Your partner		
	Yes	Perhaps	No	Yes	Perhaps	No
1 I'll be well known in my work.						
2 I'll live with my parents.						
3 I'll travel more than now.						
4 I won't have to worry about money.						
5 I'll feel old.						
6 I'll play a lot of sport.						

Discuss the statements. How many do you agree/disagree about?

Lesson 11.3 Exercise 8 (p. 97)

You work for *Flats R Us*. Look at the information below. Give your partner information as he/she asks for it, and repeat it if he/she asks you.

Flat (address): 14A Museum Avenue

Number of bedrooms: 2 small

Other rooms: large kitchen, large living room, dining room, bathroom

Floor: ground

Garden: garden

Furniture/Equipment:

      kitchen: fridge-freezer, cooker, microwave, dishwasher

      bedrooms: beds, desks, wardrobes

      living room: sofa, table, armchair, large cupboard

      dining room: table and 4 chairs

Public transport: near train station (5 min.)

Local facilities: central — shops, cinemas, restaurants all near

Rent: €100 per person per week

Review Units 4–6 Exercise 10 (p. 57)

You want information about trains to Dallas. Your partner works at the train station.

Find out about:

– *train times to Dallas.*

– *trains in the afternoon.*

– *prices.*

Choose the cheapest train.

Review Units 7–9 Exercise 3 (p. 82)

Find out information about the island of Mallorca in the Mediterranean Sea. Ask questions starting:

– *Where did … ?*

– *How long was … ?*

– *When did … ?*

Answer your partner's questions with the words in bold.

The first people were on the island **6,000 years ago**. They lived _____ _____. Later, the Greeks used Mallorca **for trade**. It was part of the Roman Empire _____ and the Romans built **roads and towns**. Finally, Mallorca became part of Spain _____.

Review Units 10–12 Exercise 12 (p. 109)

You want to buy a dining room table. Your partner is selling one. You are interested in it. Phone him/her and find out:
– the age.
– the price.
– how big is it?

Do you want to buy it?

Now, you want to sell your computer desk. Your partner phones about it. Answer his/her questions.

Computer desk

■ Only 18 months old.

■ Will sell for £14.

■ Also has chair. (Extra £3)

Lesson 12.2 Exercise 8a (p. 103)

Ask your partner questions and note the answers in the table.

Name: _____	Yes	No	Extra information?
Visit a famous place?			
Swim in a clear blue sea?			
Stay on a campsite?			
Have a beach party?			
Fly in business or first class?			
Go on holiday alone?			

INFORMATION FOR STUDENT D

Lesson 9.3 Exercise 9a (p. 79)

Lipstick

Work with your partner and prepare your talk. Follow these steps.

1 Think of an idea to use in your introduction.

Film stars love this invention.

2 Here are four facts about your invention. Make sentences with the verbs in the box. Choose three for your talk. Then check your sentences with your teacher.

> be   can invent   invent   use

a) The Egyptians / lip paint / thousands of years ago

b) 1770 / England / you / not use lipstick / because / against the law

c) An American man, Maurice Levy / the modern lipstick / 1915

d) An American woman, Hazel Bishop / kiss-proof lipstick in 1949

3 Think of four reasons to vote for your invention.

You can write on mirrors with lipstick.

4 Decide how to end your talk. Can you make a final comment about the invention?

INFORMATION FOR STUDENT C

Lesson 7.3 Exercise 9 (p. 63)

Read the information about your area and decide the advantages and disadvantages for the bookshop. Then complete the table on page 63.

The shopping mall

- Parking lot for 1,000 cars.
- 10,000 people visit every week.
- Two department stores and 50 other stores.
- Three bookstores and two music stores.
- Large stores with air conditioning.
- High rent: $800 a month.
- Closes at 8 p.m.
- Customers: families, teenagers and professional workers.
- Very safe — private security.

Lesson 9.3 Exercise 9a (p. 79)

The Post-it® note

Work with your partner and prepare your talk. Follow these steps.

1 Think of an idea to use in your introduction.

They are very important in the office.

2 Here are four facts about your invention. Make sentences with the verbs in the box. Choose three for your talk. Then check your sentences with your teacher.

> be   do   invent   sell   use

a) Two Americans / the Post-it® note / 1970

b) The average office worker / 11 Post-it® notes / every day

c) Now / 600 different Post-it® products

d) In 2000 / artist / a drawing on a Post-it® note and / for $1,000

3 Think of four reasons to vote for your invention.

They're small and they save paper.

4 Decide how to end your talk. Can you make a final comment about the invention?

SUPPLEMENTARY INFORMATION

Lesson 3.1 Exercise 1 (p. 22)

Answers

1a 2b 3b 4a 5b 6a 7b 8a

Lesson 4.4 Exercise 10a (p. 39)

Answers

Cinema 61%	Classical music concerts 13%
Theatre 25%	Modern dance events 6%
Art exhibitions 24%	Sports events 63%
Ballet and opera 16%	Pop and rock concerts 25%

Lesson 9.1 Exercise 10a (p. 75)

Inventor: _____

born 1833, Sweden

(*study*) chemistry

(*write*) poetry, novels, plays

(*try*) to make safe explosive

(*kill*) brother in an experiment 1864

(*invent*) dynamite 1866

(*start*) Nobel Prize Foundation 1895

Inventor: _____

born 1829, Germany

(*travel*) New York 1846

(*move*) San Francisco 1853

(*start*) shop for gold miners

(*sell*) equipment and clothes

(*invent*) jeans 1873

(*use*) material from Nîmes, France

(*call*) material 'denim'

Lesson 9.2 Exercise 10 (p. 77)

Answers

1 Yes, he did.

2 No, they didn't. (The Chinese made the first paper.)

3 He invented X-rays.

4 They landed on the moon in 1969.

5 He first arrived in the Caribbean Islands.

Lesson 10.1 Exercises 10b–11 (p. 85)

Compare your advice with this answer.

> Dear Nadia,
> I'm sorry to hear about your problems. I think that you should try to find a better job. Supermarkets usually pay more than restaurants. You shouldn't use your credit cards to buy things – they're very expensive. You should talk to your teachers at the university – they can help you.

Now look at these problems. What advice can you give these people?

1 I'm a student from China. I'm now living in the UK. I'm sharing a flat with three other Chinese students. We're afraid to go out after dark because we can hear a lot of police cars. We don't think that the city is safe. What should we do?
Li

2 I'm a student from Poland. I'm learning English, but I find it very difficult to remember new vocabulary. What should I do?
Veronica

3 I'm from Germany and I'm spending a year in London. I have a lot of friends and I go out a lot. I like eating in expensive restaurants and going to the theatre. The problem is, I'm an ordinary office worker and I haven't got much money. What should I do?
Klara

Lesson 11.2 Exercise 2 (p. 94)

Getting started	Latest news	FAQs	Contact us

What your answers mean:

40–60	Well done. You already lead a green lifestyle. Are there one or two things you can change to get a completely green home?
20–39	Good, but your house can be greener! Follow our advice and you can improve your score.
0–19	Do you know what green means? You should make immediate changes to help our planet. Don't wait; act now!

Done

GRAMMAR

G1 to be (affirmative)

	Contraction	Full form
I	'm	am
he / she / it	's	is
you / we / they	're	are

For speaking, use contractions with *I, he, she, it, you, we, they.*

I'm a student.
It's cold in winter.

Use *to be* with jobs, adjectives and descriptions.
He's a teacher.
The bus **is** noisy.
Buses **are** expensive in the city.

G2 to be (negative)

	Contraction	Full form
I	'm not	am not
he / she / it	isn't	is not
you / we / they	aren't	are not

New York **isn't** a capital city.
You **aren't** a teacher.

G3 to be (questions)

am	I ... ?
is	he / she / it ... ?
are	you / we / they ... ?

Use full forms (not contractions) to ask questions.
Is it expensive?
Are you a teacher?

Use full forms (not contractions) for short answers with *yes.*
Is London old? – Yes, **it is.** ✓
Is London old? – Yes, ~~it's.~~ ✗

Use contractions for short answers with *no.*
Is São Paulo a small city? – No, **it isn't.**
Are the restaurants famous? – No, **they aren't.**

G4 there is, there are (+ any)

	Singular	
	Contraction	Full form
+	there's	there is
–	there isn't	there is not
?		is there ... ?
Short answers +		Yes, there is.
–	No, there isn't.	

	Plural	
	Contraction	Full form
+		there are
–	there aren't any	there are not any
?		are there any ... ?
Short answers +		Yes, there are.
–	No, there aren't.	

Use *there is, there are* to say what is or isn't in a place. *There is* and *there are* introduce places and things.
There's an airport in the city.
There are people on the bus.

Use *any* with *there aren't* and *are there ... ?*
There aren't any cars in Venice.
Are there any cinemas in the city?

Use *a lot of* for large numbers.
There are a lot of people in Mumbai.
There are a lot of boats in the harbour.

Use full forms for short answers with *yes.*
Is there an opera house? – Yes, **there is.** ✓
Is there an opera house? – Yes, ~~there's.~~ ✗

Use contractions for short answers with *no.*
Are there any famous buildings? – No, **there aren't.**

KEY LANGUAGE

B A C	(A is) between (B and C).
A B	(A is) next to (B).
B c	(C is) in (B).
A ←→ B	(B is) opposite (A).
A B	(A is) on the left of (B).
B C	(C is) on the right of (B).

VOCABULARY

V1 Cities
Istanbul, Kraków, London, New York, São Paulo, Tokyo

V2 Adjectives
bad, beautiful, big, cheap, cold, dry, expensive, good, hot, new, noisy, old, quiet, small, ugly, wet

V3 Places in a city
airport, beach, bookshop, bridge, building site, bus station, canal, car park, church, cinema, fountain, gardens, harbour, library, market, mosque, mountain, museum, park, post office, public toilets, railway station, shopping centre, swimming pool, temple, theatre, tourist information centre, university, zoo

G1 1 **Write the correct form of *to be*. Use contractions if possible.**

1 I __'m__ a teacher.
2 She _____ a student.
3 We _____ from New York.
4 Poland and the UK _____ in Europe.
5 Brazil _____ famous for football.
6 She _____ in Kraków, in Poland.
7 Istanbul and New York _____ noisy cities.

G1,2 2 **Are the verbs correct (✓) or incorrect (✗)? Correct the wrong forms.**

1 My friend <u>aren't</u> ugly! ✗ *isn't*
2 We aren't in Brasilia – we're in São Paulo.
3 Is Tokyo a small city? – No, it isn't. It's big.
4 Are the restaurants good? – No, they are.
5 Japan isn't a cheap country.
6 Are you Spanish? – No, I am. I'm French.

G3 3 **Match questions 1–6 with answers a–f.**

1 Is it cold in winter? _____
2 Are you a student? _____
3 Are we in the east of the city here? _____
4 Are the summers dry? _____
5 Is Maria on the phone? _____
6 Is he cold? _____

a) No, I'm not.
b) Yes, she is.
c) Yes, it is.
d) No, he isn't.
e) Yes, they are.
f) No, we aren't.

G4 4 **Write the missing word in sentences 1–5.**

1 There's a famous opera house in Sydney.
2 There not any cars in Venice.
3 Is there a film at the cinema today? – No, isn't.
4 In Chicago, there any good theatres?
5 In Kyoto, there are a lot old buildings.

G1,2,3,4 5 **Choose the correct word.**

'Hello, my name [1]<u>am</u>/*is* Laura. [2]*I'm*/*I's* from Auckland. Auckland [3]<u>am</u>/*is* a city on the north island of New Zealand. There [4]*is*/*are* 1.3 million people here but it [5]*aren't*/*isn't* the capital city. In the summer it's hot and there are [6]<u>any</u>/*a* lot of boats on the sea. The city is famous for boats! [7]*Is*/*Are* there any boats in your city?'

KL 6 **Look at the map and match 1–5 with a–e.**

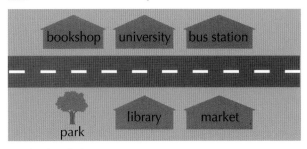

1 The bookshop is _____
2 The university is _____
3 The bus station is _____
4 The market is _____
5 The park is _____

a) next to the library.
b) on the left of the map.
c) opposite the market.
d) on the left of the university.
e) between the bookshop and the bus station.

7 **Where's the library?**
The library is _____.

8 **Speaking practice Work with a partner. Ask and answer these questions.**
Where is …
your language school?
your classroom?
your teacher?

V1 9 **Which are capital cities?**
<u>London</u> Kraków Istanbul
New York Tokyo São Paulo

V2 10 **Write the vowels (*a, e, i, o, u*) in the adjectives.**

1 The mountains are b<u>e</u>a<u>u</u>t<u>i</u>f<u>u</u>l.
2 It's h__t at the beach.
3 The library is q__ __ __t.
4 This is a b__g shopping centre.
5 Is the museum __xp__ns__v__?
6 *Marco's* is a n__w restaurant.
7 My coffee is c__ld.
8 The buses are ch__ __p.

V3 11 **Write these words in the table.**

~~museum~~ bus cinema market temple railway bookshop shopping centre

Buildings	Stations	Shopping
museum	_____	_____
_____	_____	_____
_____	_____	_____

Language reference

GRAMMAR

G1 Present simple (affirmative)

I / you / we / they	like
he / she / it	likes

The present simple verb is in the infinitive form (*live, work*) after *I, you, we* and *they*.

We live in New York.
They work for a shop.

Add *-s* to the verb after *he / she / it*.

He lives in New York.
She works for a shop.
She buys clothes for the shop.

In verbs ending in a consonant + *-y*, the *-y* changes to *-ies* after *he / she / it*.

He flies to Rome.
She studies at university.

In the verbs *go* and *do*, *-o* changes to *-oes* after *he / she / it*.

The train **goes** to London.
Philip **does** a boring job.

The verb *have* becomes *has* after *he / she / it*.

Maria **has** an interesting job.

Use the present simple to talk about things that are generally true.

I **like** the city.
We **live** in Berlin.

Use the present simple to talk about things that happen again and again.

Stephen **designs** houses.
The pilots **fly** from Paris to New York.

G2 Present simple (negative)

	Contraction	Full form
I / you / we / they	don't like	do not like
he / she / it	doesn't like	does not like

Use *do* or *does* + *not* to form the negative in the present simple.

You **don't like** airports.
They **do not speak** English.
He **doesn't go** to the cinema.
She **does not drink** coffee.

For speaking, use contractions.

My father **doesn't work**. ✓

Don't use *don't/doesn't* with the verb *to be*.

He ~~doesn't be~~ a teacher. ✗
He **isn't** a teacher. ✓

G3 Present simple questions (yes/no)

do	I / you / we / they	work … ?
does	he / she / it	

Use *do* or *does* to form a question in the present simple.

Do you live in France?
Does she study Arabic?

Use short answers with *yes/no* questions.

Do you work in an office? – Yes, **I do**. / No, **I don't**.
Does she have a lesson now? – Yes, **she does**. / No, **she doesn't**.

G4 Present simple questions (question word)

What	do	I / you / we / they	have?
	does	he / she / it	

What languages **do they study?**
What do you do?
What job **does she have?**

Don't use *do/does* with the verb *to be*.

What ~~does~~ your favourite subject **be**? ✗
What's your favourite subject? ✓
What ~~does~~ it **be**? ✗
What is it? ✓

KEY LANGUAGE

KL Asking for information (1)

What information do you want?
Where is it?
Is it (in the city centre)?
What are (the working hours)?
What does (an office assistant) do?
What (qualifications/skills) do I need?

VOCABULARY

V1 Jobs and place of work

accountant, businessman/woman, doctor, fashion buyer, lawyer, lecturer, pilot, web designer

company, court, hospital, office, plane, shop, university

V2 Studying; university

course, exam, hall of residence, qualification, score, society, staff, student, subject

V3 Office work

communication, email, event, filing, Internet, letter, meeting, photocopier, photocopying, salary, skill, work duties, working hours

(to) answer, (to) do, (to) go, (to) organise, (to) send, (to) use, (to) write

Extra practice

G1 1 Write the verb in brackets in the correct form.

1 I _work_ in a hospital. (work)
2 You _____ in China. (live)
3 Marco _____ from Holland. (fly)
4 Jake and Sandro _____ at Oxford University. (study)
5 He _____ computer programmes. (buy)
6 The boat _____ from Spain to Morocco. (go)
7 She _____ a modern computer. (have)
8 We _____ fashion designers. (meet)

G2 2 Choose the correct form.

1 They *don't/~~doesn't~~* live in India.
2 Raul *don't/doesn't* go on holiday every year.
3 She *isn't/doesn't* a pilot.
4 I *don't/not* like horse-riding.
5 We *aren't/don't* work in the city centre.
6 You *doesn't/don't* have lunch at one.
7 We *aren't/don't* like noisy offices.
8 I *don't/doesn't* go to university.

G1,2 3 Speaking practice Write sentences for yourself. Tell a partner.

I like _____
I don't like _____
I speak _____
I don't speak _____
I'm a _____
I'm not a _____
I _____
I don't _____

G3,4 4 Write the words in sentences 1–6.

| ~~do~~ do don't is does what |
| what don't where are doesn't |

1 _Do_ you work in Spain? – No, I _____.
2 _____ languages do you speak? – English and Spanish.
3 _____ you a student? – Yes, I am.
4 _____ Ricardo have a lesson now? – No, he _____.
5 _____ subjects do you study?
6 _____ he a student or a teacher?
7 _____ is the hall of residence? Is it in the city centre?
8 _____ Raul and Sophie work in the same shop? – No, they _____.

KL 5 Complete the conversation at an employment agency with a–e.

a) What
b) where is
c) what does
d) what are
e) Is it

A: I like the website manager job but ¹ _b_ the office?
B: It's in the city.
A: OK. ² _____ in the centre?
B: Yes, it is.
A: And ³ _____ the working hours?
B: Nine to five.
A: ⁴ _____ skills do I need?
B: You don't need any skills. They organise training.
A: So ⁵ _____ a website manager do?
B: Well, you work with …

V1 6 What's the job?

1 'I work in a hospital.' _doctor_
2 'We fly from Sydney to Singapore.' _____
3 She works in a court. _____
4 He designs websites. _____
5 'I teach in a university.' _____
6 'I buy clothes for a big shop in Seoul.' _____

V1,2 7 Match the words in the table and complete sentences 1–5.

live	of 100
give	in a hall of residence
do	classes
go	a course
score	to university

1 She doesn't _live_ _____. She's in a flat.
2 I want to _____ in English for business.
3 Do you _____ or to school?
4 Does your college _____ in English?
5 I need a _____ in the exam.

V3 8 Write the words in the job advertisement.

| ~~working hours~~ qualifications filing |
| duties salary |

PART-TIME OFFICE HELP
A local company needs extra help.
¹_working hours_: 11.00–14.00
² _____: $1,400 per month
Work ³ _____: photocopying and ⁴ _____.
Also some computer work.
You don't need any ⁵ _____ or experience.
We give training.

GRAMMAR

G1 Question words

What asks about a thing or an idea.
What's your favourite country?
What do you study at university?

Who asks about a person.
Who's your manager?
Who do you know in the class?

Where asks about a place.
Where do you live?
Where's the restaurant?

When asks about a time.
When is the party?
When do you start work in the morning?

How asks about the way we do something.
How do you travel to work?
How do you study languages?

Why asks about the reason for something.
Why do you want to go home?
Why do you want to meet Julia?

Which asks about a choice between a few things, usually two or three.
Which do you study, English or Spanish?
Which do you like, tea or coffee?

Sometimes we use *What … ?* and *Which … ?* with a noun.
What subjects do you study?
What cities do you visit?
Which language do you speak, Chinese or English?
Which qualification do you have, a degree or a certificate?

G2 Adverbs of frequency

100% ←----------------- 50% -----------------→ 0%					
always	usually	often	sometimes	occasionally	never

Put the adverb <u>after</u> the verb *to be*.
He'**s always** at work.
The sea **is never** cold here.

With other verbs, put the adverb <u>before</u> the verb.
I **sometimes work** in the evening.
They **often play** tennis.

Ask about routines and habits with *How often … ?*
How often do you go to the cinema?
– Occasionally.
How often do you see whales in the sea?
– We never see them.

G3 Expressions of frequency

every	
once a	day / week / month / year
twice a	
three times a	

Put the expression <u>after</u> the verb and other words.
I read the newspaper **every day**.
We go to a restaurant **once a week**.
Our family has a holiday **twice a year**.

! *once a week = weekly*
We meet **once a week**.
We meet **weekly**.

KEY LANGUAGE

KL1 Making suggestions

Why don't we (go to the dance workshop)?
Let's (go surfing this Saturday).
What about (having dinner tonight)?
I'd like to (eat a burger).

KL2 Responding to suggestions

Positive response (+)
That sounds fun/good.
That sounds interesting.
Good idea.

Negative response (–)
I don't want to do that.
That sounds boring.
I'm not sure.

VOCABULARY

V1 Words connected with water (and deserts)

lake, ocean, rain, sea (water)
cactus, desert, plant, rock, sand

V2 Animals

dolphin, penguin, seagull, shark, tuna, whale

V3 Festivals

ceremony, concert, dance, dance show, drum, drum dance, parade, race, show, workshop

V4 Classroom objects

blackboard, CD player, chair, coursebook, DVD player, English-English dictionary, notebook, pen, pencil, whiteboard

V5 Verbs

boil, change, check, close, cook, dive, drink, find, float, freeze, jump, know, make, mean, open, repeat, sleep, stop, swim, understand, wash, waste

G1 1 Complete questions 1–8 with a question word.

1 *Which* do you like, water or milk?
2 _____ do people travel to work in your city?
3 _____ does he like Kraków?
4 _____ does Jos fly to?
5 _____ job does he have?
6 _____ city do they like, Atlanta or New York?
7 _____ does she start work?
8 _____ do you know at the party?

2 Speaking practice Make questions and ask a partner.

1 What languages / speak?
   What languages do you speak?
2 What cities / like?
3 Why / study English?
4 Where / live?
5 How / travel to school?
6 When / go to sleep?
7 Who / your English teacher?

G2,3 3 Read about Youna. Choose the correct adverb or expression of frequency in sentences 1–6.

 Youna is a fashion buyer in Seoul, in South Korea. She works for a clothes shop and goes to work in her car every day.
   She goes to other countries twice a month and buys clothes. But she doesn't wear the clothes. 'They're for the shop.'
She doesn't often have free time but on Saturdays she always plays tennis. 'I like to cook but I don't often have time.'

1 She *always/occasionally* goes to work in her car.
2 She *never/often* visits other countries.
3 She *usually/never* wears the clothes.
4 She *occasionally/never* has free time.
5 She plays tennis *once a week/monthly*.
6 She *sometimes/usually* cooks.

4 Are sentences 1–8 correct (✓) or incorrect (✗)? Correct the wrong sentences.

1 I see always the dolphins. ✗ *I always see …*
2 They are never at work.
3 I every week play tennis.
4 How often do you eat at restaurants?
5 We occasionally meet for coffee.
6 He always is at school.
7 How sometimes are you in London?
8 We talk on the phone twice a week.

KL1,2 5 Write the verb in brackets in the correct form.

A: I'd like [1] *to go* (go) to the cinema on Friday.
B: That [2]_____ (sound) fun. What's the film?
A: It's *Star Wars 13*.
B: Oh no! I [3]_____ (not/want) to see that. Why [4]_____ we _____ (not/go) to a different film?
A: It's the only film this week. What about [5]_____ (have) dinner on Saturday?
B: Good idea! Let's [6]_____ (meet) at 7.00.

V1,2 6 Write these words in the table.

shark   rock   plant   dolphin   ocean cactus   whale   sand   seagull

Sea words	Desert words
*shark*_____	_____
_____	_____
_____	_____
_____	_____
_____	

V3,4 7 Match the words 1–8 with the words in the box to make combinations.

board   board   player   dance show   book   book   shop

1 dance   *show*
2 drum   _____
3 work   _____
4 note   _____
5 DVD   _____
6 white   _____
7 course   _____
8 black   _____

8 Is each combination in Exercise 7 one word or two words?

V5 9 Complete the verb for sentences 1–7.

1 How often do you d*rink* tea?
2 Water b_____ at 100 ºC.
3 In the summer, I s_____ in the sea.
4 He doesn't u_____ the word.
5 What does 'cactus' m_____?
6 Do you c_____ dinner every day?
7 Dolphins j_____ very high.

GRAMMAR

G1 Articles

a/an

The article *a/an* means *one*. We usually use *a/an*, not *one*.

> I have **a** video. (= I have one video.)

Use *a/an* with a singular noun, and to talk about a person's job.

> Hong Kong is **a** noisy city.
> George Lucas is **a** director.

Use *an*, not *a*, when the noun begins with a vowel sound (*a*, *e*, *i*, *o*, *u*).

> Monaco is **an** expensive city.
> He's **an** actor.
> But note *an hour*.

We usually say *a/an* with the schwa (ə).

> **an** actor – /ən ˈæktə/

the

Use *the* with singular or plural nouns, to talk about a specific person or thing. We know *who* or *what*.

> **The** history teacher at my school is good. (= There is only one history teacher at the school.)
> **The** Songkran Water Festival starts **the** Thai New Year. (= There is only one Songkran Festival, and one New Year.)
> **The** actors and directors meet here. (= We know which actors and directors.)

We usually say *the* with the schwa (/ə/): *the* (/ðə/) director, but before a vowel, it is the strong form /i/: *the* (/ðiː/) actor.

No article

Don't use articles with plural nouns, when you talk about people or things in general.

> **Love stories** are boring.
> **Dolphins** are famous for big jumps.

❗ Known specific = **The children** are in **the garden**.
General = **Children** are welcome at this hotel.

G2 *can, can't*

Use *can* for ability.

> Jack goes skiing. He's very good. = Jack **can** ski.
> Sheila doesn't swim. She never swims. = Sheila **can't** swim. / Sheila **cannot*** swim.

* The full form of *can't* is *cannot*.

Use *can* for permission (what is allowed).

> Only full-time students **can** use the library.

Use *can* for possibility (what is possible).

> You **can** watch television in the clubroom.

Put *can* before the main verb.

> He **can** ski. ✓
> He ~~ski can~~. ✗

Don't use *to* after *can*.

> I **can use** a computer. ✓
> I ~~can to use~~ a computer. ✗

Don't use *do/does* in a question with *can*.

> **Can she** ride a bike? ✓
> ~~Does she can~~ ride a bike? ✗

Don't use *do/does* in a negative sentence with *can*.

> We **can't** go to the gym today. ✓
> We ~~don't can~~ go to the gym today. ✗

Don't add *-s* to *can* in the *he / she / it* form.

> Rosa **can** run a marathon. ✓
> Rosa ~~cans~~ run a marathon. ✗

KEY LANGUAGE

KL1 Asking for information (2)

Can/Could you give me some information about (the resort)?
Can/Could you tell me about (the accommodation)?
Is there (a kids' club)?
Are there any (restaurants)?
Can I (play other sports)?

KL2 Answering politely

Saying *yes* politely

Yes, certainly.
Yes, of course.

Saying *no* politely

No, I'm afraid not.
I'm sorry. I'm afraid you can't.
No, I'm afraid there isn't/aren't.

VOCABULARY

V1 Types of film

action/adventure film, actor, animation, comedy, director, historical film, horror film, love story, musical (n), romantic comedy, science fiction (film), thriller, war film, western

V2 Leisure activities, sports

dance, do aerobics, do yoga, go hiking, go mountain biking , go running, go scuba diving, go swimming, go to a gym/fitness club, go wind-surfing, play basketball, play football, play tennis, ride a bike, ski

V3 Holiday resorts and entertainment

campsite, chalet, double room, family room, kids' club, painting class, satellite TV, sea view

V4 Fractions and percentages; approximation

fifth, fraction, half, percent, quarter, third

about, exactly, nearly, over

Extra practice

G1 **1** Match 1–5 with a–e.

1 Abbas Kiarostami is a _d_
2 Ariel Mateluna is an _____
3 I like _____
4 The _____
5 *Blackboards* is an _____

a) actor.
b) President is on TV.
c) interesting film.
d) film director.
e) horror films.

2 Write *a, an, the* or Ø (no article).

A: Do you often listen to [1] _Ø_ American groups?
B: Yes. In fact, I have [2] _____ new CD by [3] _____
American group. There's [4] _____ song about [5] _____
woman in New York. It's really good and [6] _____
singer is beautiful.
A: Can I listen to it?
B: Yes, of course.

3 Correct the mistakes with articles in sentences 1–8.

1 Dee is shop assistant in a big department store.
   a shop assistant
2 Festival in February in my city is really exciting.
3 I really enjoy the thrillers.
4 Let's take children with us to the party.
5 My father is a accountant.
6 A director of this film is very good.
7 Where's Luke? Is he home? – Yes, he's in a garden.
8 Let's meet in cinema in King Street.

G2 **4** Find the extra word in each sentence.

1 He can ~~to~~ sing.
2 Can does she ride a motorbike?
3 We doesn't can't go to the gym.
4 Louis can make makes films.
5 Sorry, I can't to play tonight.
6 Can you do tell me about the course?

5 Speaking practice Ask a partner questions with the words.

1 Can / speak / foreign language?
   Can you speak a foreign language?
2 Can / ride / motorbike?
3 Can / do / yoga?
4 Can / make / web page?
5 Can / run / marathon?
6 Can / play / the drums?

KL1,2 **6** Complete the conversation in a hotel with a–h.

a) Are there any
b) Yes, certainly.
c) No, I'm afraid not.
d) there isn't
e) Can you tell me
f) Can I
g) Is there
h) Could you give me some

A: Hello. [1] _h_ information about your hotel?
B: [2] _____ What do you want to know?
A: [3] _____ about the facilities? [4] _____ a swimming pool?
B: [5] _____ But there is a sauna and a fitness club.
A: Great. And is there a restaurant?
B: No, I'm afraid [6] _____.
A: [7] _____ good restaurants in the city?
B: Yes, of course. There are lots.
A: OK. [8] _____ book a room?
B: Certainly.

V1 **7** Write the type of film in sentences 1–5.

> historical ~~love story~~ thrillers
> animations westerns

1 She likes romantic comedies with a good *love story*.
2 My children like all _____, especially Wallace and Gromit.
3 A lot of boys like _____ with American cowboys.
4 I like _____ films because I learn about the past.
5 _____ are exciting.

V2 **8** Match the verb with the activity.

do	1 aerobics
	2 swimming
	3 football
play	4 yoga
	5 running
go	6 basketball
	7 tennis

V3 **9** Write words from the list V3 in this table.

Accommodation	Entertainment
_____	_____
_____	_____
_____	_____
_____	
_____	

V4 **10** Say these fractions and percentages.

> ¼   40%   ½   ¾   100%   1/5

GRAMMAR

G1   Comparative adjectives

Use comparatives to compare one person or thing with another person or thing (or to compare groups of people or things).

Adjective	Comparative
slow	slower (than)
fast	faster (than)
modern	more modern (than)
important	more important (than)

Add -er to most one-syllable adjectives.
    A bicycle is slower. (→ G3, *Spelling rules*)

Add *than* after the comparative adjective.
    A bicycle is slow**er than** a car.

Put *more* in front of most two-syllable adjectives and all adjectives with three syllables or more.
    The new office is **more modern than** the old office. ✓
    The new office is ~~moderner than~~ the old office. ✗

    Underground trains are **more expensive than** buses.

! Note these irregular comparative adjectives.
    good – **better**   bad – **worse**

    Marco's English is **better than** my English. ✓
    Marco's English is ~~gooder than~~ my English. ✗

    The coffee here is **worse than** at the restaurant. ✓
    The coffee here is ~~badder than~~ at the restaurant. ✗

G2   Superlative adjectives

Use superlatives to compare one person or thing with several people or things (more than two).
    He's **the oldest** in the class.
    My car is **the fastest** on the road.

We can also compare one group with other groups.
    Buses are **the cheapest** way to travel.

Adjective	Superlative
slow	the slowest
fast	the fastest
modern	the most modern
important	the most important

Add -est to most one-syllable adjectives.
    You have **the slowest** car. (→ G3, *Spelling rules*)

Use the article *the* before a superlative.
    Singapore is **the cleanest** city in Southeast Asia. ✓
    Singapore is ~~a cleanest~~ city in Southeast Asia. ✗

Use *most* in front of most adjectives with two syllables and all adjectives with three syllables or more.
    It's **the most beautiful** city in Europe.

! Use *in Europe / in the world / in my class* after superlatives, not *of*.

! Note these irregular superlative adjectives.
    good – **best**   bad – **worst**

    Marco's English is **the best** in the class.
    This film is **the worst** at the cinema this week.

G3   Spelling rules for comparatives and superlatives

Some comparative and superlative adjectives change their spelling.

Add -r or -st to one-syllable adjectives ending in -e.
    My sister is nice**r** than my brother.
    He's the nice**st** of my brothers.

With two-syllable adjectives ending -y, change -y to -i and add -er or -est.
    This city is ug**lier** than London.
    London Heathrow is the bus**iest** airport in the world.

With most one-syllable adjectives with a consonant + vowel + consonant spelling, double the last consonant and add -er or -est.
    big – big**g**er – big**g**est
    wet – we**t**ter – we**t**test
    sad – sa**d**der – sa**d**dest
    The UK is ~~weter~~ than Turkey. ✗
    The UK is **wetter** than Turkey. ✓
    The UK is one of the **wettest** countries. ✓

KEY LANGUAGE

KL   Buying a ticket

Traveller
Can you tell me about (the British Airways flight)?
When does it leave?
When does it arrive?
How long does it take?
How much does it cost?
Is it a good (airline)?
I'd like to book (the British Airways flight), please.

Travel agent
Would you like (standard or business class)?
How would you like to pay?
Would you like to (make a booking)?

VOCABULARY

V1   Transport

bicycle/bike, boat, bus, car, lorry, motorbike, plane, ship, taxi, train, tram, underground (train)

V2   Flying

airline, aisle seat, arrival time, business class, departures board, flight, flight attendant, in-flight service, luggage, return ticket, standard class, window seat

(to) board, (to) depart, (to) get on, (to) land, (to) leave

V3   Written work

draft, final copy, mind map, order, paragraph, sentence, topic sentence

(to) add, (to) join

Extra practice

G1 **1** **Write the adjectives in sentences 1–8 in their comparative forms.**

1 Business class is _more comfortable_ than standard class. (comfortable)
2 Kraków in Poland is _____ than Warsaw. (beautiful)
3 Buses are _____ than trams in my city. (cheap)
4 London is _____ than New York. (old)
5 My new car is _____ than my old car. (good)
6 In the city centre, a bicycle is _____ than a car. (fast)
7 Madrid is _____ than London in the summer. (hot)
8 I think the German language is _____ than English. (easy)

G2 **2** **Write the adjectives in sentences 1–6 in their superlative forms.**

1 Mount Everest is the _highest_ mountain in the world. (high)
2 Planes are the _____ means of transport. (fast)
3 Boats are the _____ means of transport. (comfortable)
4 Maths is my _____ subject at school. (bad)
5 The world's _____ spy is James Bond. (good)
6 Is the President of the USA the _____ person in the world? (important)
7 I'd like to book the _____ flight. (short)
8 Sam is the _____ man that I know. (romantic)

G1,2 **3** **Speaking practice** **Make sentences about these subjects with the comparative and superlative form.**

1 Drinks: tea / coffee / water
   I think tea is better than coffee. – But water is the best drink!
2 Animals: whales / elephants / penguins
3 Places: deserts / mountains / sea
4 Countries: Brazil / Japan / Poland
5 Sport: football / tennis / golf
6 Films: musicals / horror films / comedy films

G3 **4** **Find the extra letter in each sentence.**

1 Ice cream is niceer than bread.
2 Walking is easyier than running.
3 Tickets on aeroplanes are more expensiver than trains.
4 Blue whales are the bigggest type of whale.
5 My English is worser not better!
6 Is he a bestter actor than Tom Cruise?
7 London is the busyiest city in the UK.
8 Six o'clock is the lattest time you can come.

KL **5** **Match questions 1–6 with responses a–f.**

1 When does it arrive? _b_
2 Would you like to make a booking? _____
3 Is it a good airline? _____
4 How long does it take? _____
5 How would you like to pay? _____
6 How much does it cost? _____

a) 539 Australian dollars.
b) At 8.00 in the evening.
c) Yes, please.
d) Seven hours.
e) Oh yes. It's the best.
f) By credit card.

V1 **6** **Complete sentences 1–6 with words from the list V1. Make them true for you.**

1 I go to work by _____.
2 I can/can't ride a _____.
3 We usually go by _____ when we go on holiday.
4 In my city, _____ are the cheapest means of transport.
5 And _____ are the most expensive means of transport.
6 I like travelling by _____.

V2 **7** **Match 1–6 with a–f.**

1 I don't want a window seat, _f_
2 Is that a _____
3 Would you like business _____
4 When does it depart and _____
5 This is departures but _____
6 Please board the plane _____

a) when does it arrive?
b) return ticket?
c) you need arrivals.
d) half an hour before departure.
e) or standard class?
f) I'd like an aisle seat.

V3 **8** **Match a word or phrase in the list V3 with definitions 1–5.**

1 This is usually first in a paragraph. _____
2 This is the last draft of your writing. _____
3 It's a group of sentences. _____
4 You join these to make a paragraph. _____
5 This is a way of organising ideas. _____

GRAMMAR

G1 Countable and uncountable nouns

Nouns can be countable or uncountable.

Countable nouns	Uncountable nouns
banana doctor car phone hotel	water bread garlic sand oil

	Countable nouns	Uncountable nouns
Use of a/an	can have a/an in front of them: **A doctor** works in **a hospital**.	do not have a/an in front of them: **Garlic is** good in **salad**.
Plural form	can have a plural form: **Doctors** work in **hospitals**.	do not have a plural form and only use singular verbs: **Bread is** good for you.
some and any (→ G2 below)	can have some or any in front of the plural: **Some** restaurants are expensive. There aren't **any** hotels in the town.	can have some or any in front of them: **Some** olive oil is expensive. Is there **any** milk on the table?

Some nouns can be countable and uncountable, with different meanings.

I like **chicken** for dinner. (uncountable)
A chicken can run fast. (countable)

G2 some and any

Use some in affirmative sentences.
Yes, there are **some** strawberries.
Yes, there is **some** milk.

Use any in negative sentences.
No, there aren't **any** nuts.
No, there isn't **any** oil.

Usually use any in questions.
Are there **any** planes to Zurich today?
Is there **any** bread?

! Use some in questions to ask for or offer something.

Can you give me **some** information?
Would you like **some** chocolate?

See also Key Language: Requests and offers.

G3 much, many, a lot of

Use many and a lot of with countable nouns.
London has **many** buses
London doesn't have **a lot of** trams.

Use much and a lot of with uncountable nouns.
We have **a lot of** public transport.
We don't have **much** public transport.

Use many and a lot of in both affirmative and negative sentences.
I write **a lot of** emails to friends.*
I write **many** emails to friends.
I don't write **many** emails to friends.
I don't write **a lot of** emails to friends.

* A lot of is more common than many in affirmative sentences. Many is quite formal.

Use much in negative sentences, not in affirmative sentences.
There **isn't much** water in the desert. ✓
There is ~~much~~ water in the sea. ✗

Use much, many and a lot of in questions.
Have you got **much** money in the bank?
Do you eat **a lot of** chocolate?
Have you got **many** vegetables?

Use How many for questions with countable nouns and How much with uncountable nouns.
How many computer games have you got?
How much exercise do you do?

G4 have got

Use have got / has got in informal spoken British English. It means the same as have/has.
I've got three brothers.
I have three brothers.

! American English does not use have got / has got.

KEY LANGUAGE

KL Requests and offers

Requests
We would like / We'd like (some bread), please.
I would like / I'd like (some water).
Can/Could we have (some tea)?

Offers
Would you like (fish or meat)?

! we would = we'd   I would = I'd

! Could is more polite than can.

! Use some in offers and requests.
Would you like **some** coffee?

VOCABULARY

V1 Food and drink

banana , (roast) beef, biscuit, bread, broccoli, burger, cake, carrot, caviar, cheese, chicken, chilli con carne, chocolate, coffee, couscous, crisps, curry, fast food, fish, fruit, garlic, green tea, ice cream, lamb (kebab), meat, milk, noodles, nut, olive oil, orange, pasta, (red) pepper, pizza, potato(es), rice, salmon, sardine, strawberry(ies), sushi, tomato(es), vegetable

V2 Health and nutrition

brain, diet, energy, health, heart, illness, medicine, memory, vegetarian, vitamin

Extra practice

G1 **1** Write these nouns in the table.

~~food~~ city coffee cinema pilot
money rain film rice vitamin

Countable nouns	Uncountable nouns
_____	_food_
_____	_____
_____	_____
_____	_____
_____	

2 Sentences 1–5 are incorrect. Write them again.
1 A bread is good for you.
  Bread is good for you.

2 We work in office.
  _____

3 Green teas is a super drink.
  _____

4 Nurse work in hospitals.
  _____

5 An olive oil is good on salad.
  _____

G2 **3** Write *some* or *any* in sentences 1–10.
1 *Some* cars are expensive.
2 Are there _____ rooms at the hotel?
3 She doesn't have _____ free time.
4 There aren't _____ good restaurants in the city centre.
5 He has _____ ice cream.
6 Do you have _____ qualifications?
7 There's _____ parking at the back of the hotel.
8 There are _____ children in the street.
9 I'm sorry, there aren't _____ taxis at the moment.
10 Can I have _____ milk in my tea, please?

G3 **4** Read this interview and choose the correct words.
A: Hi Irina. Tell me about your city of St Petersburg in Russia.
B: It's a beautiful city. It has ¹*a lot of / ~~much~~* old buildings, like the castle. ²*Much/Many* tourists visit it.
A: Do you often go there?
B: No, I'm a student at the university and so I don't have ³*many/much* free time.
A: What do people do in the evening?
B: ⁴*Much / A lot of* people go to cafés and restaurants.
A: How ⁵*much/many* cafés are there in St.Petersburg?
B: I don't know exactly but there are ⁶*a lot of / much* them!

5 Speaking practice Complete questions 1–4 with your own words. Ask a partner.
1 Do you drink a lot of _____?
2 Have you got much _____?
3 How much _____?
4 How many _____?

G4 **6** Complete sentences 1–5 with the correct form of *have got*.
1 Mark *has got* two brothers.
2 His oldest brother _____ a big house in the country.
3 He _____ a beautiful wife too.
4 But they _____ any children.
5 They _____ two horses.

KL **7** You are in a café. Complete this conversation with a–f.
a) can
b) would you like
c) I'd
d) could we
e) would you
f) would like
WAITER: Hello, ¹ __e__ like some drinks?
YOU: Yes, please. ²_____ like a cola and my friend ³_____ some orange juice.
WAITER: OK. And ⁴_____ a sandwich or something to eat?
YOU: Yes, ⁵_____ have the pasta, please. And ⁶_____ we also have a salad with it?

V1 **8** Look at the list in V1. Find words to complete the table.

Fruit	Meat	Fish	Vegetables	Drinks
banana				

9 Speaking practice Ask and answer with a partner.
Which food is popular in your country?
What's your favourite food in the table in Exercise 8?

V2 **10** Re-order the letters to make a word.
1 I don't like meat. I'm a *angetevari*. *vegetarian*
2 Garlic is a natural *cinmedie*. _____
3 She has a healthy *tied* of fish, vegetables and fruit. _____
4 Green tea can protect you from *silnels*. _____
5 Eat blueberries. They help your *moremy*. _____

GRAMMAR

G1 Present continuous

Use the present continuous to describe an action happening now or around now.

They're playing tennis at the moment.

Angie can't come to the phone – **she's sleeping**.

I'm reading a really good book at the moment.

We also sometimes use the present continuous to describe a changing situation.

Our business **is growing** very quickly.

Affirmative sentences

Subject	Verb *to be*		Verb + *-ing*
	Contraction	Full form	
I	'm	am	working
you / we / they	're	are	
he / she / it	's	is	

I'm buying a new pair of jeans.

We're buying a car.

It's raining.

Negative sentences

Subject	Verb *to be*		Verb + *-ing*
	Contraction	Full form	
I	'm not	am not	waiting
you / we / they	aren't	are not	
he / she / it	isn't	is not	

I'm not watching the film now.

You aren't studying Spanish at the moment.

She isn't trying on the suit.

G2 Present continuous and present simple

The present continuous describes an action happening now. The present simple describes things that happen again and again.

I'm learning English at the moment. ✓

She does exercise every day. ✓

They ~~watch~~ TV now. ✗

! We normally use adverbs of frequency (*always*, *usually*, *never*) with the present simple and **not** with the present continuous.

I always get up at 6 a.m. ✓

~~I'm usually getting up~~ at 6 a.m. ✗

We don't use the continuous form with some verbs, e.g. *want*, *know*, *understand*, *like*.

I want a glass of water now. ✓

~~I'm wanting~~ a glass of water now. ✗

G3 Present continuous questions

Yes/No questions

Verb *to be*	Subject	Verb + *-ing*
am	I	leaving?
are	you / we / they	
is	he / she / it	

Wh- questions

Question word	Verb *to be*	Subject	Verb + *-ing*
What	am	I	doing?
Why	are	you / we / they	leaving?
Where	's (is)	he / she / it	going?

Questions in the present continuous can start with the verb *to be* or with a question word.

Are you leaving now?

When are you leaving?

The verb *to be* usually comes before the subject.

Is she working in Beijing?

Where **is she** working?

If the subject is the question word *what* + noun, the verb *to be* comes after.

What changes are happening in town centres?

KEY LANGUAGE

KL Giving advantages and disadvantages

What are the advantages/disadvantages?

Are there any advantages/disadvantages?

There are two main advantages/disadvantages.

The first/second is that ...

One/Another advantage is that ...

The disadvantage is that ...

I think / don't think (it's a nice place).

This means that ...

This is more ...

I think X is better because ....

VOCABULARY

V1 Shops and shopping

customer, discount, hypermarket, Internet shopping, market stall, online shopping, price, product, service, (department) store, supermarket

(to) buy, (to) check, (to) pay for, (to) shop, (to) spend (money), (to) spend (time), (to) try on

V2 Things we buy

books, CDs, clothes, DVDs, food, furniture, make-up, stationery

V3 US English

downtown, gas station, highway, motel, parking lot, shopping mall, store

Extra practice

G1 **1** **Complete sentences 1–8 with these verbs in the present continuous.**

| ~~talk~~ sit go buy not/work |
| do not/rain meet |

1 He *'s talking* on the phone at the moment.
2 They _____ a new house.
3 Prices _____ up again at the local supermarket.
4 She _____ some visitors at the station this morning.
5 We _____ our homework.
6 The computer _____ . There's a problem.
7 You _____ in my chair.
8 It _____ now, it's sunny!

G2 **2** **Choose the correct verb.**

My day ¹ *is / is being* always busy. For example, at the moment ² *I organise / I'm organising* dinner for some visitors from Japan. They ³ *visit / are visiting* my country for the week. My assistant usually ⁴ *helps / is helping* me but today ⁵ *she does / she's doing* a training course. Our visitors ⁶ *stay / are staying* in a hotel near the office, so ⁷ *I try / I'm trying* to book a restaurant near here. We often ⁸ *eat / are eating* in a good Indian restaurant near here, so maybe that's a good idea.

G3 **3** **Write the words in the correct order to make questions.**

1 is friend driving your
   Is your friend driving?
2 are what doing you
   _____ ?
3 are phoning you who
   _____ ?
4 going are where they
   _____ ?
5 are how feeling you
   _____ ?

G2,3 **4** **Match questions 1–6 with responses a–f.**

1 Do you often come here? *d*
2 Are you always busy? _____
3 Is he studying? _____
4 Where's he studying? _____
5 Are people buying online these days? _____
6 What do you want? _____

a) Yes, he is.
b) No, I'm not.
c) Yes, they are.
d) Yes, I do.
e) A pen, please.
f) At the University of Hong Kong.

KL **5** **Complete the conversation with sentences a–g.**

a) The second is that it's more expensive than in the city.
b) There are disadvantages in that.
c) This means that they cost more money.
d) Another is that it's more beautiful.
e) So where do you think?
f) What are the advantages in that?
g) I don't think it is.

A: I'm bored with the city. I'd like to move nearer to the sea.
B: The sea ... I don't know. ¹_____
A: Really? What are they?
B: The first is that it's often cold. ²_____
A: ³_____ Houses here are more expensive.
B: Not these days. A lot of people want a house near the beach. ⁴_____
A: Well, OK, not the sea. ⁵_____
B: Let's move to the mountains.
A: ⁶_____
B: One advantage is that it's cheaper. ⁷_____

V1,2 **6** **Choose the correct verb.**

1 How much did you *buy/pay* for the book?
2 I often *shop/spend* £100 at the hypermarket.
3 Did you *try/pay* on the suit?
4 She always *buys/checks* the prices.
5 They *buy/check* food on the Internet.
6 We can't *pay/spend* any more time and money.

7 **Read these definitions and write the word.**

1 a shop that sells all types of food _____
2 a person who buys in a shop _____
3 using a computer to shop _____
4 something that you can buy _____
5 chairs and tables, for example _____
6 a very large example of the shop in number 1 _____
7 how much you pay for something _____
8 pens, pencils and notebooks, for example _____

V3 **8** **Complete the table.**

US English	UK English
gas station	¹_____ station
²_____	motorway
parking lot	³_____ park
⁴_____	hotel (for motorists)
downtown	town ⁵_____
shopping ⁶_____	shopping centre
⁷_____	shop

GRAMMAR

G1 Past simple of *to be*

Use the past simple to talk about events and situations that are finished.

Affirmative (+)	Negative (–)		Question (?)
	Contraction	Full form	
I was	I wasn't	I was not	was I … ?
he / she / it was	he / she / it wasn't	he / she / it was not	was he / she / it … ?
you / we / they were	you / we / they weren't	you / we / they were not	were you / we / they … ?

I **was** late this morning.
You **were** in the hospital last week.
The city **wasn't** important in 2000 BC.
She **wasn't** at the shop on Saturday.
Was the food expensive? – No, it **wasn't**.

! Normally, we use *wasn't/weren't*. Use the full form *was not / were not* in formal English.

Use *there was/were* to describe something or a situation in a place in the past.

Affirmative (+)	Negative (–)		Question (?)
	Contraction	Full form	
there was	there wasn't	there was not	was there … ?
there were	there weren't	there were not	were there … ?

There was an old city in the desert.
Were there many people at the conference? – No, there **weren't**.

! Use short answers for past simple *to be* questions.

Were you early for school? – No, **I wasn't**.
Was there someone at the airport? – Yes, **there was**.

G2 *could, couldn't*

Use *could/couldn't* to talk about ability and possibility in the past.

In the past, only some people **could** read and write. Now, most people can read.
My grandparents **could** walk to their work. Now we usually drive to work.

Use *could* for *can* in the past simple.
I **can't** go tonight. → I **couldn't** go last night.

Use the infinitive without *to* after *could* or *couldn't*.
People **couldn't visit** the country. (✓)
People couldn't ~~to~~ visit the country. ✗
People couldn't ~~visits~~ the country. ✗

! Use short answers for *could* questions.

When you were one, **could you** walk? – Yes, **I could**. / No, **I couldn't**.

KEY LANGUAGE

KL1 Polite requests

Could you …	help me, please? give us (a map of the museum), please? take a photo of us?
Could you tell me …	how much it is? where (the cloakroom) is? when (the next film) is? how old it is?

A: How can I help you?
B: Could you tell me (where the cloakroom is), please?
A: Here, on the right.
B: Thank you.
A: Not at all. / You're welcome.

! We also use *Can you … ?* but *Could you … ?* is more polite.

KL2 Responding to polite requests

Positive responses
Certainly.
Yes, of course.
That's no problem.

Negative responses
I'm afraid not.
I'm afraid I can't do that.

VOCABULARY

V1 Buildings
cloakroom, courtyard, door, entrance, furniture, garden, gate, ladder, lift, painting, roof, room, stairs, wall, window

V2 Verb + preposition
chat to, focus on, go on (a trip), move onto, read about, stay in, talk to

V3 Describing objects
circle, circular, heavy, leather, length, light, long, metal, narrow, plastic, rectangle, rectangular, short, square (adj, n), weight, wide, width, wood, wooden
(to) lengthen, (to) weigh, (to) widen

Extra practice

G1 **1** **Complete the three conversations with** *was, wasn't, were* **or** *weren't.*

1

A: Sorry I ¹ _was_ late this morning.

B: That's OK. ²_____ your bus late?

A: No, it ³_____ . My train ⁴_____ late.

2

C: I didn't know it ⁵_____ Jan and Pierre's birthdays last weekend.

D: Yes, they ⁶_____ 25.

C: ⁷_____ they at the restaurant on Saturday?

D: No, they ⁸_____ . They ⁹_____ in Paris for the night!

3

E: When ¹⁰_____ your chemistry exam?

F: Last Tuesday.

E: ¹¹_____ it OK? ¹²_____ there any difficult questions?

F: There ¹³_____ two difficult questions but it ¹⁴_____ OK.

2 **Write questions with** *was* **or** *were* **for these answers.**

1 *Were you late for the class?*

No, I wasn't late for the class.

2 _____

No, the teacher wasn't here.

3 _____

I was at the cinema yesterday evening.

4 _____

Yes, it was a very good film.

5 _____

I was with my brother.

3 Speaking practice **Work with a partner. Ask and answer questions with the words below.**

> holiday   exam   party
> lesson   visit to the dentist

When was your last _____?
Where was your _____?
How was your _____?

G2 **4** **Choose the correct word.**

1 He couldn't ~~sees~~/*see* the film.

2 I'm afraid I *couldn't*/*can't* come tonight.

3 Could they ski when they were children? – Yes, they *could*/*couldn't*.

4 Ten years ago it was safe in the city. You *can*/*could* walk in the streets at night.

5 Now we *can*/*could* phone anywhere in the world but my parents *can't*/*couldn't* when they were young.

6 Sorry we *couldn't*/*can't* come last night.

7 Computers *can*/*could* do anything!

KL1,2 **5** **Write the words in questions 1–7.**

> help   when   ~~how~~   can   give   where   what

1 Could you tell me _how_ much it is?

2 Could you tell me _____ this means, please?

3 How _____ I help you?

4 Could you _____ me, please?

5 Could you tell me _____ the next show is?

6 Could you _____ us the menu, please?

7 Could you tell me _____ the cloakroom is?

6 **Now match questions 1–7 in Exercise 5 with responses a–g.**

a) Yes, of course. At 5.30 p.m. _5_

b) No, I'm afraid I can't. Ask your teacher. _____

c) Certainly. What's the problem? _____

d) Yes, I can. It's £5. _____

e) Of course. Down the stairs and turn left. _____

f) I'd like a new shirt, please. _____

g) Yes, of course. Here it is. _____

V1 **7** **Someone is describing a new house. Write in the words.**

> painting   ~~room~~   garden   gate   window   door

'This is a large ¹ _room_ and you can see the mountains through that ²_____. The ³_____ on the wall is by a local artist. Let's go through this ⁴_____. Outside there's a small courtyard and you go through this metal ⁵_____ into a ⁶_____ with plants and flowers.'

V2 **8** **Write the prepositions in sentences 1–6.**

> on   on   onto   in   ~~to~~   about

1 I like to chat _to_ my friends on the phone.

2 When do you go _____ holiday?

3 I'd like to focus _____ Phil's new idea at this meeting.

4 Did you read _____ the Chinese economy?

5 I usually stay _____ a hotel when I'm on a business trip.

6 Before I move _____ the next topic, are there any questions?

V3 **9** **Choose the correct word.**

1 I'd like a *long*/~~length~~ table.

2 This *wooden*/*wood* chair is beautiful.

3 Why is a CD *circular*/*circle*?

4 How *wide*/*width* is this room?

5 The field for baseball isn't a *rectangular*/*rectangle*. You're thinking about football.

6 How much does the baby *weight*/*weigh*?

GRAMMAR

G1 Past simple (affirmative, regular verbs)

Use the past simple to talk about finished events and times in the past.

I **worked** in Singapore in 1989.
She **lived** in Cape Town last year.
They **stayed** in a hotel last night.

With regular verbs, add -*ed* to the infinitive to make the past simple.

cook – cook**ed**
enjoy – enjoy**ed**

For verbs ending in -*e*, add -*d*.

invit**e** – invit**ed**
liv**e** – liv**ed**

! Note these spelling changes.

study – stud**ied**
carry – carr**ied**
travel – travel**led**

G2 Past simple (irregular verbs)

Many common verbs in the past simple are irregular.

do – **did**
drive – **drove**
go – **went**
have – **had**
sit – **sat**

I **sat** at the doctor's for two hours last week.
We **drove** across Europe when we were students.
→ irregular verb list page 159

! Don't add -*ed* to the infinitive or to the past form of an irregular verb.

I **went** to the meeting yesterday. ✓
I ~~goed~~ to the meeting yesterday. ✗
I ~~wented~~ to the meeting yesterday. ✗

G3 Past simple (negative and questions)

Negative sentences

| Subject | *did + not* | | Infinitive |
	Contraction	Full form	without *to*
I / he / she / it / you / we / they	didn't	did not	change

I **didn't go** out last night.
The letter **didn't arrive** this morning.
They **didn't leave** for two days.

! When we speak, and for informal writing, we use *didn't*, not *did not*.

! Do not use *didn't* with the verb *to be*.

I ~~didn't be~~ born in 1984. ✗
I **wasn't** born in 1984. ✓

Questions

Question word + *did*	Subject	Infinitive without *to*
(what) did	I / he / she / it / you / we / they	say … ?

Did he phone the police?
When did you move house?
Where did they live before?

For short answers, use *did/didn't*.

Did you play tennis with her?
– Yes, **I did**. / No, **I didn't**.
Did we agree to this price?
– Yes, **we did**. / No, **we didn't**.

! Do not use *did* with the verb *to be*.

When ~~did you be~~ born? ✗
When **were you** born? ✓

KEY LANGUAGE

KL Giving reasons

The most important reason is that …
The first/second reason is that …
The main reason is that …
One/Another reason is that …
My final reason is that …
Firstly / Secondly / Finally, …
It's important/useful because …

VOCABULARY

V1 Medical science and machines

acupuncture needles, bones, equipment, examinations, experiment, false teeth, lab(oratory), medicine, microscope, MRI scanner, scalpel, scientist, skin, teeth, tools, treatment, waiting room, X-ray machine

V2 (Everyday) inventions and machines

chewing gum, diving suit, helicopter, high heels, lipstick, parachute, Post-it® note, radio, robot, telescope, tin can, umbrella

Extra practice

G1,2 **1** **Write the past simple form of verbs 1–12.**

1 enjoy *enjoyed*
2 go _____
3 return _____
4 build _____
5 hold _____
6 work _____
7 drive _____
8 stand _____
9 help _____
10 study _____
11 travel _____
12 invent _____

2 **Complete sentences 1–8 with verbs from Exercise 1 in the past simple.**

1 I _____ from Brazil an hour ago.
2 She _____ me to carry this.
3 Many famous people _____ at Bologna University.
4 The children _____ the film.
5 Five of us _____ from Cádiz to Madrid in a really small, uncomfortable car.
6 Doctor Grey _____ in this laboratory.
7 Leonardo da Vinci _____ over 100 machines.
8 They _____ the palace in 1706.

G3 **3** **Each sentence has one word missing. Find the missing word in the box and write it in.**

~~did~~ did did did drive not was where

did
1 I ⋏ not play tennis last weekend.
2 They did see him. Did you?
3 Did you here in your car?
4 What time you leave?
5 Did you live before you lived in Morocco?
6 Did they say 'yes'? – Yes, they.
7 My brother not born in hospital.
8 Some of our friends not come to the party last night.

G1–3 **4** **Correct sentences 1–6.**

1 I ~~carryed~~ this shopping all the way from the supermarket. *carried*
2 He sitted in the hospital for two hours.
3 The Romans wored false teeth.
4 They didn't to like the food.
5 Did you enjoyed the film last night?
6 She didn't was interested in the conversation.

5 Speaking practice **Work with a partner. Compare answers to questions 1–5 with your partner.**

1 When did you leave school/university?
2 What did you do last weekend?
3 Where did your mother and father meet?
4 Why did you choose this course?
5 How long did you spend at school?

KL **6** **Complete phrases 1–4 about university with your own ideas.**

1 The most important reason for going to university is
_____

2 Another reason is that you
_____

3 It's also important
_____

4 My final reason is that
_____

7 **Now, match reasons a–d with phrases 1–4. Are they the same as your reasons?**

a) receive a qualification. *2*
b) because you learn about life. _____
c) you meet lots of interesting people! _____
d) that it's good for your education. _____

V1 **8** **Complete the table with three parts of the body and two machines.**

needles   bones   medicine   skin   laboratory
scanner   teeth   tool   microscope

Parts of the body	Machines
bones	
_____	_____
_____	

V1,2 **9** **Make words from V1 and V2. Match 1–10 with a–j.**

1 chewing   a) heels
2 diving   b) teeth
3 high   c) suit
4 Post-it®   d) machine
5 tin   e) room
6 MRI   f) needles
7 false   g) gum
8 acupuncture   h) can
9 X-ray   i) scanner
10 waiting   j) note

GRAMMAR

G1 *should, shouldn't*

Use *should* when something is the right thing to do.
> You **should** keep your money in a bank.
> He **should** call me when he gets home.

Use *shouldn't* when something <u>isn't</u> the right thing to do.
> You **shouldn't** drive over 70 kilometres per hour.
> We **shouldn't** eat there. It's expensive.

Use *Should* + subject to ask the question 'is something the right thing to do?'
> **Should I** come to the doctor with you?
> **Should we** take some money?

! Don't add *-s* to *should* after *he*, *she* or *it*.
> She **should** buy a new car. ✓
> She ~~shoulds~~ buy a new car. ✗

! Use the infinitive of the main verb without *to* after *should*.
> They **should use** a cash machine. ✓
> They should ~~to~~ use a cash machine. ✗

G2 *have to, don't have to*

Use *have to / has to* when something is necessary.
> My university is expensive so I **have to** work in the summer holiday.
> She **has to** buy some new clothes because she's got a new job.

Use *don't have to / doesn't have to* when something isn't necessary.
> We **don't have to** fly there. We can take the train.
> The game **doesn't have to** end now. I can play for another half-hour.

Use *Do* + subject + *have to* to ask the question 'is something necessary?'
> **Do you have to** leave now?
> **Does he have to** pay cash?

KEY LANGUAGE

KL Asking for and giving opinions

Asking for opinions
What's your opinion about (saving money)?
Do you think that (it's important)?
Do you agree that (it's a good idea)?

Giving opinion
In my opinion, (it's a good idea).
I think that (it's a bad idea).
Personally, I think (we shouldn't do it).

Agreeing
Yes, definitely.
Yes, I suppose it is.

Showing uncertainty
I'm not sure.
I don't know.

Disagreeing
No, not at all.

VOCABULARY

V1 Money
cash, cashpoint, cheque, coin, credit card, debt, loan, note, PIN number, purse, wallet

V2 Verbs and phrases connected with money
borrow money, (can) afford, charge interest, earn money, get a loan, lend money, pay back, refund, save

V3 Banks
bank account, bank statement, branch, insurance, interest-free, interest rate, overdraft, student account

G1 **1** **Write some advice for these problems. Use** *should* **and the words in brackets.**

1 My boss isn't nice to me. (you / get / new job)
You should get a new job.

2 I live in an ugly city.
(you / move / more beautiful)

3 My bank charges a lot of interest.
(you / change / account)

4 He often loses his wallet.
(he / be / careful)

5 He borrowed money from me. He didn't pay me back.
(you / ask / money)

6 Shopping at the supermarket is slow.
(you / shop / Internet)

2 **Write two sentences giving advice for these problems. Use** *shouldn't* **in the first sentence and** *should* **in the second. Invent the second piece of advice.**

1 I'm always late for work.
You shouldn't be late for work. You should get up earlier.

2 They go out all the time and never study.

3 He smokes 50 cigarettes a day.

4 We watch about six hours of television a day.

5 She spends all her money on clothes.

3 **Write** *Should … ?* **questions for the answers.**

1 Q: Should *I tell him* ?
A: No, it's OK. I can tell him.

2 Q: Should _____?
A: No, we can take the car. I don't want to walk.

3 Q: Should _____?
A: Yes, I think he can do the exam this term.

4 Q: Should _____?
A: Yes, a credit card is a good idea.

G2 **4** **Write the correct form of** *have to* **(affirmative, negative or question) in sentences 1–9.**

1 I _have to_ phone a friend. Can I use your phone?
2 The taxi is here. We _____ leave now.
3 It's OK. You _____ pay for the meal. We can pay.
4 It's very busy now so he _____ work long hours.
5 A birthday present _____ be expensive. It can be special and cost very little.
6 _____ we _____ decide now? I'd like time to think about the problem.
7 There isn't a lesson today so we _____ go to school.
8 I don't like Bill. _____ you _____ invite him?
9 How much interest _____ she _____ pay on the loan?

KL **5** **Write phrases a–h in the conversation.**

a) No, not
b) Do you think
c) What's your opinion
d) Personally
e) not at all
f) I'm not sure
g) definitely
h) Do you

A: ¹ _c_ about students having jobs, Ben?
B: ² _____, I think they should have a part-time job.
C: ³ _____. Students shouldn't work, really. Students have to study. They should have time.
B: But in my opinion they have time to study <u>and</u> work. There are many countries where this happens.
A: ⁴ _____ that students should pay for their education then?
B: Yes, ⁵ _____. I don't use education so why should I pay for other people?
A: Wow! ⁶ _____ agree with that, Carol?
C: ⁷ _____ at all. I think this country should have qualified people so we all have to pay for that.
A: Definitely. That's right, Ben, isn't it?
B: No, ⁸ _____ …

V1,2,3 **6** **Complete sentences 1–9 with these pairs of words.**

a) know / number
b) pay / credit
c) lend / dollars
d) afford / insurance
e) write / cheque
f) charge / interest
g) earn / money
h) get / cash
i) get / loan

1 I need to _get_ some _cash_ from the cashpoint.
2 They _____ more _____ than me but I do the same job.
3 Can I _____ by _____ card?
4 Can we _____ a _____ from the bank for a new car?
5 Can you _____ me ten _____? I left my wallet at home.
6 The banks _____ about 20 percent _____ on overdrafts.
7 I can't _____ house _____. It's too expensive.
8 Do you _____ your PIN _____?
9 You _____ a _____ for £200 and send it to us.

GRAMMAR

G1 will, won't

We use *will* ('*ll*) and *will not* (*won't*) for what we <u>know</u> about the future.

In 2050 **I'll** be 77 years old.
It **won't** be dark at 5 p.m. in October.

We use *will* ('*ll*) and *will not* (*won't*) for what we <u>think</u> about the future.

I think China **will** produce the most food in the future.
People **won't** watch TV in the future. I believe they **will** use the Internet for films and entertainment.

Use contractions '*ll* and *won't* for speaking and informal English.

In 2050 **I'll** be 77 years old.
People **won't** watch TV in the future.

Use *Will/Won't* + subject to ask questions.

Will the climate become warmer?
Won't grey whales completely disappear?

Use the infinitive without *to* after *will*.

People **will live** longer in the future. ✓
People will ~~to~~ live longer in the future. ✗

! Don't add -*s* to *will* after *he*, *she*, *it* or *there*.

She **will** have to change jobs. ✓
She ~~wills~~ have to change jobs. ✗

G2 be going to

Use *be going to* to talk about plans and intentions. These plans and intentions are not certain.

	Subject + *be* (+ *not*)	going to	Verb
+	I'm		
	he's / she's / it's		
	you're / we're / they're		start
−	I'm not		
	he / she / it isn't	going to	
	you / we / they aren't		
?	*be* + **subject**		
	am I		start ...?
	is he / she / it		
	are you / we / they		

I'm going to have a holiday in the summer.
He's going to call me in five minutes.
She **isn't going to** do it.
We **aren't going to** borrow any money next year.
Is the teacher **going to** use the book in this lesson?
Are they **going to** change the timetable?

! *She isn't going to ... = She's not going to ...*

! The plans and intentions can be personal or impersonal.

I'm going to lend him some money.
The bank **is going to** lend him some money.

KEY LANGUAGE

KL Checking understanding

Could you repeat that, please?
I'm sorry, could you say that again?
So there are (two bedrooms). Is that right?
Was that (13 or 30)?
Did you say (14 or 40)?

VOCABULARY

V1 Compound nouns

business centre, car park, Internet café, play area, police station, post office, railway station, security guard, shopping centre, sports centre, swimming pool, tennis court, theme park

V2 Green living

bath, lid, light bulb, low-energy, on/off button, saucepan, shower, solar panel, solar power, wind turbine

(to) recycle, (to) switch off

V3 Home and furniture

armchair, balcony, bathroom, bed, bedroom, bookcase, cooker, cupboard, dining room, dishwasher, fridge-freezer, kitchen, living room, sofa, table, wardrobe, washing machine

V4 Exams and tests

practice (test), relaxation, revision, test

(to) fail (an exam), (to) pass (an exam), (to) revise

Extra practice

G1 **1** **Read this dialogue between a presenter and a professor in a TV programme. Complete the dialogue with** *will, 'll* **or** *won't*.

PRES: Today I'm talking to Professor Brumsfeld about the future of transport. First of all Professor, what kind of cars [1] _will_ we drive in the future?

PROF: Some people think we [2]_____ fly in our cars but it won't happen. I really don't think so.

PRES: So, what [3]_____ we do?

PROF: Well, cars [4]_____ use petrol because the world [5]_____ have any petrol. So we need something else. Some scientists think we [6]_____ use hydrogen. The advantage is that this is cleaner than petrol and better for the environment.

PRES: So [7]_____ these cleaner cars save the planet from global warming?

PROF: No, they [8]_____. We [9]_____ need to do many other things for that.

2 **Speaking practice** **Ask a partner** *Will you ... when you're older?* **questions with the words below.**

1 children
   Will you have children when you're older?
2 another country
3 excellent English
4 new car
5 Mars or the Moon

G2 **3** **Write the words in the right order to make** *be going to* **sentences.**

1 a going I'm have to shower
   I'm going to have a shower.
2 you to TV going are watch ?
   _____
3 he anything isn't going new to do
   _____
4 is to visit John his grandmother going ?
   _____
5 aren't change going our to we plans
   _____
6 Bertrand and Tijana build a are going house to ?
   _____
7 going about find out they're to flight times
   _____
8 are we recycle going what to ?
   _____

KL **4** **A student phones about an advert for a computer. Complete the conversation between the seller (s) and the student (st) with these words in gaps 1–5.**

| say | ~~right~~ | repeat | it | was |

ST: You have a computer for sale. Is that [1]*right*?
S: a) *Yes, that's right.*
ST: Is [2]_____ a desktop or a laptop?
S: b) _____
ST: How old is it?
S: c) _____
ST: Did you [3]_____ eight or 18 months?
S: d) _____
ST: And how much is it?
S: e) _____
ST: Could you [4]_____ that, please?
S: f) _____
ST: [5]_____ that 200?
S: g) _____
ST: Oh, OK. Can I have a look at it?

5 **Complete the dialogue in Exercise 4 with these responses in lines a–g.**

A laptop.   Eighteen.   One-eight months.
I'd like £200.   ~~Yes, that's right.~~   Yes, it was.
Two hundred pounds.   About 18 months.

V1 **6** **What word is missing from each group to make compound nouns?**

1 business, shopping, sports _____
2 car, theme _____
3 police, railway_____

V2,3 **7** **Find words in V2 and V3 to write next to these headings.**

1 bedroom: *wardrobe,*_____
2 kitchen: _____
3 living room: _____
4 bathroom: _____

V4 **8** **Write the words in sentences 1–6.**

| revise | practice | pass | relaxation | revision | fail |

1 I _____ grammar every day because I have a test once a week.
2 She didn't do any _____. That's the reason she failed.
3 I'm sure that Klaus will _____ his exam. He's very good at English.
4 But it's possible that Elena will _____ the exam, as her English isn't very good.
5 The teacher gave us a _____ test today.
6 _____ the night before an exam is the best way to prepare.

GRAMMAR

G1 Present perfect (regular verbs)

We use the present perfect when we talk about an experience in the past, but we don't say when we did it.

	Subject + *have* (+ *not*)		Past participle
	Contraction	Full form	
+	I've / you've / we've / they've	I / you / we / they have	worked
	he's / she's / it's	he / she / it has	
–	I / you / we / they haven't	I / you / we / they have not	
	he / she / it hasn't	he / she / it has not	
?	*have* + subject		(ever) worked ... ?
	have I / you / we / they		
	has he / she / it		

! Note that regular past participles are the same as the past simple form of the verb (add *-ed* to the end of the infinitive).

I've **visited** a lot of countries.
She's **talked** to the class.

We **haven't studied** the present perfect.
My father **hasn't changed** a lot in the last 20 years.

Have you ever **watched** a musical at the theatre?
Has he phoned about the flat?

Use short answers (without the main verb) to answer questions.

Have you talked to your teacher? – Yes, **I have.** / No, **I haven't.**

G2 Present perfect (irregular verbs)

Many common verbs are irregular, and the past simple and the past participle can be different.

eat – ate – **eaten**
write – wrote – **written**
drive – drove – **driven**
be – was/were – **been**
go – went – **gone**
do – did – **done**

I've **eaten** sushi.
They've **driven** a sports car.

! I've **been** to France. = I've gone to France and I've come back.
He's **gone** to France. = He's gone and he hasn't come back.

→ irregular verb list page 159

G3 Present perfect and past simple

We use the present perfect when we do not give (or don't know) the exact time we did something. We use the past simple when we give (or know) the exact time we did something.

He's **travelled** to many countries.
In 1990, he **travelled** around the world.

We add more information with the past simple.

I've **been** to Mexico twice. I **went** there **in 1997** and then I **went** again **in 2003**. I **stayed** there **for three months** that time.

! Do not use past time adverbs (*yesterday, last night, a year ago*) with the present perfect.

He's travelled through the jungle **last year**. ✗
He's **travelled** through the jungle. ✓
He **travelled** through the jungle **last year**. ✓

I've eaten sushi **last night**. ✗
I've **eaten** sushi in Japan. ✓
I **ate** sushi **last night**. ✓

Have you finished the essay **at the weekend**? ✗
Have you finished the essay? ✓
Did you finish the essay **at the weekend**? ✓

→ irregular verb list page 159

KEY LANGUAGE

KL Linkers, sequencers and fillers

also, let me see, perhaps, so, then, well, what else?

VOCABULARY

V1 Adjectives

awful, bare, brick-red, close to, crowded, disgusting, empty, fascinating, kind, lonely, pale, religious, still, tall, universal, unpleasant, watery, well-educated

V2 Adjective + noun

bare feet, bare wall, crowded city, crowded train, empty bottle, empty room, lonely life, lonely person, pale colour, pale face, still lake, still water

G1,2 1 Write these verbs in sentences 1–8 using the present perfect.

| drive | go | look | watch | eat | ~~learn~~ | talk | be |

1 They *have learned* a lot with the new teacher.
2 _____ you _____ at the holiday photographs?
3 _____ she _____ a Porsche?
4 They _____ Spanish food but not Japanese food.
5 _____ you _____ that new TV travel programme?
6 _____ they _____ about our new idea?
7 I _____ very busy.
8 Michael _____ to Bermuda. He doesn't want to come back.

G2 2 Correct the verbs in sentences 1–6.

1 Sally has never ~~drove~~ a Lamborghini. *driven*
2 Have you ever see a dolphin?
3 Russell has went to the hospital. He'll be back at 6.00.
4 We haven't have dinner. Would you like to eat with us?
5 Have you ever growed flowers in your garden?
6 David Attenborough has maked a lot of TV programmes about the natural world.

G3 3 Choose the correct verb form.

1 I *made / have made* a cake for us yesterday morning.
2 Can we give these customers a table? They *went / have been* here many times before.
3 We *ate / have eaten* alligator on holiday in Florida last year.
4 *She left / She's left* for work at 8.30.
5 I don't think *he was / he's ever been* to the opera.
6 My football team *didn't play / hasn't played* very well last Saturday.
7 You *didn't meet / haven't met* my sister. This is her first visit.
8 My parents *have never been / never went* abroad. They want to go to Australia this year.

4 Match questions 1–5 with responses a–e.

1 Did you spend your childhood in the country? *b*
2 Have you ever studied Chinese? _____
3 Were you ever lonely? _____
4 Have you ever been to the house in Florence? _____
5 Did you have a good time last night? _____

a) No, I haven't.
b) No, I didn't. We moved to the city when I was two.
c) Yes, we have. We've been several times.
d) Yes, I did. It was a great evening.
e) Yes, I was sometimes.

KL 5 Write the words in gaps 1–4 in this dialogue.

| perhaps | also | so | ~~let~~ |

A: What's the hottest place you've ever been to?
B: [1] *Let* me see. Erm ... [2]_____ it was when I went on holiday to India. We went to Delhi and then the south. That was hot. What about you?
A: Well, I've been to the Sahara desert [3]_____ that was the hottest.
B: I'm sure!
A: I've [4]_____ been to Mexico but it wasn't as hot as the desert.

V1 6 Write the missing vowels (a, e, i, o, u) in the adjectives.

1 This food tastes d *i* sg *u* st *i* ng. Send it back.
2 The printer is __mpty. Put some paper in.
3 Budapest is a f__sc__ n__t__ng city.
4 A very k__nd person gave me some water.
5 I'm not a w__ll-__d__c__t__d person but I have a very good job.
6 I was in a car accident yesterday. It was a very __npl__ __s__nt experience.

V2 7 Match these adjectives and nouns, and then complete sentences 1–5.

bare	life
crowded	colour
empty	train
lonely	bottle
pale	feet

1 I took a very *crowded* *train* into the city yesterday.
2 We want a _____ _____ on the walls in the bedroom – maybe a light blue.
3 Don't walk on the street with _____ _____. It's dangerous.
4 Oh, another _____ _____. Can you get some more olive oil from the cupboard?
5 My aunt had a very _____ _____. Her husband died when she was 25 and she didn't get married again.

AUDIOSCRIPTS

CD 1
Lesson 1.1 Track 1.2

1

Teacher, Pavel

T: Good morning. Come in. What's your name?
P: Pavel.
T: OK, Pavel. Have a seat. Where are you from?
P: From Kraków, in Poland.
T: Oh, OK. Tell me something about Kraków.
P: Well, it's a beautiful city. It's very old. It's in the south of Poland. It isn't the capital of Poland – that's Warsaw.
T: Is it a big city?
P: No, it isn't. It's quite small.
T: Anything else?
P: It's cold in winter. And er ... for you, it's very cheap!
T: OK, good, Pavel. We're on page ...

2

Teacher, Ayla

T: Hello! Come in. Are you Ayla?
A: Yes, that's right.
T: OK. Where are you from, Ayla?
A: Istanbul, in Turkey.
T: OK, what's Istanbul like?
A: Sorry?
T: Tell me something about Istanbul.
A: Oh, OK. It's a big city, very beautiful, but very noisy! The mosques are very famous.
T: I see. What about the weather?
A: It's hot in summer and it's wet in winter, but spring and autumn are nice.
T: Are the restaurants good?
A: Yes, they are, very good!

Lesson 1.2 Track 1.3

1

Hello! I'm Yukako and I'm from Kyoto. Kyoto's in the west of Japan. My city's old and there are a lot of old buildings. There are a lot of temples. They're very quiet. I love the old buildings.

2

Hi there! I'm Pablo. I'm from Lima, in Peru. In my city there are hundreds of cafés. They're great. I love them.

3

Hi. I'm Stefan and I'm from Chicago, in the United States. In the city there are a lot of museums. I love the museums in Chicago.

4

Hello. I'm Peter and I'm from Cape Town in South Africa. In Cape Town there's a beautiful mountain and there are a lot of beaches. The beaches are fantastic. I love them.

Lesson 1.3 Track 1.5

1 (railway station)   4 (swimming pool)
2 (zoo)   5 (building site)
3 (car park)   6 (bus station)

Track 1.6

School administrator, 2 students

SA: Good morning everyone. Welcome to Cambridge and to the Cam English School. Right, now, please look at your maps. There are a lot of interesting places in the city centre. First of all, please find Trinity Street and King's Parade – they're on the left of your map. There are a lot of beautiful colleges on these streets. Opposite Trinity College there's a good bookshop and a small post office.
   In the middle of the map, between Trinity College and the main post office, there's the main shopping area, with the market and the shopping centre. The market's nice, with food and clothes and a lot of other things. And it's cheap! The shopping centre's ... well ... to tell you the truth, it's ugly, but there are a lot of shops.
   On the right of the map, there's the bus station, next to the park. It's quite busy in the mornings and evenings. Take the bus from there to the railway station, or to London. Any questions so far?
S1: Yes. Is there a library?
SA: Yes, there is. It's in the shopping centre. On your map, there's a person with a book.
S1: Oh, yes. Thank you.
S2: Excuse me, is there a zoo?
SA: No, I'm afraid there isn't, not in the city. OK then, that's all for now. Don't forget – tomorrow at three o'clock, there's a guided tour of the city. Have a good time and learn a lot of English!

Lesson 1.4 Track 1.9

A B C D E F G H I J K L M N O P Q R S
T U V W X Y Z

Track 1.10

1 A H J K
2 B C D E G P T V
3 F L M N S X Z
4 I Y
5 Q U W
6 O
7 R

Lesson 2.2 Track 1.11

Teacher, Gina

T: Gina, do you have time for me to ask a few questions?
G: Of course. What are they about?
T: Well, it's a survey about student life – your studies, your home life and your free time.
G: OK, fine.
T: Right, well, first of all, about your studies. Do you study English at the weekend?
G: Yes, I do. On Sundays, I study for about an hour.
T: Do you bring a dictionary to class?
G: No, I only have a big old dictionary at home.
T: Do you have a computer?
G: Yes. It's our family computer.
T: And at the school, do you use the library and study centre?
G: No, I don't. I don't have time in the week.
T: OK. Now some questions about work, travel and home. You study, but do you also have a job?
G: A job – no, I don't. But I have children! That's a job really.
T: Yes, true. Do you travel to school by train, bus or car?
G: By bus. It's cheap.
T: Do you live alone, with family or with friends?
G: You know that answer! With my family.
T: Indeed, sorry. One or two questions now about your free time. Do you meet your classmates outside school?
G: Yes, I do. We go to a café after class every day, for a quick coffee and a chat.
T: Do you play sports?
G: No, I don't! I don't like sports!
T: OK, and finally, what other things do you do in your free time?
G: I don't have a lot of free time – I'm a mother, you know! In the little time I have, I read books.
T: OK. Thank you for your time, Gina.

Lesson 2.3 Track 1.12

Agent, Petra

A: Hello. How can I help you?
P: Hello. Can you tell me about the office *assistant* job, please?
A: Certainly. Let me find the information. Let me see ... Right. The office assistant job ... with DP Computer Export?
P: Yes, that's right.
A: OK. What information do you want?
P: Well, first of all, where is it? Is it in the city centre?
A: Yes, it is. It's a *modern* office and there's good *transport*.

P: Fine. What are the working hours and salary?

A: Well, you work from Monday to Friday, from nine o'clock to half past five. And the salary is … let me see … yes … it's 1,000 pounds a month.

P: OK, but what does an office assistant do? What are the work duties?

A: Well, in this job you *answer* the phone, you do the *filing* and you do the *photocopying*. You also write and send *emails* and *letters*. OK?

P: Yes, thank you. What qualifications do I need?

A: Well, you need a school *certificate* and basic English. I'm sure you have those.

P: Yes, I do. And what skills do I need?

A: Erm … you need good *computer* skills and good *communication* skills. OK?

P: Yes, that's fine. Thank you.

A: So, are you interested in the job?

P: Erm, well, … the salary isn't very good … Do you have any other jobs?

Track 1.13

1 What information do you want?
2 Where is it?
3 Is it in the city centre?
4 What are the working hours and salary?
5 What does an office assistant do?
6 What are the work duties?
7 What qualifications do I need?
8 What skills do I need?

Lesson 2.4 Track 1.17

A email, pilot, visit
B complete, design
C company, organise
D accountant, designer, location

Lesson 3.1 Track 1.18
(Tracks 1.19 and 1.20)

Presenter, Dr Simmonds

P: Dr Simmonds, my idea of a desert is a very hot place with a lot of sand. Is this correct? I mean, what *is* a desert, exactly?

S: Well, there are different kinds of desert – hot deserts and cold deserts. And hot deserts aren't always hot; the temperature changes, for example, from 38 degrees to ten degrees …

P: Ten degrees! That's cold! When are deserts that cold?

S: At night. They're hot during the day but cold at night.

P: Mmm, interesting.

S: Also, only about 30 percent of the world's deserts are sand – a lot of deserts are just rocks and stones. But all deserts have one thing in common: they're very dry, with a maximum of 250 mm of rain a year.

P: Really? So, why are deserts dry?

S: Well, for a number of reasons. Sometimes they're a long way from the sea and rain doesn't reach them. Sometimes mountains stop the rain.

P: OK, so there isn't any water – so how do animals and plants live in deserts?

S: Life in deserts isn't easy. A lot of desert animals sleep in the day and come out at night to look for food. The kangaroo rat gets all its water from its food. And desert plants have water in them. The Saguaro cactus in North America has five tonnes of water in its body and it sometimes lives for 200 years.

P: Wow! What about people? How do they live in the desert?

S: Desert people often live in groups, and move from place to place. They often live at the edges of deserts, not in the middle. The Aborigines of Australia eat desert plants and animals and live that way, but it's a hard life!

Lesson 3.3 Track 1.21

Andy, Cassie, Li

A: Right then, does anyone have any ideas for the last few spaces? Cassie?

C: Well, what about having a music show on Friday evening? There aren't any other music shows in the festival. Is that OK, Li?

L: Yes, I think that's a good idea. Let's have traditional music and modern music. I know a Malaysian pop band – and that traditional Cambodian group wants to come again.

A: Excellent. And let's have the dance workshop on Saturday afternoon. What do you think?

L: Erm, … I'm not so sure, Andy.

C: Yeah, … I don't agree with you.

A: You don't? Why not?

C: Well, Andy, the traditional boat races are very popular, and the dance workshops need a lot of people. I'd like to have the dance workshop in the morning, and I'd like to have the international food market in the afternoon. People often go to the market during the races and before the barbecue.

A: OK. I agree. What about Saturday evening? What would you like to have then, Li?

L: Why don't we have a drum concert then? The Burmese drum circles are very exciting.

A: Great idea, Li. That way people either watch a film or watch the drum concert, if they don't come to the barbecue, of course.

L: Fantastic. Right, that's all then. Let's go and get something to eat.

A: Great. I'm starving. Let's go for a burger.

C: A burger? Huh, OK.

Track 1.22

C: I'd like to have the dance workshop in the morning, and I'd like to have the international food market in the afternoon. People often go to the market during the races and before the barbecue.

A: OK. I agree.

L: Fantastic. Right, that's all then. Let's go and get something to eat.

A: Great. I'm starving. Let's go for a burger.

C: A burger? Huh, OK.

Track 1.23

a) OK.   b) OK.
1 Yes, …
2 Excellent.
3 OK. I agree.
4 Great idea, Li.
5 Fantastic.
6 Great.

Lesson 3.4 Track 1.25

1d
– What does 'glacier' mean?
– A large river of ice that moves down a mountain.

2f
– What part of speech is 'glacier'?
– It's a noun.

3a
– How do you spell 'glacier'?
– G-L-A-C-I-E-R.

4b
– Where is the word stress in 'glacier'?
– It's on the first syllable.

5g
– How do you pronounce it?
– /ˈglæsiə/

6e
– How do you say 'glacier' in Polish?
– *Lodowiec*.

7c
– What is *lodowiec* n English?
– In English, it's 'glacier'.

Review 1–3 Track 1.26

Interviewer, Marek

1f
I: Who do you live with?
M: With my mother and father in Gdańsk.

2e
I: Are you a student or do you work?
M: I'm a student.

3b
I: Is there a university in your city?
M: Yes. There is. It's famous in Poland.

4d
I: What do you study?
M: English and Art.

6c
I: Where exactly is your city?
M: Gdańsk is in the north of Poland.

8h
I: Does the city have an airport?
M: Yes, it does.

9g
I: When do tourists usually visit your city?
M: In the summer. The winter is very cold.

10a
I: Why do they visit the city?
M: They want to see the old town in the centre. It has beautiful buildings.

Track 1.27
Fabio, Gill
F: Hello. Are you Gill?
G: Yes, that's right.
F: I'm Fabio. Is it your first day here?
G: Yes, it is.
F: What's your job?
G: I'm not sure exactly. I'm an assistant, with some computer work and filing, I think.
F: Well, don't worry. When do you have lunch?
G: At 12 o'clock.
F: That's now! Why don't we go together?
G: That sounds good. Where do you usually eat?
F: It depends. What do you want?
G: Something small. And a coffee.
F: OK. I know a quiet café. Let's go there.
G: Good idea! Is it in the centre?
F: Yes, it's next to the post office.
G: OK. Let's go.

Lesson 4.2 Track 1.28
Interview 1
Gym assistant, Lisa
GA: Hello. We're doing a survey of our customers. Can I ask some questions?
L: Erm, yes, that's OK.
GA: Thank you. First, what's your name?
L: Lisa. Lisa White.
GA: And how often do you come to the club, Lisa?
L: Three times a week, usually.
GA: Do you use the running machines?
L: Yes, I do.

GA: Right, can you run ten kilometres in an hour?
L: Oh no, I can't. Maybe in 70 or 80 minutes.
GA: That's good. And do you work out in the gym?
L: Yes, I do, twice a week.
GA: OK, and what weight can you lift?
L: Well, I don't usually lift a lot, but I can lift 35 kilos.
GA: Do you use the swimming pool?
L: No, I don't.
GA: Really? Why not?
L: Well, erm, I can't swim, so I don't use it.
GA: Can't you? We offer lessons here, you know.
L: I know, I know, but I'm scared of water.
GA: I see. Well, I'm sure our trainer can help you …

Interview 2
Gym assistant, Dan
GA: What's your name?
D: Dan. Dan Tobin.
GA: And how often do you come to the club, Dan?
D: Twice a week, usually.
GA: Do you use the running machines?
D: Yes, I do.
GA: Can you run ten kilometres in an hour?
D: Oh, yes, I can. Easy. I can run that in about 30 minutes.
GA: Really? That's fast! And do you work out in the gym?
D: Yes, but only once a week.
GA: OK. What weight can you lift?
D: I can lift 50 kilos.
GA: Mmm, that's good. And do you use the swimming pool?
D: Yes, I do. I usually swim two kilometres, but I can swim five kilometres.
GA: Really?
D: Oh yes, I'm super fit!
GA: Yes, clearly. Can we test your fitness today? We have a machine …
D: Oh, is that the time? I can't stay, I'm afraid, I have an important meeting. Bye.
GA: But I have … oh …

Track 1.29
1 Can I ask some questions?
2 Right, can you run ten kilometres in an hour?
3 I can lift 35 kilos.
4 Oh, yes, I can.
5 I can run that in about 30 minutes.
6 I can swim five kilometres.

Track 1.30
1 No, I can't.
2 I can't swim.
3 Can't you?
4 I can't stay, I'm afraid.

Lesson 4.3 Track 1.31
Sarah, Travel agent
S: Hello.
TA: Hello, can I help you?
S: Yes, please. Can you give me some information about the Sarong Holiday Resort?
TA: Yes, certainly. What would you like to know?
S: First of all, can you tell me about the accommodation, please?
TA: Yes, of course. All the rooms are double rooms. Some of the rooms have a sea view.
S: I see. Are there any family rooms?
TA: No, I'm afraid not. They can put extra beds in your room for children.
S: And what restaurants are there in the resort?
TA: There are five different restaurants – Thai, Chinese, Indian, Italian and American. You can eat breakfast, lunch and dinner in four of them. I'm afraid you can't have breakfast in the Indian restaurant.
S: The advert says that the resort offers water sports. Can I play other sports, tennis, for example?
TA: I'm sorry. I'm afraid you can't. They only have water sports at the resort.
S: I see. Finally, I've got two young children. Is there a kids' club in the day?
TA: No, I'm afraid there isn't. There's a babysitter service in the evenings. The babysitter looks after your children in your room and you can go to the cinemas and restaurants.
S: Right. Thank you very much for your help and the information.
TA: You're welcome, madam. Do you want to make a reservation?

Track 1.32
1
S: Can you give me some information about the Sarong Holiday Resort?
TA: Yes, certainly. What would you like to know?

2
S: First of all, can you tell me about the accommodation, please?
TA: Yes, of course. All the rooms are double rooms.

3
S: Are there any family rooms?
TA: No, I'm afraid not.

4
S: Can I play other sports, tennis, for example?
TA: I'm sorry. I'm afraid you can't.

5
S: Is there a kids' club in the day?
TA: No, I'm afraid there isn't.

AUDIOSCRIPTS

Lesson 4.4 Track 1.34
1 The number of people in the UK is 60,500,000.
2 The number of people in Australia is 20,100,000.
3 The number of countries in the world is 192.
4 The number of languages in the world is 6,000.
5 The number of tigers in the world is 7,000.

Track 1.35
a) one hundred; a hundred
b) a hundred and forty
c) two thousand
d) two thousand three hundred
e) two thousand three hundred and forty-five
f) five million
g) five million six hundred thousand
h) five million six hundred and seventy thousand

Lesson 5.1 Track 1.36
1 Plane travel is safer than car travel.
2 The Suez Canal is longer than the Panama Canal.
3 Buses are more expensive in London than in São Paulo.
4 Lorries are bigger in the USA than in the UK.
5 Chicago O'Hare Airport is busier than Paris Charles de Gaulle Airport.

Lesson 5.2 Track 1.37
1

Hello. I'm Mei and I work in Beijing. I think the best way to get around Beijing is by motorbike. I've got a small motorbike and it's the quickest and cheapest way for me to travel. In Beijing, the buses are really crowded and I don't like them at all. The metro is the fastest way to travel, but it's not very large. Many people use bikes, but my motorbike is faster than a bike! It takes me 30 minutes to get to work.

2

Hi, my name is Fuad and I study at Cairo University. Travelling around my city is not very easy because the roads are very small and very busy. The metro here is quite small and my college isn't on a metro line. That's a pity because the metro is the most comfortable way to travel in Cairo. I travel by bus to college. It's the cheapest way to travel, but it's also the most popular, so the buses are very crowded. I never get a seat and it takes about an hour to get to my college!

3

I'm Sandra, and I live in Amsterdam. Every day I cycle to university. It only takes me about 20 minutes. A bike is the cheapest way to travel, of course, and it's also very popular here, because the city is very flat. In the city centre, trams are the best way to get around – I always use them when I go shopping. Many tourists travel on the canal boats, but I don't because they're the most expensive way to travel.

Lesson 5.3 Track 1.38
1 Check the departures board and see when the flight leaves.
2 I'd like a return ticket to Rio, please.
3 I usually travel in standard class, but sometimes my company pays and then I fly business class.
4 This airline has really good in-flight service. The flight attendants are really helpful.
5 I always ask for a window seat. I love the view of the clouds.
6 I always ask for an aisle seat because I've got long legs!

Track 1.39
Travel agent, Sasha.
TA: Hello.
S: Hello, it's Sasha Kaplinski here.
TA: Hello Sasha. I've got your email about New York.
S: Great! I'd like to book the trip now. Have you got some details for me?
TA: Well, I've got two flights for you, one is with Oz Air, the other one is with Top Air.
S: Can you tell me about the Oz Air flight first? When does it leave?
TA: OK. Well, the flight leaves at eight in the morning and it arrives at seven in the morning, their time.
S: OK. How long does that flight take?
TA: It takes 14 hours.
S: Fourteen, that's not bad. And how much does it cost?
TA: Erm, it costs 300 Australian dollars.
S: That's a good price. Is it a good airline?
TA: Oh yes. The in-flight service is very good.
S: Fine, and what about the second flight?
TA: The second one is with Top Air. This is a very good airline. Their in-flight service is excellent – it's better than Oz Air's. You can have a head massage and the food is great.
S: Sounds good. When does it leave? And when does it arrive?
TA: Well, it leaves at six in the evening and gets there at 5 p.m., their time.
S: How much does it cost?
TA: This one costs 600 Australian dollars.
S: I see. How long does it take?
TA: It also takes 14 hours.
S: Mmm, that's good, but it's expensive.
TA: Do you want to make a booking now?
S: Erm, I think so. Yes.

Track 1.40
TA: Do you want to make a booking now?
S: Erm, I think so. Yes.
TA: OK. One moment please. Right, so, can I have your full name, please?
S: Sasha Andrei Kaplinski. That's K-A-P-L-I-N-S-K-I.
TA: Thank you. And which airline would you like to travel with?
S: I'd like to book the Oz Air flight, please.
TA: OK. When do you want to travel?
S: Next Tuesday.
TA: Next Tuesday, that's the 1st of October, and what about the return flight?
S: One week later, please.
TA: OK, on the 8th, that's no problem. So, would you like business or standard class?
S: Oh, standard class. The company doesn't want to spend a lot of money.
TA: Fine, and finally, would you like a window or an aisle seat?
S: Oh, can I book that now?
TA: Yes, you can.
S: Excellent. Can I have a window seat, please?
TA: Certainly. OK, that's all. How would you like to pay?
S: Oh, by credit card please, the company credit card.
TA: OK, can I have the card number, please? ...

Lesson 6.2 Track 1.41

Track 1.41
Interviewer, David
I: Hello, David. Before you can join the Kids' Fitness Club, we interview you about your lifestyle – about what you eat and what you do in your free time. OK?
D: Fine.
I: Right. Have you got a large family? Do your parents work?
D: Well, I've got a sister, she's two years older than me, and yeah, both of my parents work. Dad's a policeman and Mum's a teacher.
I: OK. How much exercise do you do in your free time?
D: Exercise?
I: Yes, do you play any sports, for example?
D: Oh, no, not really. At school we have one sports lesson a week, but in my free time I don't do much.
I: Do you walk to school or cycle?

D: No ... Dad takes me to school in the car. I haven't got a bike.

I: Fine. So, how much TV do you watch?

D: I don't know, about four hours.

I: Four hours a week. That's good.

D: No, four hours a day.

I: I see. Erm, next, how many computer games have you got?

D: I don't know, a lot. I play them all the time. About 30.

I: OK, well, what about your diet? How much fruit do you eat? How many vegetables do you have each day?

D: Well, Mum gives me an apple every day, but sometimes I don't eat it. Vegetables? Perhaps one or two. I don't eat them at school, they're boring.

I: And how many pizzas or burgers do you eat?

D: Oh, I don't know. About three burgers and a pizza each week, sometimes more. I eat a lot of chocolate and sweets ... oh, and I love crisps. Crisps are vegetables, aren't they?

I: Well, not really, but ...

D: So, can I join the club?

I: Sure, but why do you want to join?

D: Well, I know I'm overweight and I want to change that. And the gym sounds fun – my friends say you can watch TV when you're on the bikes.

I: That's true. But you need to change your diet as well.

D: My diet?

I: What you eat. You need to eat more fruit and vegetables.

D: Yeah [yes], whatever. Do the TVs show MTV?

Track 1.42
1 How much exercise do you do?
2 How much TV do you watch?
3 How many computer games have you got?
4 How much fruit do you eat?
5 How many vegetables do you have each day?
6 How many pizzas or burgers do you eat?

Lesson 6.3 Track 1.43
Jane, Tariq
J: Good morning, Event Catering Services. How can I help?
T: Hi, it's Tariq here, from the university.
J: Ah, hi Tariq. This is Jane. How are you?
T: Fine thanks. And you?
J: Great. So, how can I help you this time?
T: Well, there's a conference at the university next week and I'd like to

order some food for the conference lunch.
J: OK, so, what would you like for the first course?
T: Well, have you got any tomato soup?
J: Yes, we have. How much would you like?
T: We'd like 50 cans, please.
J: That's fine. And for the main course?
T: Could we have 50 chicken salads, please, 50 vegetarian pizzas and 40 lamb kebabs?
J: Oh Tariq, I'm sorry. I'm afraid we haven't got any chicken salads at the moment. We can provide cheese salads.
T: OK, can we have 50 cheese salads then?
J: Sure, no problem.
T: Thanks. For dessert, we'd like 100 ice creams and 50 apple pies.
J: That's no problem. Would you like some water or fruit juice?
T: Yes, please. Could we have 50 large bottles of still water and some small bottles of apple juice?
J: How many bottles of juice would you like?
T: Oh, 100, please.
J: Fine, anything else? Would you like some coffee?
T: No, thank you.
J: Some tea?
T: No, thanks. That's everything.
J: OK. And when do you want the delivery?
T: Ah yes, well the conference is ...

Track 1.44
1 Could you send me some coffee?
2 I'd like 50 lamb kebabs, please.
3 Can we have 40 bottles of water, please?
4 Would you like some bread?
5 We'd like some chicken salads, please.

Review 4–6 Track 1.46
1
Interviewer, Man
I: Right, thank you for coming. First of all, what sports do you like?
M: Most sports really. I play a lot of football at the weekend and go running every morning.
I: That's good. And do you have any qualifications in fitness training?
M: No, but I'm good at using weights.
I: Can you teach yoga?
M: Erm ... no, I can't but I can teach aerobics ...

2
Interviewer, Woman

I: OK. I'd like to ask you some questions. First of all, do you often use a gym?
W: Yes, I use the fitness machines every week and I also teach yoga at a local college.
I: Great. We also have a lot of international clients. Can you speak any other languages?
W: Yes, I can. I can speak some Spanish.
I: OK. And can you drive?
W: No, I can't, I'm afraid. But I ride a bike everywhere and I go cycling every morning ...

Track 1.47
Traveller, Employee
T: Hello, could you give me some information about trains to Seattle?
E: Yes, certainly. What would you like to know?
T: First of all, when do they leave?
E: The first train is at ten in the morning and the next train is at 12.
T: Is there a train in the afternoon?
E: I'm afraid there isn't. There's a train in the evening.
T: OK. How much does a ticket cost?
E: The first train is 34 dollars. The other trains are 40.
T: I'd like two tickets for the first train, please. First class, please.
E: That only has standard class seats, I'm afraid.

CD 2
Lesson 7.1 Track 2.2
1 I can't talk now, I'm trying on some trainers.
2 Call me back later. I'm driving.
3 Can you see me? I'm standing at the corner, opposite the bank.
4 Can I call you back? The waiter's waiting for me to order.
5 We're just arriving at the bus station. See you in five minutes.
6 I'm in the car park. I'm putting the food in the car.

Track 2.3
1
Shop assistant, Customer
SA: Do they fit?
C: Yes, they feel fine.
SA: Walk around the shop and check they're OK. There's a mirror over there. How do they feel?
C: OK, but perhaps the left one is a little small.
SA: Right, well, try a bigger size.

2
SA: Can I help you?
C: Yes, I'm looking for *Birds Without Wings*.
SA: I'm afraid we don't have that one in the shop.

c: Oh, I see. That's a pity. I really want to read it.

sa: We can order it for you.

c: Really? Great! Thanks very much.

sa: That's fine. Can I have your name ...

3

sa: OK, so that's 15 pounds. How would you like to pay?

c: By credit card, please.

sa: Fine.

c: Here you are.

sa: Thank you. Can you enter your number please?

c: Of course.

sa: Great. Here's your receipt, and here's your shirt. I've only got a large bag, I'm afraid.

c: That's fine. Thank you very much. Bye.

Lesson 7.2 **Track 2.4**

Presenter, Linda

p: Good afternoon and welcome to our weekly shopping programme *Shopaholic*. Now, are you an online shopper? Or do you prefer to queue at the supermarket? Linda Stanley of *Consumer World* magazine is with us in the studio to talk about Internet shopping. Hello, Linda.

l: Hi there!

p: First of all, Linda, is Internet shopping becoming really popular now?

l: Yes, it is. It's becoming part of our lives. More and more people are buying online.

p: Mmm, so what are they buying?

l: Books and CDs are the most popular things, and then travel. People are also spending a lot of money on health and beauty, and food and drink. For example, they're using the online services of supermarkets for big or heavy things like bottles of water.

p: Interesting. And <u>how</u> are people using the Internet to shop? I mean, how do they start?

l: Well, people are usually online for 12 to 18 months before they try online shopping. They usually start with something simple like books.

p: Yes, it's great for books. Are people comparing prices on the Internet now?

l: Yes, they are. It's easy to compare prices – there are special websites for this. So the Internet is giving people a lot of power.

p: I see. I guess men enjoy using the Internet. What about women? Are <u>they</u> using the Internet for shopping?

l: Yes, they are. Definitely. More and more women are shopping online. The great thing about the Internet is

this: it's 24/7. You can shop online all day, every day. This is very good news for busy women with jobs and children.

p: Of course. And what are companies doing to get business on the Internet?

l: Well, some companies are offering big discounts to get new customers. You can get a Harry Potter book, for example, for half price.

p: Is this the end of traditional shopping – you know, people going to shopping centres and supermarkets?

l: No, I don't think so – not just yet, anyway. Perhaps in the future. Right now, people are moving between the Internet and real shops to save time and money.

p: Well, it all sounds very exciting. Thanks for coming in and telling us about it, Linda.

l: My pleasure.

Lesson 7.3 **Track 2.5**

Brad, Zara

b: So, what advantages does downtown have?

z: Well, first of all, I think it's a nice place for people to visit, and there are some interesting local shops.

b: Oh yeah? What are they?

z: Well, there are some cafés and there's a music shop, and also an art shop. This means that people there are interested in the books we sell.

b: OK. Are there any more advantages?

z: Yes, another advantage is that the area is safe – crime is low. And, of course, there's a bus station.

b: Right. What about the disadvantages?

z: I think there are two main disadvantages. One disadvantage is that the rent is high and the other is that a lot of people go to the shopping mall outside the town. This means that sometimes there aren't very many customers downtown.

b: I see. So, the area is a nice one, but the rent is expensive and most people go to the mall.

z: Yes.

b: Mmm. What do you know about the shopping mall?

z: Well, it's ...

Lesson 7.4 **Track 2.7**

Track 2.7

Teacher, Nicolas

t: Are you ready to give your talk, Nicolas?

n: Of course.
   Good afternoon everybody. In this short talk, I'd like to tell you about

my favourite store – Harrods, the huge department store in London. The building is beautiful, especially at night, when there are hundreds of lights outside. It's open every day of the week, including Sundays. There are seven floors, I think. You can find everything in Harrods: clothes, watches, books and DVDs, children's toys, things for your home and sports equipment. You can even buy a famous green Harrods shopping bag. And Harrods can order anything you want! It's famous for its fantastic food halls, and there are about 25 cafés and restaurants. One of the most interesting things is that there's even a doctor in the store – as well as a bank. To finish, I think Harrods is the best department store in the world! That's all. Thank you.

Lesson 8.1 **Track 2.9**

1 The city was lovely.
2 There were gardens everywhere.
3 It was very safe, too.
4 The people were kind.
5 The women were beautiful.
6 The streets were busy.
7 There was an interesting market.

Lesson 8.2 **Track 2.10** **(Tracks 2.11 and 2.12)**

Tutor, Nathan, Marjorie

t: OK everyone! Today's presentation is by Nathan and Marjorie. Start when you're ready, Nathan.

n: OK. Hello everyone. Our presentation is called *A Smaller World* and it's about technology and cultural change. The talk focuses on technology that makes the world smaller, for example television.

m: First of all, can you imagine life without cars and planes? Before the invention of these means of transport, people could only travel by train or boat, and they couldn't travel very fast. Now, with cars and planes, we can travel further and faster. Some people even live in one country and work in another because they can fly to work. Fifty years ago, people certainly couldn't do that. And of course, many people fly thousands of miles to go on holiday, and while their grandparents could only read about distant places, they see them. Before we move onto the next type of technology, it is important to remember that planes and cars do have their negative points. They can be dangerous and they cause a lot of pollution, and this also changes the way we live.

N: OK. Second, communications technology, like television and the Internet, certainly makes the world smaller. We stay in our house or office, but we can see news and shows from all around the world. With the Internet, we can write and chat to people all over the world. This is an incredible invention. We can find anything we want in seconds. It makes the world smaller, and it makes it faster! But do these things have any negative points? Well, yes, they do. Nowadays, people spend more time using the technology than they do meeting other people. We're spending more and more of our time in our houses, talking to strangers in other countries, than we are with our friends and neighbours. My grandmother could name all the people in her street, but I don't even know the names of my neighbours!

M: So, you can see that technology changes our way of life and culture, in both positive and negative ways. A lot of technology makes the world a smaller place, but does it make it a better place?

T: OK. Thank you Nathan and Marjorie, that was great. Are there any questions?

Lesson 8.3 Track 2.13

1

Visitors, Richard, Jessica
V1: Excuse me.
R: Yes, madam. How can I help you?
V1: Could you tell me where the cloakroom is, please?
R: Certainly, madam. Can you see those stairs over there?
V1: Yes, I can.
R: Well, go down those stairs and then turn left. The cloakroom is next to the toilets.
V1: Thank you.
R: You're welcome.

2

V2: Excuse me, could you help me, please?
J: Yes, of course. What would you like?
V2: Well, I'd like to go on a guided tour. Could you tell me how much it costs?
J: Certainly, sir. Are you interested in the long or the short tour?
V2: Oh, the short one, please.
J: OK, well a short tour costs two pounds.
V2: Oh that's cheap, could you tell me how much the long one costs?
J: Yes, of course. That's five pounds. Which would you like?
V2: Erm, the short one please.

3

V3: Excuse me.
R: Yes madam, how can I help?
V3: Well, I'd like to see a film about the Egyptian Mummies. Could you tell me when the next film starts?
R: Of, course, let me just check … erm, yes, it starts at 2.30.
V3: At 2.30?
R: Yes, madam. That's right.
V3: OK. Isn't there one before that?
R: I'm afraid not, madam. We only show the film in the afternoon.
V3: OK, thank you.
R: You're welcome.

4

V4: Excuse me.
J: Yes, sir, how can I help?
V4: I'm really interested in this statue. Could you tell me how old it is?
J: Mmm, let me see … Yes, this is a Roman statue, it's about 2,000 years old. It's a statue of Venus, the goddess of love.
V4: I see, it really is lovely. Thank you.
J: Not at all.

5

V5: Excuse me.
R: Yes, madam?
V5: We're visitors. Could you give us a map of the museum, please?
R: Of course, madam. Where do you come from?
V5: Italy. Why?
R: Well, would you like the map in Italian or English?
V5: Oh, could you give us both please, so we can practise our English?
R: Certainly. There you are.
V5: Thank you very much.
R: Not at all. Enjoy your visit.

6

V6: Excuse me.
J: Yes, sir?
V6: I'm here with my friends. Could you take a photo of us? Next to the mummy?
J: Oh. I'm afraid not, sir. You can't take photographs in the museum.
V6: Really? Oh dear, I only want you to take one quick photo.
J: I'm afraid I can't do that. Why don't you take one outside, after your visit?
V6: OK, we can wait.
J: Thank you. Enjoy the rest of your visit.
V6: Thank you.

Track 2.14

1 Could you help me, please?
2 Could you tell me when the next film starts?
3 Could you give us a map of the museum, please?

Track 2.15

1 Could you open the door, please?
2 Could you take my coat, please?
3 Could you tell me when the museum closes?
4 Could you tell me what this means, please?
5 Could you tell me where the shop is?

Lesson 9.1 Track 2.16

1 Leonardo started his studies of art in 1468.
2 He finished these studies in 1472.
3 He wanted money so he started work as an engineer.
4 Leonardo worked as an engineer for 32 years.
5 He lived in Milan from 1472 to 1500. / He stayed in Milan from 1472 to 1500.
6 He returned to Florence after 28 years in Milan. / He moved to Florence after 28 years in Milan.

Track 2.18

Alfred Nobel was born in 1833 in Sweden. He studied chemistry but he also wrote poetry, novels and plays. He tried to make a safe explosive, but, unfortunately, he killed his brother in an experiment in 1864. He invented dynamite in 1866. In 1895 he started the Nobel Prize Foundation.

Levi Strauss was born in Germany in 1829. He travelled to New York in 1846 and moved to San Francisco in 1853. He started a shop for gold miners: he sold equipment and clothes. In 1873 he invented jeans – he used a material from Nîmes in France and called it 'denim'.

Lesson 9.2 Track 2.19

Presenter, Stephen Bayley
P: Welcome to this week's edition of *Understanding Science*. With me in the studio is Professor Stephen Bayley of Nottingham University. Professor Bayley, I'd like to start by asking you this question: what is the most important medical invention of the last 30 years?
SB: Well, that's a difficult question because there are a lot of important inventions. Certainly, one of the most important is the MRI scanner.
P: The scanner? Can you tell us something about it?
SB: Yes, well, basically it's a big box with a hole in the middle …

Track 2.20

P: ... And how does it work?

SB: Well, you lie in the hole and the scanner takes pictures of you. Like an X-ray machine, the MRI scanner can look into our bodies, but normal X-ray machines can only show the hard parts of our bodies, the bones and teeth for example, while the MRI scanner can show both the hard and soft parts of the body, so it's more useful. It can take a picture of the whole body and you get the pictures very quickly. It's not dangerous, either, like X-ray machines.

P: That's good. When did scientists invent it?

SB: Well, it didn't happen overnight. In 1945, scientists discovered NMR – Nuclear Magnetic Resonance. In the 1950s an American scientist named Felix Bloch did some experiments in the lab and understood the importance of NMR for looking inside the human body.

P: So did Felix Bloch invent the MRI scanner?

SB: No, he didn't. Another American, Raymond Damadian, and his team built the first full-body MRI scanner.

P: When did they do that?

SB: In 1977.

P: And when did doctors start to use this new machine?

SB: A few years later. In 1984, hospitals around the world bought their first MRI scanners.

P: It all sounds fantastic. Are there any problems with the scanner?

SB: Well, it isn't good for people who don't like small spaces!

Lesson 9.3 Track 2.21

Hello and welcome to *The nation's favourite everyday invention*, the show that tells you the story behind the everyday objects that we use in our daily lives. Each week, we tell you some key facts about the inventions and I tell you why I think they are wonderful or important. At the end of each programme, you can vote for your favourite invention. Simply send a text message to 0810 40 50 60, giving the name of your personal choice. So, vote for an invention and let's find our national favourite.

Track 2.22

The first of today's everyday inventions is that classic symbol of the English businessman – the umbrella. Nowadays, everyone has got one, but before 1750, men never carried umbrellas. So, what's the story of the umbrella, or brolly? Here are today's four facts.

First, many hundreds of years ago, rich and important people in hot countries such as China, India and Egypt used umbrellas. These rich people did not use their umbrellas in the rain, they used them in the sun. Of course, poor people worked in the sun, but they didn't have umbrellas.

Secondly, the Chinese invented the first umbrellas for use in the rain. They put oil and wax on their paper umbrellas.

Thirdly, umbrellas reached Britain about 400 years ago, but, at first, only women had umbrellas: men didn't like them. In 1750, Jonas Hanway, a British traveller, was the first man to use an umbrella on the streets of England. Other men followed his example and the umbrella at last became very popular in Britain.

And finally, the first umbrella shop, James Smith and Sons, opened in London in 1830, and it's still open today.

And did you know that over 7,000 people lose an umbrella on London Transport every year, and all these umbrellas go to the Lost Property office. That's a lot of umbrellas!

Track 2.23

So, why vote for the umbrella?

Well, the most important reason is that it's one of the oldest inventions in the world. People found it very useful thousands of years ago, and we still find it useful today.

Secondly, the umbrella is a great invention because it's got several different uses. We can use it in the rain, we can use it in the sun and we can use it as a walking stick.

Thirdly, vote for the umbrella because umbrellas bring colour to our grey, rainy streets.

My final reason is that umbrellas are very cheap to make and cheap to buy.

So, that's the wonderful umbrella. When it rains, the rich and the poor can all stay dry. It's an invention for everyone. If you think this is the greatest everyday invention, vote now by sending a text message to ...

Track 2.24

1 Well, the most important reason is that it is one of the oldest inventions in the world.

2 Secondly, the umbrella is a great invention because it's got several different uses.

3 Vote for the umbrella because umbrellas bring colour to our grey, rainy streets.

4 My final reason is that umbrellas are very cheap to make.

Lesson 9.4 Track 2.26

Hedy Lamarr was very famous in the years before the Second World War. She was born in Vienna, Austria, in 1913. As a child, she grew up in Vienna. Later, when she was a teenager, she went to acting school in Berlin. Then, in 1932, she acted in the European art film *Extase*, and she became famous. The next year, she married Fritz Mandl, the first of her six husbands. Mandl sold weapons to Adolf Hitler in the years before the war. During her marriage, she learnt many things from her husband, but after four years, she left him and she went to London. After that, she went to America and she became a Hollywood star. At that time, people called her the most beautiful woman in the world. In the summer of 1940, she met George Antheil, a composer. She and George developed a radio communications system for submarines in 1942. In 1966, she wrote a book about her life, *Extase and Me*. She died in 2000.

Review 7–9 Track 2.27

Manager, Customer

M: Hello. I'm the manager of this supermarket and today we're talking to some of our customers. Do you have five minutes?

C: Yes, OK.

M: Great. What are you buying today? Food or clothes?

C: Food and clothes. I always buy food on Mondays and today I'm also looking for some clothes for my children.

M: OK. And do you usually pay by credit card?

C: Yes, I do but I'm using cash today.

M: I see. And on average how much do you spend here every week – under or over 100 pounds?

C: Oh, probably over 100 pounds.

Track 2.28

Shop assistant, Customer

SA: Hello, can I help you?

C: Yes. Could you show me some mobile phones, please?

SA: Certainly. We have over 15 different designs. Which phones would you like to see?

C: I don't know. There are so many!

SA: This one is the best.

C: Why?

SA: Well, it has two main advantages. The first advantage is the camera and the second is that you can watch TV on it.

C: Yes, but that means it's the most expensive. Sorry, but I'd like something simpler.

SA: That's no problem. This model is half the price.

C: Does it have games?

SA: No, I'm afraid not, but it has a camera.

Lesson 10.1 Track 2.29

Sue Cutler

Good afternoon, everyone. How are you today?

My talk this afternoon is about how to stay safe in the city.

First of all, let me tell you that the city of Sheffield is actually one of the safest cities in the UK. Most other big cities are much more dangerous than here. So don't be scared! But we should always be careful and look after ourselves and our possessions.

We can talk about our personal safety later, but let's start by saying something about looking after our money. Here are a few things you should and shouldn't do. A lot of this is common sense, of course, and I'm sure you already do most of these things in your own countries.

Track 2.30

Sue Cutler, 3 Students

SC: Anyway, here goes, starting with the things you should do. Number one – you should be careful in crowded places. By this, I mean on trams, on buses, in busy markets and shopping streets. Pickpockets – that's people who steal your wallets, purses, cameras and so on – pickpockets love crowded places. So take care.

The next thing is about cards, credit cards and debit cards. You should keep your PIN number safe and secret – only you should know it. Cashpoints are usually outside banks. When you use them, have a look at who is behind you. Are they too close? Are they interested in what you're doing? Don't let anyone see you put in your PIN number.

Another important point. If you carry a bag, carry your bag carefully. Make it difficult for someone to take it off you. And if you carry just a wallet, you should keep it in your jacket, in an inside pocket, not in the back pocket of your trousers.

Now, that brings us to some things you <u>shouldn't</u> do. You shouldn't carry a lot of cash about with you. By that, I mean lots of big notes, and coins. You can replace traveller's cheques and credit cards. But you can't replace lost cash.

Next, you should never take your money out of your wallet or purse in busy public places. This one is obvious, isn't it? Don't attract the attention of thieves by counting your money on a busy street! OK. Any questions so far?

S1: Should I wear a money belt when I go out?

SC: Well, most people here don't wear money belts. Also, money belts are often uncomfortable so I don't think that it's necessary, but it's up to you, I suppose.

S2: Last night, some of us went out to a café. One of the girls had her mobile phone on the table all the time. Is that OK?

SC: Well, no, she shouldn't do that. That's really not a good idea. She should keep it in her bag.

S3: Should I leave money in my university room?

SC: The rooms are generally very safe, but, no, you shouldn't really have a lot of cash in your room, just in case. Any other questions? OK, now let's move on to talk about personal safety ...

Lesson 10.3 Track 2.31

Researcher, Katie, David

R: Excuse me, I'm working for a bank and we're doing a survey about money. Can I interview you?

K: Well, actually we're rather busy.

D: Yes, we're doing the shopping and we have to be back at the car park in ten minutes.

R: I understand, but it's only a short interview, and you can win a holiday to Thailand.

K: Really? Well, I don't see any problems.

D: But darling, we should finish the shopping.

K: Five minutes isn't a problem, is it, David? So, what's the first question?

R: Right, well, if you're sure. Erm, what's your opinion about having credit cards?

D: Well, personally, I think that they're a bad idea. It's very easy to spend more than you can afford.

R: And you, madam, what's your opinion?

K: Well, in my opinion, they're great. They give you a chance to buy expensive things when you want them. You don't have to wait for them.

R: OK madam, and do you think that saving money is important?

K: Erm, yes, I suppose it is, but to be honest, I don't save very much each month. I prefer to spend my money now.

R: And sir, do you think that saving money is important?

D: Oh yes, definitely. When you're old, you can't live without money, so I save something every month, for my pension.

R: Right. Do you think that borrowing money from friends is a good idea?

D: Oh, no, not at all. I think that it's a terrible idea because if you forget to pay them back, well, things can get very difficult, can't they?

R: Mmm, I guess so. And you, madam, do you think that it's a good idea?

K: Well, I'm not sure. It's cheaper than borrowing from banks. But you have to be careful, you shouldn't borrow a lot or often, and of course, you have to remember to pay your friend back!

R: OK. Finally, do you agree that people should give money to charity every month?

K: No, not at all. I believe that the government should look after everyone. My money is my money.

R: And you, sir? Do you agree that we should give money to charity?

D: Well, yes, I do. We should give some money, but we aren't very rich so I can't always give something, but I do try, when I can.

R: Well, thank you very much ...

Track 2.32

R: OK madam, and do you think that saving money is important?

K: Erm, yes, I suppose it is, but to be honest, I don't save very much each month. I prefer to spend my money now.

R: And sir, do you think that saving money is important?

D: Oh yes, definitely. When you're old, you can't live without money, so I save something every month, for my pension.

AUDIOSCRIPTS

Lesson 10.4 Track 2.33

Part 1

Sue Cutler

Right, I expect you want to open a bank account while you're here, so this next part of my talk is about the banks in Britain and their student services. There are four main or high street banks in Britain. They are, first of all, NatWest, that's spelt N-A-T-W-E-S-T. Secondly, Barclays, that's B-A-R-C-L-A-Y-S. Thirdly, HSBC, H-S-B-C and finally, Lloyds TSB. That's two words. LLOYDS, double L-O-Y-D-S, then T-S-B, Lloyds TSB. All of these banks offer student bank accounts and there are some differences between these accounts.

OK, so, first of all, the NatWest student account. This account offers an interest-free overdraft. As well as this, you can get a credit card and the interest rate for that is about 18.9 percent per year. Also, the bank offers discounts on train fares in Britain.

Track 2.34

Part 2

The second account is with Barclays. Like the NatWest account, there's an interest-free overdraft. In addition, this bank offers a credit card with an interest rate of 19.9 percent, so it's more expensive than the NatWest card. With this account, students also get free mobile phone insurance. I imagine that's popular with many of you.

Track 2.35

Part 3

Right, now the HSBC account. This account also has an interest-free overdraft. In addition, there's a credit card and the interest rate is 18.9 percent. As well as this, students get a free driving lesson.

Finally, the Lloyds TSB student account offers an interest-free overdraft. Also, students get a credit card with an interest rate of 17.9 percent. Unfortunately, this account doesn't offer any discounts or free services.

So, that's an overview of the four main banks and their student accounts. Are there any questions?

Lesson 11.1 Track 2.36

1 I'll be rich.
2 You'll have three children.
3 She'll buy a sports car.
4 He'll live alone.
5 It'll make them happy.
6 We'll speak excellent English.
7 They'll go to Australia.

Lesson 11.2 Track 2.37

Interviewer, Martin, Simon, Vicky

1

I: What was your score?
M: I got 36, but my flatmate, Richard, only got 25.
I: Right, and what are you going to do? What changes are you going to make?
M: Well, I'm going to have showers in the future, no more lovely hot baths for me. Richard is going to make more changes.
I: Oh yes, what's he going to do?
M: Well, he's going to recycle things, like paper and glass. At the moment he doesn't recycle anything, which is terrible. Also, he's going to turn things off, especially his CD player as he always leaves that on standby. Oh, and he's going to cover his saucepans when he's cooking – but that isn't very often!

2

I: What was your family's score?
S: Yes, well, we got 40, but we're going to make some big changes anyway.
I: Oh yes, such as?
S: Well, we're going to buy a solar panel and some low-energy light bulbs. We think that the solar panel will be a great idea for us because we'll save money. The children are young, so they can't do a lot, but they're going to recycle their paper – they do a lot of pictures and drawings. We aren't going to have showers because we haven't got a shower at the moment – only a bath.

3

I: What was your score?
V: Oh, it was very good, I got 35.
I: I see, and what are you going to do to go greener?
V: Oh, I'm too old to change a lot. I'm not going to do anything new. I recycle everything, I turn everything off. What more can I do? Solar panels are very expensive.
I: Why don't you buy green electricity?
V: Oh, I'm not sure, is that easy to do?
I: Yes, it is now. We can find a company for you and you don't need to change anything in your house.
V: That sounds a good idea. Let me think about it.

Track 2.38

1 I'm going to find out about green electricity.
2 She isn't going to buy a wind turbine because it's expensive.
3 We aren't going to change anything. We're already very green.
4 They're going to turn off their TVs with the on/off button.

5 Are you going to make any changes?
6 He's going to cycle to work every day.

Lesson 11.3 Track 2.39

Estate agent, Conor

EA: Hello, Find-a-Flat-Fast. How can I help?
C: Ah, hello. I'm looking for a flat to share with a friend. Hello, can you hear me?
EA: Yes, I can. How many bedrooms do you want?
C: Two bedrooms.
EA: OK, let's see. I've got one here, it looks lovely – two bedrooms, kitchen, living room, two bathrooms ... ground floor with a garden ... , but there's no furniture, just a cooker and fridge-freezer in the kitchen.
C: That's OK. How much is the rent?
EA: It's 150 euros a week per person.
C: Oh, that's expensive. We're students.
EA: OK, here's another one. It's got two bedrooms, and both are large. There's a small kitchen, a dining room and a living room. There's also a large bathroom.
C: Right. What floor is the flat on?
EA: It's on the fourth floor, and I'm afraid there isn't a lift.
C: I'm sorry, could you repeat that, please?
EA: Sure. It's on the fourth floor.
C: And there isn't a lift?
EA: That's right.
C: OK, erm ... what furniture is there?
EA: Well, in each bedroom there's a bed, a desk and a wardrobe. In the kitchen there's a cooker, a fridge-freezer and a washing machine. There's a table with chairs in the dining room and a sofa in the living room.
C: Just a moment. So, there's a cooker, a fridge-freezer and a washing machine. Is that right?
EA: Yes, it is.
C: What about the local area? Is it near public transport?
EA: Well, there's a bus stop about 15 minutes away.
C: I'm sorry, could you say that again?
EA: Sure. There's a bus stop about 15 minutes away.
C: A bus stop. OK. And, was that 15 or 50 minutes?
EA: Fifteen, one five.
C: What about trains?
EA: I'm afraid there isn't a local station.
C: Mmm, and how much is it?
EA: It's 90 euros a week, per person.
C: I'm sorry, did you say 19 or 90 euros?
EA: No! It isn't that cheap! It's 90, nine zero. Would you like to see the flat?

C: Well, we really need a flat near a train station, so I don't think that we will. But thanks for your help. Goodbye.

EA: Goodbye.

Track 2.40

4 ... was that 15 or 50 minutes?
5 I'm sorry, did you say 19 or 90 euros?

Track 2.41

1
– It's on the fourth floor.
– I'm sorry, was that the fourth or the fifth floor?

2
– The rent is 150 euros.
– Did you say 150 or 15?

3
– It's got a living room.
– Was that a living room or a dining room?

4
– There's a sofa in the living room.
– Did you say there is or there isn't a sofa?

5
– It hasn't got a balcony.
– Did you say it has or hasn't got a balcony?

Lesson 12.1 Track 2.42

Peter, Kirsty

P: G'day.

K: Hi there!

P: My name is Peter Knight. I'm doing research into people who grow up in different countries and I'm talking to people here at the university today. Is it OK if I ask you a few questions?

K: Sure, go ahead.

P: Well, first, tell me, have you ever lived abroad?

K: Yes, I have.

P: Oh, that's lucky for me! What's your name?

K: Kirsty Andrews.

P: OK, Kirsty. Which countries have you lived in?

K: Erm ... England, Oman and Japan. That's it, I think.

P: Why have you lived in so many places?

K: Because of my Dad's job.

P: I see. And ... erm ... what's your favourite country?

K: Australia! No, seriously, I really like Japan. It's amazing! It's so different.

P: Can you speak Japanese?

K: A little bit, yeah [yes].

P: Have you ever worked in any of these countries?

K: No, I haven't.

P: OK. Next question. Has your experience changed you in any way?

K: OK. Let me see ... well ... I know a lot more about the differences between cultures ... and I don't think that my way is the best way or the only way.

P: What about friends? I mean, do you see your old friends from the different countries?

K: Yeah, that's a problem. My best friend is in Japan. She's visited me once or twice here and we send emails all the time but I still miss her a lot.

P: I can understand that. Right ... final question ... are there any other countries you'd like to live in?

K: Well, I've never lived in a poor country. I think it could be an important experience. Maybe an African country, or something like that. And I haven't lived in South America. I'd like to spend some time there. Maybe I'll do these things after graduation.

P: Right ... I'll let you get on with your lunch. Thanks a lot for your time, Kirsty.

Track 2.43

1 We've visited a lot of interesting places.
2 I've changed a lot in the last ten years.
3 She's talked to people from a lot of countries.
4 He's watched films in different languages.
5 They've moved house several times.

Lesson 12.3 Track 2.44

Interviewer, Woman

I: What's the tallest building you've ever seen?

W: The tallest building? Well ... let me see ... erm ... I haven't seen many really tall buildings, but last year I went to New York and I visited the Empire State Building, and I really liked it. Erm ... I first saw the building from the plane. That was fantastic; it made me think of the film *King Kong*. Then I visited the building the next day. It's very tall and it's also beautiful, I think. It's different from most tall buildings because erm ... it's made of bricks and has a lot of windows. Other tall buildings are all glass, so it's very different, and that's why I think that it looks beautiful. Anyway, I went to the top of the building in the lift, and the view from the top is wonderful. You can see all of Manhattan in every direction – the yellow taxis look so small, like tiny insects! Well, what else? Oh yes, I also went up

the building at night. That was great – you can see all the lights of New York City below your feet. That was a very special moment for me. So, that's the tallest building I've seen.

Lesson 12.4 Track 2.45

OK, now I'm going to talk about technology and learning. First of all, the Internet. There are several ways you can use it to improve your English, because you can read, listen and write.

Writing practice is excellent for your learning; it's almost as important as speaking. On the Internet there are two places where you can write – message boards and live chat rooms. Live chat rooms are great for improving your fluency, because you have to write quickly. It's like a conversation. A message board is good for both fluency and accuracy because you can think and prepare before you write. Both are excellent for communication practice.

Now, the Internet is a good place to practise your listening. You should visit a good news site, such as the BBC, and watch the short video clips. Before you watch, you can read about the story, and then you can watch the clip as many times as you want. Often these are short and you can watch clips about news and sports, even music. In order to improve your listening, you have to be an active listener: make notes, try to write down the main points, try to write down new vocabulary.

Finally, on the Internet there are many sites for English language learning. Have you visited the website for this book? There are extra practice exercises and reading materials. The BBC World Service also has an excellent site for learning English, with special message boards for learners.

The best thing about the Internet is that it gives you the chance to do things with the language, and that's very important. All right? Good, now I'm going to talk about ...

Track 2.46

In conclusion, the important thing is to do lots of different things:
'We remember 20 percent of what we read, 30 percent of what we hear, 40 percent of what we see, 50 percent of what we say, 60 percent of what we do and 90 percent of what we read, hear, see, say and do. So, follow my advice and enjoy practising your English outside the classroom.

Review 10–12 Track 2.47

2 Men

1

м1: Hello.

м2: Hello. I'm interested in the bike for sale.

м1: OK. Great. Well, it's about two years old.

м2: Sorry, did you say two?

м1: Yes. And it's 50 pounds.

м2: Sorry, was that 15 or 50?

м1: Fifty. It's a mountain bike.

м2: That sounds good.

м1: What else do you want to know about it?

м2: Erm, I don't know really.

м1: Well, would you like to see it then?

м2: Yes, I could come this afternoon ...

2

Man, Woman

м: Hello.

w: Hello. I'm interested in the CD player for sale in the paper.

м: OK. Well, it's new. It's still in the box.

w: Sorry, what did you say?

м: It's in the box. I've never opened it.

w: Oh. And how much is it?

м: I paid 50 pounds for it. So it's 30 pounds. OK?

w: Sorry, can you repeat that?

м: It's 30 pounds.

w: OK. Could I come and see it?

м: Sure.

w: Where do you live exactly?

Sound-spelling correspondences

In English, we can spell the same sound in different ways, for example, the sound /iː/ can be 'ee', as in *green*, 'ea' as in *read* or 'ey' as in *key*. Students of English sometimes find English spelling difficult, but there are rules and knowing the rules can help you. The chart below gives you the more common spellings of the English sounds you have studied in this book.

English phonemes

Consonants

Symbol	Example	Symbol	Example
p	park	s	sell
b	bath	z	zoo
t	tie	ʃ	fresh
d	die	ʒ	measure
k	cat	h	hot
g	give	m	mine
tʃ	church	n	not
dʒ	judge	ŋ	sing
f	few	l	lot
v	view	r	road
θ	throw	j	yellow
ð	they	w	warm

Vowels

Symbol	Example	Symbol	Example
iː	feet	əʊ	gold
ɪ	fit	aɪ	by
e	bed	aʊ	brown
æ	bad	ɔɪ	boy
ɑː	bath	ɪə	here
ɒ	bottle	eə	hair
ɔː	bought	ʊə	sure
ʊ	book	eɪə	player
uː	boot	əʊə	lower
ʌ	but	aɪə	tired
ɜː	bird	aʊə	flower
ə	brother	ɔɪə	employer
eɪ	grey	i	happy

Sound	Spelling	Examples
/ɪ/	i y ui e	this listen gym typical build guitar pretty
/iː/	ee ie ea e ey ei i	green sleep niece believe read teacher these complete key money receipt receive police
/æ/	a	can man pasta land
/ɑː/	a ar al au ea	can't dance* scarf bargain half aunt laugh heart
/ʌ/	u o ou	fun sunny husband some mother month cousin double young
/ɒ/	o a	hot pocket top watch what want
/ɔː/	or ou au al aw ar oo	short sport store your course bought daughter taught bald small always draw jigsaw warden warm floor indoor
/aɪ/	i y ie igh ei ey uy	like time island dry shy cycle fries die tie light high right height eyes buy
/eɪ/	a ai ay ey ei ea	lake hate shave wait train straight play say stay they grey obey eight weight break
/əʊ/	o ow oa	home cold open show throw own coat road coast

* In American English the sound in words like *can't* and *dance* is the /æ/ sound, like *can* and *man*.

IRREGULAR VERB LIST

Infinitive	2nd Form (Past Simple)	3rd Form (Past Participle)
be	was/were	been
become	became	become
begin	began	begun
break	broke	broken
bring	brought	brought
build	built	built
buy	bought	bought
can	could	been able
catch	caught	caught
choose	chose	chosen
come	came	come
cost	cost	cost
dig	dug	dug
do	did	done
draw	drew	drawn
drink	drank	drunk
drive	drove	driven
eat	ate	eaten
fall	fell	fallen
feed	fed	fed
feel	felt	felt
find	found	found
fly	flew	flown
forget	forgot	forgotten
get	got	got
give	gave	given
go	went	gone/been
grow	grew	grown
have	had	had
hear	heard	heard
hold	held	held
hurt	hurt	hurt
keep	kept	kept
know	knew	known
learn	learned/learnt	learned/learnt

Infinitive	2nd Form (Past Simple)	3rd Form (Past Participle)
leave	left	left
let	let	let
lose	lost	lost
make	made	made
mean	meant	meant
meet	met	met
pay	paid	paid
put	put	put
read /ri:d/	read /red/	read /red/
ride	rode	ridden
ring	rang	rung
run	ran	run
say	said	said
see	saw	seen
sell	sold	sold
send	sent	sent
shine	shone	shone
show	showed	shown
sing	sang	sung
sit	sat	sat
sleep	slept	slept
speak	spoke	spoken
spend	spent	spent
stand	stood	stood
steal	stole	stolen
swim	swam	swum
take	took	taken
teach	taught	taught
tell	told	told
think	thought	thought
throw	threw	thrown
understand	understood	understood
wear	wore	worn
win	won	won
write	wrote	written

Elementary and Pre-intermediate levels

Ian Lebeau studied Modern Languages at the University of Cambridge and Applied Linguistics at the University of Reading. He has nearly 30 years' experience in ELT – mainly in higher education – and has taught in Spain, Italy and Japan. He is currently Senior Lecturer in English as a Foreign Language at London Metropolitan University.

Gareth Rees studied Natural Sciences at the University of Cambridge. Having taught in Spain and China, he currently teaches at London Metropolitan University and University of the Arts. He also develops English language materials for the BBC World Service Learning English section and he makes films which appear in festivals and on British television.

Intermediate and Upper Intermediate levels

David Falvey studied Politics, Philosophy and Economics at the University of Oxford and did his MA in TEFL at the University of Birmingham. He has lived in Africa and the Middle East and has teaching, training and managerial experience in the UK and Asia, including working as a teacher trainer at the British Council in Tokyo. He is now Head of the English Language Centre at London Metropolitan University. David is co-author of the successful business English course *Market Leader*.

Simon Kent studied History at the University of Sheffield. He has 20 years' teaching experience including three years in Berlin at the time of German reunification. Simon is co-author of the successful business English course *Market Leader*. He is currently Senior Lecturer in English as a Foreign Language at London Metropolitan University.

David Cotton studied Economics at the University of Reading and French Language and Literature at the University of Toronto. He has over 30 years teaching and training experience, and is co-author of the successful *Market Leader* and *Business Class* coursebooks. He has taught in Canada, France and England, and been visiting lecturer in many universities overseas. He is currently visiting lecturer at London Metropolitan University.

Far left: Simon Kent
Centre left: David Falvey
Centre: Gareth Rees
Centre right: Ian Lebeau
Far right: David Cotton